101 MASTERPIECES

OF

NEW YORK CITY

ALSO BY VALERIE ANN LEEDS

Marguerite Zorach: A Life in Art
Robert Henri: The Painted Spirit
Robert Henri in Santa Fe: His Work and Influence
Leon Kroll: Revisited
Ernest Lawson

101 MASTERPIECES

OF

NEW YORK CITY

MUST-SEE WORKS OF ART & ARCHITECTURE
IN THE NEW YORK METROPOLITAN AREA

VALERIE ANN LEEDS

WITH MELINA V. KERVANDJIAN
AND CONTRIBUTIONS BY FEAY S. COLEMAN

INTRODUCTION BY JOHN YAU

MANUFACTURED IN THE UNITED STATES OF AMERICA

A TRADE PAPERBACK ORIGINAL PUBLISHED BY
ALYSON BOOKS
245 WEST SEVENTEENTH STREET
NEW YORK, NY 10011

DISTRIBUTION IN THE UNITED KINGDOM BY
TURNAROUND PUBLISHER SERVICES LTD.
UNIT 3, OLYMPIA TRADING ESTATE,
COBURG ROAD, WOOD GREEN
LONDON N22 6TZ ENGLAND

FIRST EDITION: JANUARY 2009

09 10 11 12 13 14 15 16 17 a 10 9 8 7 6 5 4 3 2 1

ISBN: 1-59350-098-X
ISBN-13: 978-1-59350-098-6

LIBRARY OF CONGRESS CATALOGING-IN-PUBLICATION DATA ARE ON FILE.

COVER DESIGN BY VICTOR MINGOVITS
BOOK DESIGN BY VICTOR MINGOVITS

To Kevin,
and also to my parents
for making everything possible.

CONTENTS

CONNECTICUT
||||||||||||||||||||||||||||||||||||||||||||||||||||||||||||||||||||||||||||||||||||||||||||||||||||||||||||||||||||||||||||

PREFACE

WHILE LIFE LISTS HAVE BECOME increasingly in vogue in recent years, I was surprised to find that such a compilation of notable art and architecture destinations in the New York metropolitan area had never been published. The 101 destinations that are presented here (plus mention of additional others worthy of visiting) have been selected with an eye toward accessibility. The criteria were that destinations must have exceptional artistic significance and must be located in Manhattan and the surrounding areas and be within an easy day trip of the city. The regions outside of Manhattan that are covered encompass the Hudson River valley, Long Island, the Boroughs, New Jersey, and southern Connecticut. While some places such as The Metropolitan Museum of Art and the Museum of Modern Art (MOMA) are quite well known, others are unfamiliar to the general public and are often overlooked even by art cognoscenti.

The 101 selections were the result of a deliberative process, and the iconic nature of single works of art, as well as the overall importance of the collections, architectural significance of buildings, institutions, and landscape designs, as well as regional considerations were weighed with regard to the final list. With the inherent limitations of this publication, it is in no way intended to be comprehensive, but is meant to highlight a range of new experiences and possibilities for readers with an interest in art and architecture. The resulting compilation obviously reflects personal choices by the authors and the elimination of many important destinations; this is an unfortunate part of any selection process. This publication could have easily included several hundred destinations, but would then hardly function as an introductory portable guide. Thus, many significant institutions and works are not represented, including such obvious omissions of notable institutions as the Jewish Museum and the American Folk Art Museum. To keep the list to 101, it was unfortunately necessary to eliminate many worthy sites.

My particular gratitude is extended to Richard Fumosa, editor at Alyson Books, for proposing the idea of this guide to me after long talking about working on a project together. His expertise, enthusiasm, and help throughout the process were vital. Melina V. Kervandjian warrants a particular note of appreciation for her stellar effort. She was an able collaborator, co-authoring this publication and assuming responsibility for most all of the entries relating to painting and sculpture. Without her knowledge, insight, can-do spirit and willingness to delve into this project on a short timeline, it would never have been realized. Gratitude is also extended to Feay S. Coleman who contributed several entries and who offered her particular expertise on architecture, gardens, and decorative arts.

Before planning your trips, it is advisable to check Web sites as information is subject to change. It is the sincere hope that this guide will introduce some unknown local and regional treasures to art enthusiasts in their leisure hours, hopefully even reintroducing some places with a new perspective that may even be located right around the corner.

VALERIE ANN LEEDS

■ INTRODUCTION ■

NEW YORK CITY and its neighboring cities and towns offer the greatest concentration of art and innovative architecture in America. Let's take two obvious examples—the 22-story Flatiron Building (1902) that occupies the triangular block formed by Twenty-third Street, Fifth Avenue, and Broadway, and the 102-story Empire State Building at the intersection of Fifth Avenue and Thirty-fourth Street. A mere ten blocks separates these historic landmarks, and yet it's difficult to imagine finding in such close proximity two more different skyscrapers constructed during the first decades of twentieth century. That is the beauty of New York; it all fits together somehow.

The Flatiron Building was designed by architect Daniel Burnham in the Beaux-Arts style, complete with a limestone and glazed terra-cotta façade. Through the use of a steel skeleton, Burnham was able to transform the classical style into something new, as well as erect a structure far higher than its nineteenth-century predecessors. More than a century after it was built, the Flatiron Building still attracts many visitors who gaze at its prow-like front facing north (the walls are around 6 1/2 feet apart at their narrowest point), as the city's recent construction of viewing areas flanked by Broadway and Fifth Avenue attest. There are always people straining to get a better view, as well as shutterbugs trying to find the perfect photograph. The Flatiron Building is just one of the many treasures of Manhattan.

Erected less than thirty years later (and in 410 days), the Art Deco-style Empire State Building has 6,500 windows, 73 elevators, and its own zip code (10118). Today, more than 20,000 people work there every day. Is it any wonder that the Empire State Building was named by the American Society of Civil Engineers as one of the Seven Wonders of the Modern World?

New York City's magic and magnificence reminds me of one of those Russian dolls that contains another doll, which doll contains still another.

Once you begin looking—starting with facades, moving on to the lobbies, and, in the case of historic landmarks and museums, the collections—you quickly learn that the city has a daunting abundance of riches. Valerie Ann Leeds's *101 Masterpieces of New York City* is a rare combination of reliable guide and a wondrous celebration of the city's treasures.

Even after living in New York City for more than thirty years, I am continually reminded that there is so much about this continually changing city that remains to be discovered. For example, the Metropolitan Museum of Art—housed in a building with distinguished reconstruction programs and add-ons that have continued up to 1991—has more than two million works of art in its collection. There are nineteen curatorial departments, each with its experts and very particular focus. This is where generations of artists have gone to learn from different masters, and where you can pass the time in galleries filled with art from antiquity to the present—and, for inveterate people-watchers, there are always interesting individuals from different countries and walks of life.

Just north of the Metropolitan Museum of Art is Frank Lloyd Wright's spectacular spiral masterpiece, the Solomon R. Guggenheim Museum (1959). Whatever you think of Wright's inimitable design—and it is difficult to be neutral about it—the Guggenheim established the possibility that a museum itself could be seen as a work of art. Wright was none too subtle about his intention when he said that he wanted his building to make the Metropolitan Museum of Art "look like a Protestant barn."

To see what younger, contemporary architects have done, go to the Bowery and visit the New Museum of Contemporary Art (2005-7), a seven-story structure that resembles a stack of shiny metal boxes casually balanced on top of each other. Like the Met and the Guggenheim, the New Museum is iconic—and, like its forbearers, it is a destination for both longtime residents and people from far and near visiting Manhattan for the first time.

Valerie Ann Leeds deserves our thanks for not limiting her attention to the city's world-famous wonders, but also detailing less familiar ones that can be discovered on the edges of Upper Manhattan and even farther away. I had not known of the Morris-Jumel Mansion or that it is New York City's oldest surviving home (built in 1765, and remodeled in 1815). I learned that "[t]he first floor includes a parlor in which Madame Eliza Jumel married Aaron Burr in 1833." Being transported through history is one of the pleasures that happens throughout this book. Open to any page and you will learn something new, even from entries about buildings you have been to and thought you knew a lot about. Here Leeds describes one historic attraction:

> The Dyckman Farmhouse is a typical Dutch Colonial farmhouse and the only remaining one of its kind in Manhattan. Situated in Inwood, the farm had occupied an area of several hundred acres bordering the Harlem River and originally had many cherry, peach, and apple trees. Once the largest farm in Manhattan, it now occupies the corner of Broadway and 204th Street and includes a small garden park—a country oasis amid the city.

Thankfully, Leeds doesn't confine herself to what lies within the borders of New York City, but travels to the nearby countryside and easily reached cities. Among Connecticut's many treasures to which she directs our attention is New Haven's Yale University Art Gallery (1951–54), which, as Leeds points out, was Louis I. Kahn's first public commission. It is one of only three museums he designed, the others being the Kimbell Art Museum (1972) in Fort Worth, Texas, and the Yale Center for British Art (1969–74), which is a few blocks away from the gallery. The visitor to New Haven will also be able to see Paul Rudolph's Art and Architecture Building (1959–63), Eero Saarinen's Ingalls Rink (1953–58) and the Ezra Stiles and Morse Colleges (1958–62), and Gordon Bunshaft's Beinecke Rare Book and Manuscript Library(1963). One can use Leeds's book to plan trips just to see Saarinen's buildings, for example, or to see those of James Renwick.

For someone like myself, who enjoys both actual travel and being an armchair traveler, *101 Masterpieces of New York City* is the perfect book. It has something for everyone. Each of Leeds's entries is concise, impeccable, and replete with all kinds of information, from the background history to the hours a building is open to the public. I knew that one of my favorite museums, the Wadsworth Atheneum (1842) in Hartford, Connecticut, is America's oldest public museum—but I didn't know its fascinating back story. I certainly didn't know that Washington Square Park was built over a cemetery, and that "the remains of more than 20,000 people rest under the square," or that "St. Paul's Chapel (1766) is New York's oldest public building in continuous use and one of the finest examples American Georgian architecture." This is living history as well as our cultural legacy. Begin reading this book, and you won't put it down. It is much more than a guide—it is a love letter to a city and the people who made it.

JOHN YAU

101 MASTERPIECES

OF

NEW YORK CITY

Central Tibetan Thanka of Guhyasamaja, Akshobhyavajra (17th century), Rubin Museum of Art, New York.

NEW YORK CITY

UPTOWN

■ **AMERICAN ACADEMY OF ARTS AND LETTERS**
633 West 155th Street
Audubon Terrace
ARCHITECT: William Mitchell Kendall (act. 1882–1941),
  of McKim, Mead, and White, 1923

■ **ADMINISTRATION BUILDING**
ARCHITECT: Cass Gilbert (1859–1934), 1930

■ **NORTH GALLERY AND AUDITORIUM**
ARCHITECT: Charles Pratt Huntington (1871–1919), 1907

■ **FORMER AMERICAN NUMISMATIC SOCIETY**
PHONE: (212) 368-5900
WEB SITE: www.artsandletters.org
E-MAIL: academy@artsandletters.org

MODELED ON THE Académie française, the American Academy of
Arts and Letters, founded in 1904, celebrates individuals who have made
significant contributions in the fields of arts, letters, poetry, music, painting,
sculpture, and drama. The seven founding members of the institute were
William Dean Howells, Augustus Saint-Gaudens, Edmund Clarence Stedman,
John La Farge, Mark Twain, John Hay, and Edward MacDowell, who then
nominated others until the full membership body was attained. The current

academy represents the merger in 1976 of the National Institute of Arts and Letters and the American Academy of Arts and Letters. The Academy resides in a complex of three Beaux-Arts granite and limestone buildings on Audubon Terrace. The land that comprises the Terrace was donated by academy member Archer M. Huntington, and was the former property of the noted naturalist and artist, John James Audubon.

The Administration Building on West 155 Street, completed in 1923 and designed by William Mitchell Kendall from the firm, McKim, Mead, and White, holds executive offices, members' room, portrait gallery, library, and several exhibition galleries, including the south gallery. The adjoining building, designed by Cass Gilbert and completed in 1930, contains the north gallery. The third building, completed in 1907, is the former headquarters of the American Numismatic Society, and was acquired to expand the academy. This building, the east wing, was one of the first structures on Audubon Terrace and was designed by Charles

Detail of the filigree work of a Gothic arch, Central Park Bridge, spanning a bridle path south of the tennis courts.

Pratt Huntington, the same architect who designed the Hispanic Society, the Geographical Society, and the former building of the Museum of the American Indian, that were originally on the Audubon Terrace.

Bronze doors (1930), designed by Academician Herbert Adams, and leading from Audubon Terrace to the Academy's north and south galleries, depict classical figures representing Arts, Letters, Poetry, Music, Painting, Sculpture, Inspiration, and Drama. Academician Adolph A. Weinman's bronze doors, at the 155th Street entrance to the Administration building were installed in 1938. They are dedicated to the novelist Mary E. Wilkins Freeman, one of the Academy's first female members, and to the women writers of America.

The Academy presents two exhibitions annually and is open only when exhibitions are mounted, in March/April and May/June—call or check the Web site for dates. The gallery is open during exhibitions and the hours are: Thursday through Sunday, 1 p.m. to 4 p.m. except Saturdays and Sundays of holiday weekends. The galleries are located on Audubon Terrace. Enter through the gates between 155th and 156th Streets on the west side of Broadway. Admission is free.

■ CENTRAL PARK, 1858

Central Park South (59th St.) to 110th St. at the northern end and
from 5th Ave. on the East Side to Central Park West (8th Ave.) on
the West Side.
Frederick Law Olmsted (1822–1903)
and Calvert Vaux (English, 1824–1895)

CENTRAL PARK, the result of a winning design by Frederick Law Olmsted and Calvert Vaux, opened to the public in 1858, distinguishing it as the first landscaped public park in the United States. Work continued on the park for some time and by 1863, the park encompassed 843 acres, occupying six percent of Manhattan Island.

In 1853, the state of New York authorized the city to acquire over 700 acres in midtown Manhattan. There was rough, irregular terrain with swampy areas and large rocky outcroppings between 59th and 106th Streets and between Fifth and Eighth Avenues. Based on the European model of large public parks seen in London and Paris, a Central Park Commission was formed and in 1857 it held a design competition. The "Greensward Plan," the result of a collaboration between Olmsted and Vaux, was the one selected as the winner from thirty-three entries. Olmsted and Vaux's conception had contrasting types of landscape areas, including pastoral, picturesque, and formal aspects, while also allowing traffic to run through the park, with four sunken roads crossing the width of the park. Criticism was lobbed at the plan, which forced the designers to add pedestrian, carriage, and esquestrian drives that allowed for further circulation within the park. Along with Jacob Wrey Mould (1825–1886), Vaux added many bridges and archways to counteract the varying grades of the landscape. Belvedere Castle, 1865, located midpark at 79th Street, was another collaboration between Vaux and Mould, and was conceived as a Victorian whimsy, a purely decorative structure that would provide visitors with an elevated vantage point.

Olmsted and Vaux created a bucolic setting that encompasses many aspects of the English landscape tradition, which views nature as a release from crowded urban environs. Central Park is conceived on a plan of four quadrants: the South End (which runs from 59th Street to the 72nd Street crosstown drive); the Great Lawn (which runs from 72nd Street to 85th Street; the Reservoir (which runs from 85th to 97th streets); and the North End. Highlights in the South End include the Zoo, which opened in 1871 and can be found between 63rd and 66th streets off Fifth Avenue; the Carousel; the Sheep Meadow; Literary Walk; the Mall; the Bandshell; and Bethesda Terrace. In the Great Lawn section are Conservatory Water (the boat pond); the Boathouse; Belvedere Castle; Turtle Pond; the Ramble; and the Lake. In the uppermost section attractions include Lasker Pool and the Ravine.

The Mall and Bethesda Terrace represent the more formal elements within the park design of Olmsted and Vaux. The environment for a promenade is an integral aspect of park design and the designers felt the need to balance the natural features, such as the Ramble and the Lake, with the Mall. In designing the Mall and the Literary Walk (which runs approximately from 66th to 72nd streets at the southern end of the mall), they planted rows of American elms, which enclose the mall and create a natural ceiling. The southern end of the Mall is often referred to as Literary Walk as it contains statues of literary figures, including Shakespeare, Sir

Walter Scott and Robert Burns. Creating a park out of the natural topography of the selected area posed many challenges to the designers. Poor soil for trees and shrubs forced them to transport enormous amounts of soil from New Jersey. To achieve the effects laid out in their design, much manual digging was necessary, as was the blasting of large areas of rock, and the fabrication of six manmade bodies of water fed by city water.

Central Park is also home to a great many important sculptural works. Among its sculptural highlights is the iconic work, the **SHERMAN MONUMENT** (1903), located in Grand Army Plaza at 59th Street and Central Park South. Augustus Saint-Gaudens (1848–1907) depicts General William Tecumseh Sherman, the Union military hero of the Civil War, on horseback on his way to battle in 1864. He is accompanied by Nike, the goddess of victory. Sitting atop a pedestal by Charles McKim, the Sherman Monument was Saint-Gaudens's last great work.

Also at Grand Army Plaza is the **PULITZER FOUNTAIN**, executed by sculptor Karl Bitter (1867–1915) in 1916. Joseph Pulitzer, the newspaper publisher, left money for a fountain to be erected and Bitter and architect Thomas Hastings were commissioned to create the fountain. To make the plaza symmetrical, the Sherman monument was moved sixteen feet to its present location to allow for symmetrical positioning of the fountain. The fountain sculpture represents Pomona, the Roman goddess of abundance.

At the Artists' Gate, located at the park entrance at 59th Street and Avenue of the Americas, is a sculpture of José Martí (1959) by American sculptor Anna Vaughn Hyatt Huntington (1876–1959). The sculpture is one of three monuments to Latin American heroes at the Artists' Gate Plaza. Martí was a Cuban patriot, journalist, and poet who fought for the liberation of Cuba from Spanish rule. The statue shows Martí as he was mortally wounded, his horse rearing.

At the Merchants' Gate, located at West 59th Street at Columbus Circle, is the **MAINE MONUMENT** (1901–1913), by Attilio Picarelli (1866–1945). The monument commemorates the more than 260 American sailors who died in 1898 in an explosion on the USS *Maine* in the Havana harbor in Cuba. Cuba was under Spanish rule and by 1898 Spain was at war with the United States. William Randolph Hearst's newspaper called for public sponsorship of a monument to honor the sailors. Substantial donations for the memorial were collected, resulting in the Beaux-Arts-style monument that marks the west entrance to the park. The monument's gilded figures represent the Columbia Triumphant featuring a seashell chariot of three hippocampi that are part horse and part sea-creature, which are supposedly fabricated from metal recovered from the guns of the Maine.

American sculptor Paul Manship (1885–1966) is also well represented in Central Park. Positioned at the entrance to the zoo in Central Park is Manship's Lehman Gates (1960–61), featuring a bronze male figure and two goats dancing atop granite pedestals. Two other boys on other pedestals are playing pipes within the connecting curvilinear vegetal and bird designs

Balto, *the sled dog, a favorite of all ages in Central Park by Frederick George Richard Roth (1925)*

of the gate. Manship's other sculpture in Central Park is his **GROUP OF BEARS** (1952) at the Pat Hoffman Friedman playground, inside the Park at Fifth Avenue and 80th Street. Other versions of the sculpture can be found in the American Wing at **THE METROPOLITAN MUSEUM OF ART** and the Bronx Park Zoo. He is also the sculptor of the iconic Prometheus Fountain at **ROCKEFELLER CENTER** (see p. 69) At the path west of the Mall near 66th Street is **THE INDIAN HUNTER** (1866), one of several sculptures in the park by John Quincy Adams Ward. It depicts a Native American with a bow and a fierce hunting dog. When this work was shown at the Paris University Exposition of 1867, it established Ward's reputation. It was placed in Central Park in 1869 and was the first sculpture by an American sculptor in the park. Along the Literary Walk, Ward's full-length statue of **WILLIAM SHAKESPEARE**, which was dedicated in 1872, sits on a pedestal by Jacob Wrey Mould. On Central Park West Drive opposite 67th Street is another well-known example of Ward's, **THE LONE SENTRY** (1869), and on Pilgrim Hill, inside the park at 72nd Street near Fifth Avenue is his **THE PILGRIM**, of 1884, on a granite pedestal by Richard Morris Hunt. This work was commissioned by the New England Society of New York on the occasion of their 75th anniversary to honor the early colonists who landed on Plymouth Rock in 1620.

BALTO, 1925, by Frederick George Richard Roth (1872–1944) is one of the park's most popular works. It is located on East Drive near 66th Street. It is dedicated to the sled dogs that led several dogsled teams through a snowstorm in the winter of 1925 in order to deliver medicines that would stop a diphtheria epidemic in Nome, Alaska. Larger than life-size, the dog statue is sited on a rock outcropping on the main path to the zoo. (Balto was also the subject of an animated/live-action film (1995) produced by Steven Spielberg.)

The Bethesda Terrace, considered the central focal point of the park, overlooks the Lake and the shores of the Ramble. **THE BETHESDA FOUNTAIN** contains a prominent sculpture, **ANGEL OF THE WATERS** (1873) by Emma Stebbins (1815–82), which features a lily representing purity in the hand of the angel. The four figures below represent Peace, Health, Purity, and Temperance. Stebbins, the sister of the president of the board of the Commissioners of Central Park, was the first woman to receive a sculptural commission in New York City.

Located at Fifth Avenue between 70th and 71st Streets is the Beaux-Arts **RICHARD MORRIS HUNT MEMORIAL** (1898) executed by Daniel Chester French (1850–1931) in honor of the architect's dedication to the cause of art in America. Hunt's work can be seen in the façade of **THE METROPOLITAN MUSEUM OF ART** (see p. 28) several blocks north, as well as the pedestal of the Statue of Liberty. French, on the other hand, is perhaps best known for his monumental sculpture of a seated Abraham Lincoln inside the Lincoln Memorial in Washington, D.C.

The bronze standing figure of the orator and statesman **DANIEL WEBSTER** by sculptor Thomas Ball (1819–1911) can be found at the convergence of two park drives near the Strawberry Fields Memorial, near West 72nd Street. Ball had executed a number of variants of this sculpture, but this larger-than-life-size bronze was commissioned and presented by Gordon W. Burnham in 1876.

The large sculpture depicting **ALICE** from Lewis Carroll's 1865 classic, *Alice's Adventures in Wonderland,* is one of several destinations in the park specifically designated for children. Located on East 74th Street on the north side of Conservatory Water, the literary figure is represented perched on a large mushroom, reaching toward the pocket watch held by the March Hare, host of the tea party. The Cheshire Cat is peering over her shoulder while the Dormouse and the Mad Hatter surround her. The sculptor José de Creeft (1882–1984) executed the work, which was unveiled in 1959 as a memorial to Margarita Delacorte. Alice is said to resemble the artist's daughter. De Creeft is best known as a modernist and for his part in the direct carving movement in America.

Among the most notable works in Central Park is **CLEOPATRA'S NEEDLE**, a 3,500-year-old Egyptian obelisk behind **THE METROPOLITAN MUSEUM OF ART** (at 82nd Street and Fifth Avenue). The monument is from Heliopolis, dating to about 1500 B.C. It was moved to Alexandria around 12 B.C. by the emperor Augustus. The lower corners of the stones had been broken off, so Roman bronze supports in the form of sea crabs were placed under them. Two of the originals are in the Metropolitan Museum of Art, but the other two were stolen prior to coming to America. The obelisk was transported to the United States in 1879 and was erected in the park.

The **BURNETT MEMORIAL FOUNTAIN**, dedicated to the author Frances Hodgson Burnett, who wrote *The Secret Garden,* was placed in the park in 1936. The sculpture was created by Bessie Potter Vonnoh (1872–1955) between 1926 and 1936, and was placed in the **CONSERVATORY GARDEN** when it reopened in 1936. When Frances Hodgson Burnett died in 1924, some of her friends wanted to honor her memory by creating a storytelling area in Central Park. They chose the Conservatory Garden as the site for the memorial, and it is believed that the two figures, a reclining boy playing the flute and a young girl holding a bowl, represent the two main characters from *The Secret Garden*. The memorial is located in the Conservatory Garden in the south garden at 104th Street and Fifth Avenue.

The park is open from 6:00 a.m. until 1:00 a.m. Park Drive is closed to vehicular traffic on weekdays from 10:00 a.m. to 3:00 p.m. and from 7:00 p.m. to 7:00 a.m; on weekends, it is closed from 7:00 p.m. Friday to 7:00 a.m. Monday; on holidays, it is closed from the night before at 7:00 p.m. to 7:00 a.m. the day after.

COOPER-HEWITT, NATIONAL DESIGN MUSEUM
2 East 91st Street
ARCHITECT: Babb, Cook and Willard (active 1899–1902)
PHONE: (212) 849-8400
WEB SITE: http://cooperhewitt.org
E-MAIL: chtours@si.edu

THE COOPER-HEWITT, National Design Museum, a branch of the Smithsonian Institution since 1967, was founded in 1897 and is the nation's foremost museum devoted exclusively to historic and contemporary design. Housed in the former mansion of the industrialist Andrew Carnegie, the home was designed by the architectural firm of Babb, Cook & Willard and built between 1899 and 1902. Designed in the fashion of a comfortable Georgian country house, the mansion also includes one of the only large private gardens in Manhattan, which offers a beautiful retreat from the hustle and bustle of the city. The Cooper-Hewitt's complex, which houses more than 250,000 objects in addition to a first-rate library devoted to the study of design, also includes two historic townhouses, renovated to serve museum needs.

The Cooper-Hewitt's collection is international in scope. The institution is meant to serve as a repository of design through the ages, as well as an active and continually growing and changing resource that provides inspiration for contemporary designers working in various media.

The collection, which spans twenty-four centuries, comprises a wide range of objects, and among its highlights are drawings by such Renaissance masters as Michelangelo (1475–1564) and other works on paper such as Italian and French drawings and prints pertaining to ornament, decorative arts, and architecture from the seventeenth to the nineteenth centuries; furniture by Charles (1907–1978) and Ray (1912–1988) Eames and Frank Lloyd Wright (1867–1959); lighting by Ingo Maurer (b. 1932); graphic design by Edward McKnight Kauffer (1890–1954), Paula Scher (b. 1948), and other contemporary designers; textile designs by the Wiener Werkstätte; Russel Wright (1904–1976) dinnerware; a large and important collection of American nineteenth- and early-twentieth-century art that includes drawings and prints by Frederic E. Church (1826–1900), Winslow Homer (1836–1910), Daniel Huntington (1816–1906), and Thomas Moran (1837–1926), housed in the Henry Luce Study Room for American Art; and more recent designs for environmentally responsible housing and transportation.

In addition to displaying objects from the permanent collections, the Cooper-Hewitt also holds important temporary exhibitions featuring and addressing both historical and contemporary design, and it also sponsors the National Design Triennial, a showcase for experimental innovations by contemporary designers.

Located on Museum Mile, at the corner of 91st Street and Fifth Avenue, the Cooper-Hewitt is open Monday through Thursday 10 a.m. to 5 p.m.; Friday 10 a.m. to 9 p.m.; Saturday 10 a.m. to 6 p.m.; Sunday 12 to 6 p.m. Weather permitting, the garden entrance on 90th Street is open May through September. Admission fees apply.

■ DYCKMAN FARMHOUSE, 1784
4881 Broadway at 204th Street
PHONE: (212) 304-9422
WEB SITE: www.dyckmanfarmhouse.org
E-MAIL: info@dyckmanfarmhouse.org

THE DYCKMAN FARMHOUSE is a typical Dutch Colonial farmhouse and the only remaining one of its kind in Manhattan. Situated in Inwood, the farm had occupied an area of several hundred acres bordering the Harlem River and originally had many cherry, peach, and apple trees. Once the largest farm in Manhattan, it now occupies the corner of Broadway and 204th Street and includes a small garden park—a country oasis amid the city.

The house was rebuilt around 1784 by William Dyckman, a descendent of one of the early settlers of New Amsterdam, after the original structure was destroyed by the British during their occupation of Manhattan between 1776 and 1783.

The house has a pitched gambrel roof and walls composed of wood, brick, and fieldstone, reflecting Dutch architectural influence. Much of the wood is hand hewn, and handmade nails are evident as are binding materials of mud and marsh grass. There is a summer kitchen at the southern end that may date to an earlier time. The grounds also include a smokehouse and military hut that were utilized during the British occupation.

The farmhouse museum contains rooms open to the public, such as a parlor and Colonial kitchen. The interior boasts Dyckman family and period furnishings assembled by a later generation of Dyckmans, who took over the property in 1915, restoring and then donating it to the city to avert development.

Museum and grounds are open to the public Wednesday through Saturday 11:00 a.m. to 4:00 p.m. and Sunday, 12:00 p.m. to 4:00 p.m. It is closed on Mondays and Tuesdays. There is a nominal entry fee and children under the age of ten are free. Reservations are required for groups of ten or more.

THE FRICK COLLECTION (1913–14)

1 East 70th Street
ARCHITECT: Thomas Hastings (1860–1929)
PHONE: (212) 288-0700
WEB SITE: www.frick.org
E-MAIL: info@frick.org

THE INDUSTRIALIST Henry Clay Frick commissioned the American architect Thomas Hastings, who also designed The New York Public Library with his partner, John Merven Carrère, to build a private residence that drew from eighteenth-century domestic architectural sources. Frick, an important collector of beautiful furnishings, decorative art, and masterworks by many of the greatest European artists, presented his impressive collection throughout his home and in rooms and galleries designed specifically for their display.

Frick, who died in 1919, bequeathed the residence and the collection to a board of trustees, which oversaw the transformation of the space by the architect John Russell Pope (1874–1937). The Frick Collection opened to the general public in 1935. Although its scale and scope cannot compare to large museums like the Metropolitan Museum, the quality of the works in this relatively small collection affords it an important place in the art world.

Among the Frick's extraordinary religious paintings is Giovanni Bellini's (c. 1430–1516) **ST. FRANCIS IN THE DESERT** (c. 1480). Considered by many Bellini's greatest work, *St. Francis in the Desert* is an arresting image of the dramatic moment when the Saint receives the stigmata. Jan van Eyck's (active 1422–1441) **VIRGIN AND CHILD WITH SAINTS AND DONOR** (c. 1441) exemplifies the Flemish artist's amazing attention to detail and his deft handling of paint.

The Frick has a particularly strong collection of portraits. In the magnificent and imposing late **SELF-PORTRAIT** (1658), Rembrandt van Rijn (1606–1669) demonstrates his painterly virtuosity and pictures himself as a confident, almost monarchic presence. Jean Auguste-Dominique Ingres's (1780–1867) outstanding **COMTESSE D'HAUSSONVILLE** (1845) is one of the French master's finest portraits. Ingres captures the accomplished countess's intelligence and beguiling sensuality in a painting that also exhibits the highly finished surfaces and the mastery of rendering fabric and texture for which he is well known.

The Frick owns three of the only thirty-five to forty paintings known to have been executed by the Dutch painter Johannes Vermeer (1632–1675). **MISTRESS AND MAID** (c. 1665–70), one of the Collection's most noteworthy genre paintings, depicts a private, domestic moment where a

Johannes Vermeer's Officer and Laughing Girl *(c.1665–1660)*

wealthy woman is surprised by the contents of a letter brought by her maid. The psychological and class drama is rendered with the greatest attention to formal detail. Vermeer's **OFFICER AND LAUGHING GIRL** (c. 1655–1660) is a particularly fine example of his handling of and preoccupation with the treatment of light, which is again apparent in **GIRL INTERRUPTED AT HER MUSIC** (1658–59), where the relationship between the viewer and the object of the gaze is complicated by the fact that the "interrupted" girl manages to in turn interrupt the viewer's process of looking with her own steady gaze.

French eighteenth-century painting is also well represented, most notably in the Fragonard Room, where Jean-Honoré Fragonard's (1732–1806) series, **THE PROGRESS OF LOVE** (1771–73), is the focus. In fact, Frick ordered that the room be totally rebuilt after purchasing the large paintings, which illustrate the four ages of love (from flirtation, to a secret meeting, to consummation or marriage, culminating in settled happiness).

In the area of landscape painting, the Frick houses several jewels, including John Constable's (1776–1837) **THE WHITE HORSE** (1819), the first of the English painter's famous "six-footers," large, six-foot canvases painted to be displayed at the Royal Academy.

The Frick is open Tuesday through Saturday 10:00 a.m. to 6:00 p.m.; Sundays 11:00 a.m. to 5:00 p.m.; closed Mondays and holidays. Admission fees apply. Audio tours are included in admission.

GENERAL GRANT NATIONAL MEMORIAL (GRANT'S TOMB), 1891–97

Riverside Drive at 122nd Street
ARCHITECT: John H. Duncan (1855–1929)
PHONE: (212) 666-1640

GRANT'S TOMB, as the memorial has become known, is the largest tomb in North America and the largest mausoleum in the Western Hemisphere. It houses the remains of General Grant and his wife, Julia Dent Grant. It is dedicated to the life and accomplishments of General Grant, who led the Union victories at the battles of Vicksburg and Chattanooga during the Civil War and eventually to General Robert E. Lee's surrender at

Appomattox. Grant served two terms as the eighteenth president of the country, from 1869 to 1877.

The memorial, in Riverside Park, overlooks the Hudson River from Morningside Heights. It was designed by architect John H. Duncan, who won a design competition for the project. The success and popularity of Grant's Tomb launched him on a successful career. The Neoclassical structure, composed of limestone, marble, and granite, is said to be modeled after the Mausoleum at Halicarnassus (Greek Ionia), and also recalls Napoleon Bonaparte's resting place, Les Invalides, and the Panthéon in Paris. There is a majestic domed rotunda under which Grant and his wife are entombed in twin black polished sarcophagi.

The monument was funded with donations of over $600,000 from about 90,000 people—the largest fundraising effort to date in America. The monument became one of the country's most popular destinations in the early twentieth century; however, during the intervening decades, Grant's Tomb eventually lost its luster as a destination. In the 1990s, however, there was great renewed interest in the Civil War, and a restoration campaign was initiated, which culminated in the monument's rededication in 1997.

As a result of the popularity of Grant's Tomb, Duncan became one of the most popular American architects of the period and was commissioned to design a number of buildings and projects in the area, including New York townhouses for wealthy clients such as Otto H. Kahn, Arthur Lehman, and the Goelets; some remaining examples of his dwellings can be seen on the Upper East Side at 21 East 84th Street; and 1132 and 1134 Madison Avenue.

Duncan also designed a war monument celebrating the Battle of Trenton, which was dedicated in 1893. Located in Trenton, New Jersey, at Warren and Broad Streets, the **TRENTON BATTLE MONUMENT** is a granite column with plaques by artists Thomas Eakins and Karl Niehaus that depict Washington and his army crossing the Delaware; the Battle of Trenton; and the surrender of the Hessians. Call (609) 737-0623 for more information.

The Grant Memorial is open 9:00 a.m. to 5:00 p.m. daily with the exception of Thanksgiving Day, Christmas Day, and New Year's Day. It is sometimes closed due to extreme inclement weather. Admission is free.

■ GRACIE MANSION, 1788

East End Avenue at 88th Street
PHONE: (212) 570-0985 or (212) 570-4751
WEB SITE: www.nyc.gov/html/om/html/gracie.html

IN 1799, A PROSPEROUS New York merchant named Archibald Gracie built a sixteen-room country house overlooking a bend in the East River, 5 miles north of the city, where he would catch the breezes off the river. He enlarged the house in 1802–4 and sold it in 1823 due to financial failures. It had several owners before it was acquired by the City of New York in 1896. Additional acreage was added that form the nearly fifteen-acre Carl Schurz Park, where the mansion is situated.

The house is styled as a country home for an elegant gentleman of his day, with fine architectural details characteristic of the Federal style. The fanlight lunette over the front door and the sidelights are typical of the era. The foyer has a *trompe l'oeil* painted floor, which makes it appear to be made of marble. The central design suggests a compass, paying homage to Gracie's business as a shipping merchant. The library has retained much of its original character; the mantel and the dentil molding date to the construction of the house in 1799. The yellow parlor dates to an early nineteenth-century addition.

The Gracie family entertained dignitaries, including Louis Philippe (later the king of France), John Quincy Adams, James Fenimore Cooper, and Washington Irving, among others. There were other country houses located nearby, including the John Jacob Astor house, whose residence was near 87th Street between York and East End Avenues.

After decades of use as a concession stand and restrooms for the park, Gracie Mansion was restored and became the first home of the Museum of the City of New York. When the museum moved to another location, Gracie Mansion became a historic house museum run by the Parks Department. Parks Commissioner Robert Moses convinced city authorities to designate it as the official residence of the mayor, and in 1942, Fiorello H. La Guardia became Gracie Mansion's first resident mayor.

The house was enlarged in 1966 with the addition of the Susan E. Wagner Wing, which includes a grand ballroom and two intimate reception rooms. It is the only house of its day in Manhattan still inhabited as a residence; it underwent a major restoration in the early 1980s.

Tours of Gracie Mansion are given at 10:00 and 11:00 a.m. and 1:00 and 2:00 p.m. on Wednesdays only from March to mid-November. Prebooking your guided tour is compulsory and reservations should be made least three weeks ahead. There is a nominal admission fee; students are free

Another structure of the period located not far away and worthy of a visit is the **MOUNT VERNON HOTEL MUSEUM AND GARDEN** located at 421 East 61st Street, which was constructed in 1799 as a carriage house for a twenty-three-acre estate on land that was owned by Abigail Adams Smith, daughter of John Adams. The carriage house was later converted to the Mount Vernon Hotel in 1826, which became a popular country resort for New Yorkers living in the crowded southern end of the island.

■ SOLOMON R. GUGGENHEIM MUSEUM, 1959

1071 Fifth Avenue (at 89th Street)
ARCHITECT: Frank Lloyd Wright (1867–1959)
PHONE: (212) 423-3500
WEB SITE: www.guggenheim.org
E-MAIL: visitorinfo@guggenheim.org

THE GUGGENHEIM MUSEUM, originally known as the Museum of Non-Objective Painting, was founded by the wealthy American industrialist Solomon R. Guggenheim. Its first home opened to the public in 1939 to display modern and contemporary art. The Guggenheim Museum in New York, which focuses primarily on modern and contemporary painting and sculpture, would expand over the years to include four other important collections in addition to Solomon Guggenheim's own collection of European abstract art by such artists as Vasily Kandinsky (1866–1944). Important additions to the Guggenheim were made with the accessioning of the Justin K. Thannhauser collection of Impressionism and Post-Impressionism; Karl Niendorf's group of works by the German Expressionists; Katherine S. Dreier's collection of the historic avant-garde; and Dr. Giuseppe Panza di Buomo's Minimalist, Environmental, and Conceptual art collection.

In 1959, the Guggenheim moved to its current home, a tour-de-force of twentieth-century architecture by the renowned American architect Frank Lloyd Wright. Wright's spiral-shaped building appears from the outside as a white architectural ribbon that subtly unfurls and becomes increasingly wider as the building reaches higher. In designing a home for modern and contemporary art, Wright deliberately turned his back on more traditional conceptions of museum architecture, which were often rooted in classicism or in the art and architecture of the past more generally. Wright said that his building would make the nearby Metropolitan Museum of Art "look like a Protestant barn."

Although celebrated for its innovations, Wright's design has been criticized because its internal spiral space, which has somewhat concave walls, makes it difficult to hang and display art, and because the narrow, artificially lit exhibition niches tend to be too dark, despite the natural light that pours in through the rotunda's extraordinary skylight. There is also the argument that such a remarkable architectural feat can overshadow the art within; however Wright's design in many ways set the tone for an important trend in twentieth- and twenty-first-century museum architecture, where it can be said that the museum building has become a work of art—an integral part of the collection itself, as demonstrated by more recent designs such as Frank Gehry's (b. 1929) Guggenheim Museum Bilbao (1997). And despite the logistical difficulties it may pose, Wright's building ultimately functions as a rather spectacular stage for the exhibition of the collection as well as the temporary shows mounted by the museum each year.

The Guggenheim's Impressionist and Post-Impressionist holdings include several major works from the period by such artists as Édouard Manet (1832–1883), Camille Pissarro (1830–1903), Paul Cézanne (1839–1906), and Vincent van Gogh (1853–1890). Manet, the painter of the infamous OLYMPIA (1863; Musée d'Orsay, Paris), who provocatively confronted the viewer with her unwavering gaze, rethinks the relationship between viewer and object in the Guggenheim's BEFORE THE MIRROR (1876). Manet depicts a corseted woman, most likely a courtesan, who turns her back to the viewer while her impressionistically painted, ambiguous reflection faces the viewer. The painting exhibits the lightened palette and short, quick brushstrokes, which mark the shift of Manet's later canvases toward Impressionism.

Three strong paintings reflect key developments in landscape painting during this period include Pissarro's **THE HERMITAGE** (c. 1867), a *plein-air* painting that registers the influence of realism and the Impressionistic interest in capturing light effects; van Gogh's **MOUNTAINS AT SAINT-RÉMY** (1889), a personalized and expressive landscape painted during a period of recovery after a mental breakdown; and Cézanne's **BIBÉMUS** (c. 1894–95), with its application of patches of color with short brushstrokes that establish both flatness and depth.

A particularly important component of the Guggenheim's twentieth-century collection is a large group of works by the Russian-born Vasily Kandinsky, who was a founder of Der Blaue Reiter (The Blue Rider), a group of German Expressionist artists working in Munich from 1911 until 1914, disbanding because of the outbreak of World War I. The scope and depth of the Kandinsky collection, which is the largest in the United States, offer a significant glimpse into the development of Kandinsky's oeuvre, beginning with such early works as **BLUE MOUNTAIN** (1908–09), featuring his signature horse and rider motif against an abstract landscape in a painting saturated with color. Kandinsky, who was concerned with art's spiritual and transformative powers, would move to develop a more abstract yet still symbolic visual vocabulary, producing such paintings as **IMPROVISATION 28** (1912). In later years, influenced in part by the Suprematist and Constructivist movements of the Russian avant-garde, with which he became familiar upon returning to Russia after the outbreak of World War I, paintings such as **IN THE BLACK SQUARE** (1923) began to display geometric abstractions.

In addition to the remarkable Kandinsky collection, German Expressionism is also well represented by such paintings as Franz Marc's (1880–1911) exuberant and brightly painted **YELLOW COW** (1911). The Dresden-based German Expressionist group Die Brücke (The Bridge) offered a vision of the modern world that was coarser, darker, and more blunt than that offered by Kandinsky's and Marc's Der Blaue Reiter paintings. In **ARTILLERYMAN** (1915), Ernst Ludwig Kirchner (1880–1938), perhaps the best-known member of the group, depicts a group of naked soldiers, whose angular bodies are claustrophobically packed together in a shower monitored by a fully clothed officer.

Given Solomon R. Guggenheim's interest in early-twentieth-century abstraction, it is natural that the museum has a strong group of works representing central artistic movements of the period. Notable among them is its collection of Cubist works by such masters as Pablo Picasso (1881–1973) and Georges Braque (1882–1963). Picasso and Braque fractured form to offer various perspectives simultaneously in faceted and often ultimately complicated and flattened compositions like Braque's **VIOLIN AND PALETTE** (1909) or Picasso's **ACCORDIONIST** (1911). In slightly later works such as **MANDOLIN AND GUITAR** (1924), Picasso's conception of Cubism evolved from the earlier Analytic Cubist paintings, toward the development of Synthetic Cubism, where instead of breaking down form and using a darker, almost monochromatic palette, he adopted a brightened color scheme and overlapping forms, in a technique that brings to mind collage. In addition to Picasso's Cubist works, the museum also displays the artist's great range with such extraordinary works as the melancholy **WOMAN IRONING** (1904) from his moody Blue Period and the sensual, abstracted rendering of **WOMAN WITH YELLOW HAIR** (1931).

The Guggenheim's paintings by Piet Mondrian (1872–1944) effectively capture the range and trajectory of his career. Mondrian was influenced by Cubism and was a member of the Dutch De Stijl movement, which practiced pure abstraction and sought to reduce form and color to express a utopian understanding of harmony and order. **TABLEAU 2** (1922), which employs primary colors within a network of rectangles and a central square outlined in black on a white background, and the extremely simplified black-on-white **COMPOSITION NO. 1** (1930), are two especially strong examples of Mondrian's work at the museum that reflect his use of the synecdochic grid.

Like Mondrian, Fernand Léger (1881–1955) was influenced by the Cubists, and his palette is also a simplified, reductive one. Léger's **THE GREAT PARADE** (1954) is a huge canvas (almost 10 feet by 13 feet) for which he made over a hundred preparatory studies. In an effort to create a truly popular art, Léger turned to a mechanical aesthetic, a nod to the importance of industrialization and the central role of the worker in an increasingly modernized and urbanized world.

New York boasts several masterworks by Marc Chagall (1887–1985), including the Guggenheim's **PARIS THROUGH THE WINDOW** (1913) and **GREEN VIOLINIST** (1923–24). Although Chagall's paintings reflect a response to contemporary artistic movements such as Orphic Cubism, characterized by overlapping vivid colors to express sensations, his work is also fantastically lyrical and highly personal.

Important examples of post-1945 work at the Guggenheim by artists associated with or influenced by the development of Abstract Expressionism include Jackson Pollock's highly gestural and haunting **OCEAN GREYNESS** (1953), one of his last significant works; Mark Rothko's (1903–1970) luminous and contemplative, stacked rectangular fields of color in such works as **UNTITLED (VIOLET, BLACK, ORANGE, YELLOW ON WHITE AND RED)** (1949); and Clyfford Still's **1948** (1948), with its earthy colors applied thickly with a palette knife.

Key movements and artists from the second half of the twentieth and from the early twenty-first centuries are also addressed by the collection. The Pop artist Andy Warhol's (1928–1987) **ORANGE DISASTER #5** (1963), with its eerie repetition of an empty electric chair, makes a statement about violence and the media by drawing from newspaper photographs. Photographer Cindy Sherman's **UNTITLED FILM STILL #15** (1978) is one of a significant series of sixty-nine fictional "film stills" that she assembled to explore the role of female sexuality in movies and their powerful influence on modern culture. The German painter Anselm Kiefer's (b. 1945) **LES REINES DE FRANCE** (1995), a layered painting consisting of emulsion, acrylic, sunflower seeds, photographs, gold leaf, and cardboard on canvas, offers an almost celebratory consideration of French history and France's female monarchs that contrasts sharply with Keifer's darker, earlier works such as **SERAPHIM** (1983–85), which addresses in symbolic terms the horrors perpetrated by the Nazis.

The Guggenheim's strong sculpture collection spans the twentieth century (and beyond, as the museum continues to grow its collection with the accessioning of contemporary art of various media). The museum holds works by the giants of twentieth-century sculpture, including Constantin Brancusi (1876–1957), Alexander Calder (1898–1976), Louise Nevelson (1899–1988), Alberto Giacometti (1901–1966), Louise Bourgeois (b. 1911), Donald Judd (1928–1994), Claes Oldenburg (b. 1929), Richard Serra (b. 1939),

David Smith (1906–1965), and Eva Hesse (1936–1970), among others.

The Romanian-born Constantin Brancusi is especially well represented with such masterworks as the marble **MUSE** (1912), which reflects his interest in simplifying form. Reducing his muse, with her ovoid-shaped head, to a few simple details, sinuous lines, and smooth surfaces, Brancusi seeks to convey an ideal. Louise Nevelson's huge **WHITE VERTICAL WATER** (1972), which comprises twenty-six sections and is 18 by 9 feet, offers an organized, almost architectural view of nature with its multiple compartments and neutralizing use of a single color; at the same time, Nevelson balances such organization by rendering organic the sculpture's component parts. Alexander Calder's large mobile **RED LILY PADS** (1956) is composed of delicate discs that gently float and literally move over the viewer as they are shifted by the air that surrounds them. Donald Judd's Minimalist **UNTITLED** (1969), a vertical stack of ten highly polished copper rectangular, box-like forms, juts out from the wall into the viewer's space, exploring mathematical repetition, the relationship of the part to the whole, and the dynamic physical relationship between viewer and object.

The museum's significant examples of installations and multimedia works include several works by Joseph Beuys (1921–1986), such as **TERREMENTO** (1981), which commemorates the loss of life in an earthquake in a small city outside of Naples. The installation, also a political statement in favor of independence for this Italian region, consists of a typesetting machine, an Italian flag, felt, nine blackboards with chalk and drawings, a metal container with fat and lead type, a cassette recorder, and a brochure.

Wright's spiral-shaped building is an incredible space for site-specific installations, and the Guggenheim frequently displays work that engages in a thought-provoking dialogue with the building itself. Richard Long's (b. 1945) 28-foot-in-diameter **RED SLATE CIRCLE** (1980), for example, which comprises 474 stones from a New York quarry, recalls the spiral when installed in the rotunda while evoking, in a very earthy and primordial way, endless paths and rocky terrains far away from the city. Other artists who have engaged in such a physically transformative dialogue with the building include Jenny Holzer (b. 1950), who lined the winding inner spiral with selections from her famous LED. **TRUISMS** series in a 1989 retrospective, and Dan Flavin (1933–1996), whose narrow, fluorescent light column **UNTITLED**

(TO TRACY, TO CELEBRATE THE LOVE OF A LIFETIME) (1992) rose through the center of the rotunda to cast it in a warm pink glow.

The Guggenheim is open Saturday to Wednesday 10 a.m. to 5:45 p.m.; Friday 10 a.m. to 7:45 p.m.; closed Thursdays. Admission fees apply. On Friday evenings beginning at 5:45 p.m. the museum has a "Pay What You Wish" program, where admission is by donation. The last tickets are issued at 7:15 p.m. The Guggenheim participates in the City Pass program, which offers a discounted rate for a combined ticket to six top attractions in the area (American Museum of Natural History, Empire State Building, Museum of Modern Art, The Metropolitan Museum of Art, Circle Line Sightseeing Cruises or Statue of Liberty).

There are parking garages within walking distance from the museum: Impark Parking located at 40 East 89th Street (between Madison and Park Avenues) and Sylvan Parking is located at 60 East 90th Street (between Madison and Park Avenues). Both lots offer a discounted rate to museum visitors with a parking ticket validated at the museum's membership desk.

THE HISPANIC SOCIETY OF AMERICA MUSEUM AND LIBRARY
613 West 155th Street
PHONE: (212) 926-2234
WEB SITE: www.hispanicsociety.org

THE HISPANIC SOCIETY OF AMERICA, founded by the philanthropist Archer Milton Huntington, is dedicated to collecting and making available to the public a wide-ranging collection of art, artifacts, and books relating to Spain, Portugal, and Latin America. The museum's Beaux-Arts-style building on the Audubon Terrace, named for the famous painter and naturalist, John James Audubon, whose farm once occupied the site, opened in 1908. Huntington, who helped develop the Audubon Terrace, envisioned the larger site as an important cultural center, and, indeed it housed and continues to house several cultural and academic institutions, including the American Academy of Arts and Letters.

The museum collection includes works by the great Spanish masters, including El Greco (1541–1614), Francisco de Zurbarán (1598–1664), Diego Velázquez (1599–1660), Bartolomé Esteban Murillo (1618–1682), and

Francisco Goya (1746–1828). The collection is also remarkable for its scope; in addition to Spanish masterworks, the museum possesses artifacts such as two complete Spanish sixteenth-century tombs, featuring remarkable sculptural programs complete with marble life-sized effigies of the deceased noblemen for whom the tombs were realized.

Among the most significant works in the Hispanic Society collection is Goya's **THE DUCHESS OF ALBA** (1797). The Duchess of Alba was an especially well-known (and somewhat notorious) woman in Spain's aristocratic circles, within which she was famous for her great beauty and sensuality and for her free-spirited ways. Here, Goya presents the confident Duchess standing against a sketchily suggested spot within the Andalusian countryside. Wearing a black mantilla over her head and a lace dress punctuated by the gold blouse and shoes and the red sash at her waist, the unconventional duchess is shown in the costume of a maja—or in the garb of a stylish, somewhat bohemian woman of the lower classes who strolled the boulevards uninhibited by aristocratic social expectations, enjoying the sights, sounds, and entertainments offered by the city.

Historians have long-believed that Goya and the duchess, whom he rendered several times, had been involved in a significant love affair. In fact, scholars point to the Hispanic Society's painting as a testament to their intimate relationship. Most noteworthy are the Duchess's two rings quite prominently displayed on her right hand: on her middle finger is an oval-shaped ring inscribed "Alba"; the ring on the adjacent index finger reads, "Goya." And, on the sand to which she points very emphatically, is the artist's signature preceded by the word, "Solo," arranged upside-down, more for her eyes than the viewers', as if to delare that for her there is "Only Goya" ("Solo Goya").

Another highlight at the Hispanic Society is the Sorolla Room, which features Joaquín Sorolla y Bastida's (1863–1923) exceptionally detailed fourteen-panel mural series, **VISION OF SPAIN** (1913–1919), a light-filled, celebratory perspective of the people, geography, and traditions of the regions of Spain. The room will reopen after renovations in early 2010.

The sculptor Anna Hyatt Huntington (1876–1973), Archer Huntington's wife, is responsible for the sculptures from Spanish history and literature that grace the museum's North terrace. The most noteworthy of these is **EL CID** (1927), the charging equestrian statue that features the famous Castilian nobleman and soldier who was known for his prowess in fighting the Moors in the eleventh century.

The museum is open Tuesday through Saturday 10:00 a.m. to 4:30 p.m.; Sunday 1:00 to 4:00 p.m.; closed on Mondays. Free 45-minute tours are offered at 2:00 p.m. on Saturdays. Admission is free.

There is limited metered parking on Broadway and free parking on 155th Street between Broadway and Riverside Drive (check signs for alternate side regulations). There is a parking garage on 153rd Street between Broadway and Riverside Drive.

LOW MEMORIAL LIBRARY, 1897
Columbia University
West 116th Street between Broadway and Amsterdam Avenue
ARCHITECT: Charles McKim (1847–1909)
  of McKim, Mead, and White

THE DOMED MONUMENTAL Low Library is the jewel and centerpiece of the Columbia University campus, whose original axial plan was conceived by the prominent architectural firm of McKim, Mead, and White. The building is modeled on the Roman Pantheon and the Greek Parthenon and is conceived in the shape of a Greek cross. It sits higher than the campus, and its entrance is dominated by a series of stairways that lead up to a monumental portico lined with grand Ionic columns; the portico is topped by a beautiful coffered ceiling. The interior is also stunning and presents a domed granite rotunda—the largest in North America—with green Irish marble columns and classicized decorative details. It is one of New York's finest examples of American Renaissance architecture. It is now dedicated to administrative use, including the visitors' center, as the building did not adequately meet the needs of its original use as a library.

The library is named for Abiel Abbot Low, father of its donor, Seth Low, class of 1870, who served in various capacities as mayor of Brooklyn, president of the university, and mayor of New York City.

In front of the building is a major sculpture of an enthroned seated figure whose hand is extended in a welcoming gesture—the *Alma Mater*. It was created by noted American sculptor Daniel Chester French (1850–1931) in 1903 and has become an emblem of the University.

■ THE METROPOLITAN MUSEUM OF ART

1000 Fifth Avenue at 82nd St.

ARCHITECT: Calvert Vaux (1824–95) and Jacob Wrey Mould
   (1825–86); Richard Morris Hunt (1827–1895)

PHONE: (212) 535-7710

WEB SITE: www.metmuseum.org

E-MAIL: customer.service@metmuseum.org

THE METROPOLITAN MUSEUM OF ART, which was established in 1872, houses a massive and encyclopedic collection of about three million objects, including paintings, sculpture, decorative arts, and artifacts such as armor, costumes, and musical instruments, just to name a few. After occupying two temporary sites, the Met hired the American architects Calvert Vaux and Jacob Wrey Mould to design a permanent home on the east side of Central Park. The original redbrick neo-Gothic structure by Vaux and Mould that opened in 1880 has been expanded many times, including a substantial addition made in 1901 by Richard Morris Hunt, who was responsible for the Beaux-Arts-style façade and the central pavilion, and the north and south wings (1911) by the famed architectural firm of McKim, Mead, and White. Currently, the museum is almost a quarter mile long and more than two million square feet.

A visit to the Metropolitan Museum, like a visit to the Louvre in Paris, can be overwhelming because of the sheer size of its physical space and of its incredible collections, which offer a comprehensive history of art with examples of the highest quality. Visitors might want to pace themselves either by allowing several hours or by making briefer visits over the course of a few days, perhaps focusing on a handful of its seemingly endless galleries in order to better savor and appreciate its numerous masterworks.

In viewing the museum's ancient collections, one often has the sense of being virtually transported geographically and chronologically. The museum has completely reassembled an actual sandstone Egyptian cult temple within its galleries. The **TEMPLE OF DENDUR** (c. 15 B.C.), which would have been submerged in the 1960s during the construction of the Aswan High Dam in Egypt, was a gift to the United States as a token of gratitude for its campaign to save Nubian monuments. The simple, classical temple was built on the banks of the Nile during the reign of the Roman Emperor Augustus to honor the goddess Isis and two deified sons of a local Nubian chieftain.

The Metropolitan's extraordinary Greek and Roman collection boasts sculptures, painted vases, and even Roman wall paintings. Treasures include the archaic Greek **KOUROS**, a sculpture from the early sixth century B.C. of a young male nude with long stylized hair and a perfectly balanced and idealized body, indicating that he has been depicted in his prime. And just as the Temple of Dendur transports the visitor to ancient Egypt, the

The Temple of Dendur *has its very own wing at The Metropolitan Museum of Art.*

reconstruction of the **CUBICULUM FROM BOSCOREALE** (40–30 B.C.) allows viewers to envision themselves within the Roman villa outside of Pompeii, the original home of these excavated wall paintings that are full of naturalistic garden scenes and exquisitely detailed architectural vistas.

Within the Islamic galleries, visitors will stumble upon the eighteenth-century Syrian **NUR AL-DIN ROOM**, yet another of the Metropolitan Museum's extraordinary array of period rooms. With its rich wood paneling painted in gesso, its stained-glass windows that filter in light, and the operating fountain that trickles water over geometrically patterned marble, the room, a former reception area for the patriarch of a wealthy family in Damascus, offers a multisensory experience and allows the eye to wander over a variety of textures and materials.

The Metropolitan's exceptional collection of Medieval and Gothic art and architecture is primarily housed at its location in Fort Tryon Park, known as **THE CLOISTERS**. A detailed description of the Cloisters and its many treasures is offered below.

Sandro Botticelli's (1445–1510) distinguished **THE ANNUNCIA-TION** (c. 1485) is among the numerous highlights of the Metropolitan's Renaissance collection. A mature, highly unified composition by the Florentine master, *The Annunciation* is an exemplar of the Renaissance values of symmetry and balance, as illustrated by the almost-perfect mirroring of the figures of Mary and the archangel Gabriel.

Other extraordinary Renaissance works at The Metropolitan include Giotto's (1267–1337) **THE EPIPHANY** (c. 1320), a carefully considered dual narrative composition on a gold ground; Raphael's (1483–1520) brilliantly colored and modeled **MADONNA AND CHILD ENTHRONED WITH SAINTS** (1504–5); the exquisite **MADONNA AND CHILD ENTHRONED WITH TWO ANGELS** (c. 1437) by Fra Filippo Lippi (c. 1406–1469); and Agnolo Bronzino's (1503–1572) **PORTRAIT OF A YOUNG MAN** (c. 1540), perhaps one of Bronzino's finest portraits, which perfectly captures the aloofness and pride of his sitter, who was likely a member of the artist's literary circle.

The Northern European Renaissance collection is also exceptionally represented by such masterworks as the small but powerful diptych (perhaps once part of a triptych) **THE CRUCIFIXION** and **THE LAST JUDGMENT** (1425–30) by Jan van Eyck (active c. 1422, d. 1441) of the Netherlands.

Highly detailed and expressive, the two vertical panels subtly organized with horizontal bands of imagery, graphically represent physical suffering, grief, and the chaos and horrors of the Last Judgment, presided over by the triumphant and enthroned Christ surrounded by his followers. In addition to Van Eyck's diptych, the Northern European Renaissance collection's highlights include Dieric Bouts's (active c. 1457, d. 1475) **VIRGIN AND CHILD,** an incredibly sensitive representation of the emotional and physical bond between mother and child; and Pieter Bruegel the Elder's (active c. 1551, d. 1569) **THE HARVESTERS** (1565), a picture of contemporary rural labor within a highly detailed, naturalistic landscape.

The museum's seventeenth-century collection of European painting and sculpture includes some of the most celebrated works of the period, including Nicolas Poussin's (1594–1665) dramatic and monumental **THE RAPE OF THE SABINE WOMEN** (1633–34); **YOUNG WOMAN WITH A WATER JUG** (early 1660s), one of only about thirty-five known works by the Dutch master Johannes Vermeer (1632–1675); El Greco's (1541–1614) striking **VIEW OF TOLEDO** (c. 1597), with its spectacular sky achieved through a vivid contrast of light and dark; several important works by Rembrandt van Rijn (1606–1669), including a wonderful late **SELF-PORTRAIT** (1660) and his famous imagining of **ARISTOTLE WITH A BUST OF HOMER** (c.1653) that brings together two literary giants of ancient Greece; and Gian Lorenzo Bernini's (1598–1680) marble **BACCHANAL: A FAUN TEASED BY CHILDREN** (1616–17), a magnificent example of the dynamic movement, detail, emotion, and even sensuality that is characteristic of the best of Baroque sculpture; and Adélaïde Labille-Guiard's (1749–1803) beautiful and historically significant **SELF-PORTRAIT WITH TWO PUPILS** (1785), a rare eighteenth-century painting depicting a woman painter at work as both artist and teacher.

Antonio Canova's (1757–1822) Neoclassical marble sculpture of the triumphant **PERSEUS WITH THE HEAD OF MEDUSA** (1804–6), whose pose brings to mind the renowned classical Apollo Belvedere (350–325 B.C.) sculpture at the Vatican, is one of the many highlights of the Metropolitan's eighteenth-century European collection. The museum's paintings from the period are equally exceptional, and among the most notable are **THE DEATH OF SOCRATES** (1787), one of the Neoclassical master Jacques-Louis David's (1748–1825) most recognized works; Jean Auguste Dominique

Ingres's (1780–1867) **PRINCESSE DE BROGLIE** (1851–53), among the last and finest of his aristocratic portraits, which displays his virtuosity and mastery of representing luxurious textures and materials; and two masterpieces of English landscape painting, John Constable's (1776–1837) naturalistic and picturesque **SALISBURY CATHEDRAL FROM THE BISHOP'S GROUNDS** (c. 1825) and Joseph Mallord William Turner's (1775–1851) more romantic **THE GRAND CANAL, VENICE** (1835).

The nineteenth-century galleries are noteworthy for such works as Rosa Bonheur's (1822–1899) monumental **THE HORSE FAIR** (1851–53) and Gustave Courbet's (1819–1877) provocative and sexual **WOMAN WITH A PARROT** (1865–66), together with Édouard Manet's (1832–1883) own **WOMAN WITH A PARROT** (1866), a response to Courbet's controversial nude. The collection also possesses numerous masterpieces by the Impressionists and Post-Impressionists, including Claude Monet's (1840–1926) studies of light effects within scenes of contemporary leisure in such

images as **WOMEN IN THE GARDEN** (1866) and **LA GRENOUILLÈRE** (1869); the Pointillist **CIRCUS SIDESHOW** (1887–88) by Georges-Pierre Seurat (1859–1891); and several portraits, landscapes, still-life paintings, and genre scenes such as **THE CARD PLAYERS** (early 1890s) by Paul Cézanne (1839–1906), among others.

The American collection is also first-rate and includes wonderful examples of eighteenth-century portraiture by artists such as John Singleton Copley (1738–1815), Ralph Earl (1751–1801), and Gilbert Stuart (1755–1828), whose highly ornamented and detailed **MATILDA STOUGHTON DE JAUDENES** (1794) is among his finest. Other American treasures include **THE OXBOW** (1836), one of the most celebrated paintings by the acknowledged father of the Hudson River School, Thomas Cole (1801–1848), a panoramic view that captures the grandeur of the Connecticut River and its unique oxbow formation after a

John Singer Sargent's elegant masterpiece, Madame X *(1883–84)*

thunderstorm; the iconic history painting **WASHINGTON CROSSING THE DELAWARE** (1851) by the German-born Emmanuel Leutze (1816–1868); John Singer Sargent's (1856–1925) notorious **MADAME X** (1883–84), which he once called, "the best thing I have done"; and several outstanding works by Mary Cassatt (1844–1926), including her confident **PORTRAIT OF THE ARTIST** (1878) and **LADY AT THE TEA TABLE** (1885), which exhibits her command of color, composition, and a nuanced and thoughtful consideration of women in domestic settings.

The giants of twentieth-century art are also well represented at the museum, with such works as Pablo Picasso's (1881–1973) portrait of **GERTRUDE STEIN** (1906), an almost sculptural, substantially modeled representation of the famous American writer; Henri Matisse's (1869–1954) joyous celebration of color, form, and movement in **NASTURTIUMS WITH "DANCE"** (1912); prominent examples of abstraction, such as Jackson Pollock's **AUTUMN RHYTHM (NUMBER 30)**, Willem de Kooning's (1904–1997) **ATTIC** (1949), and Robert Motherwell's (1915–1991) **ELEGY TO THE SPANISH REPUBLIC, 70** (1961); renowned photographs such as Edward J. Steichen's moody **THE FLATIRON** (1904); and highpoints of modern sculpture such as David Smith's (1906–1965) stainless steel **BECCA** (1965). The Met's twentieth-century collection also includes a number of fine examples of decorative arts and furnishings; Frank Lloyd Wright's (1867–1959) **LIVING ROOM FROM THE FRANCIS W. LITTLE HOUSE** (1912–14) is among the museum's unsurpassed collection of period rooms.

The Asian galleries are also remarkable for their scope and quality, with works such as the extremely large and detailed sculpture of the serene and regal **STANDING BODHISATTVA MAITREYA** (c. second–early third century) from Pakistan; the sensuously elegant **STANDING MAITREYA** (ninth–tenth centuries) from Nepal; extraordinary examples of Chinese scroll painting, including the panoramic landscape **SUMMER MOUNTAINS** (c. 1023–56) and the historical landscape **EMPEROR MING-HUANG'S FLIGHT TO SHU** (twelfth century); and the Japanese six-panel screen, **BATTLE OF THE HEIJI ERA** (c. 1600), which offers the traditional bird's-eye view found in Japanese painting and which is noteworthy for its expositional and dramatic qualities and for its exceptional composition and detail.

In the Met's numerous non-Western galleries, visitors will find a range of diverse and high quality works from various regions of the continent of Africa, including a lovely, heart-shaped, simplified and abstracted **FACE MASK** (nineteenth–twentieth century) from Gabon; displayed in the Oceanic rooms are a number of striking memorial poles (mbis) carved by the Asmat people of West New Guinea; and the Pre-Columbian collection includes sculpture, artifacts, and beautiful painted vessels such as the eighth-century Mayan **VESSEL WITH MYTHOLOGICAL SCENE**, which depicts a detailed image of the underworld.

The Metropolitan Museum of Art is open Tuesday through Thursday 9:30 a.m. to 5:30 p.m.; Friday through Saturday 9:30 a.m. to 9 p.m.; and Sunday 9:30 a.m. to 5:30 p.m. It is closed on most Mondays; check the museum's Web site for certain holiday exceptions. Admission with a suggested donation. The Metropolitan Museum participates in the City Pass program, which offers a discounted rate for a combined ticket to six top attractions in the area (American Museum of Natural History, Empire State Building, Museum of Modern Art, Guggenheim Museum, Circle Line Sightseeing Cruises or Statue of Liberty).

The museum's parking garage is located at 80th Street; discounted rates are available with parking ticket validation at the Uris Center Information Desk near the 81st Street entrance.

■ **THE CLOISTERS**
Fort Tryon Park
PHONE: (212) 923-3700
WEB SITE: www.metmuseum.org (choose Cloisters collection link)
E-MAIL: cloisters@metmuseum.org

LOCATED IN FORT TRYON PARK, near the northern tip of Manhattan, the Cloisters, a branch of The Metropolitan Museum, is home to some of the finest examples of art and architecture from medieval Europe. The space itself is meant to transport the visitor back to the Middle Ages. The museum's building and its cloistered gardens have been assembled in part by piecing together actual medieval architectural and sculptural elements imported from five French cloisters and other monastic sites in southern France.

The Cloisters was initially established by the American sculptor George Grey Barnard (1863–1938), who made his living as a dealer of medieval art. Bernard managed to export from France a shipload of Romanesque and Gothic art and architecture and sculpture right before a French law went into effect prohibiting the removal of France's "cultural heritage." He used these materials to open a public museum, which he named the Cloisters. John D. Rockefeller Jr. later purchased Bernard's entire collection and funded the creation of a new museum in Fort Tryon, which he donated to the Met and opened to the public in 1938. The new museum building was designed by Charles Collens (1873–1956), who designed the building in a generalized and simplified medieval style and who incorporated architectural and sculptural elements exported by Bernard. Joseph Breck (1885–1933), a curator of decorative arts and assistant director of the Metropolitan, and James J. Rorimer (1905–1966), who would later be named director, were primarily responsible for the interior. The Cloisters collection contains approximately 5,000 works of medieval European art, most of which date from the twelfth through the fifteenth centuries.

Among the highlights of its manuscript collection are an early fifteenth-century French illuminated book of hours, **LES BELLES HEURES DE JEAN DUC DE BERRY** (15th century), by the Limbourg brothers and the **BOOK OF HOURS OF JEANNE D'ÉVREUX**, Queen of France (c. 1325–28) by Jean Pucelle. **LES BELLES HEURES**, a private devotional book, is a sumptuously illuminated manuscript that demonstrates a synthesis of Northern and Italian stylistic and iconographic concerns. Jean Pucelle's book of hours is noteworthy for its stylistic innovations and for its humorous marginalia, peripheral illustrations that helped juxtapose the profane with the central sacred imagery of the manuscript.

The Annunciation Tryptich
*(detail) by Robert Campin
(c. 1425)*

Robert Campin's (d. 1444) **THE ANNUNCIATION TRIPTYCH** (The Merode Altarpiece, c. 1425), is an extraordinary example of fifteenth-century Southern Netherlandish painting which reflects a remarkable attention to detail. Through his mastery of architectural details and illusionistic effects, Campin simulates the experience of looking through a tripartite window in this altarpiece.

THE UNICORN TAPESTRIES (1495–1505) is a beautiful group of seven wool and silk Southern Netherlandish tapestries, complexly woven using silver and gilded threads to render magical scenes featuring the mythical unicorn.

The gilded silver RELIQUARY SHRINE (second quarter of the fourteenth century), attributed to Jean de Touyl (d. 1349), is noteworthy for its gorgeous Gothic architectural details, including arches, vaults, and sculptural decorations. Scenes from the life of the Virgin Mary and the infant Christ have been rendered with translucent enamel panels, evoking stained glass windows.

In addition to displaying the art and architecture of the Middle Ages, the Cloisters tries to recapture medieval horticultural practices with gardens planted in accordance with information found in a variety of scientific treatises and other archival materials and with ideas borrowed from the visual information provided by the art of the period.

The Cloisters is open Tuesday to Sunday 9:30 a.m. to 4:45 p.m. (November to February); 9:30 a.m. to 5:15 p.m. (March to October). It is closed January 1, Thanksgiving Day, and December 25. Collection tours are at 3:00 p.m. Tuesday through Friday and on Sunday; tours are free with museum admission, which is a suggested donation. No reservations necessary. Free city parking is available in Fort Tryon Park.

■ MORRIS-JUMEL MANSION (ROGER AND MARY PHILIPSE MORRIS HOUSE), 1765; REMODELED CA. 1810
65 Jumel Avenue, 160th Street at Edgecombe Avenue
PHONE: (212) 923-8008
WEB SITE: www.morrisjumel.org

LOCATED ON A BREEZY hilltop known as Mount Morris in Upper Manhattan, the Morris-Jumel Mansion is New York's oldest home. The residence also has historical significance for having served as headquarters to

General Washington in September and October of 1776. After Washington's departure, the mansion hosted various British and Hessian military leaders, and served as an inn before reverting back to a country residence.

The Morris estate, which originally encompassed more than 130 acres, had views of the Harlem River, the Bronx, and Long Island Sound to the east, New York City and the harbor to the south, and the Hudson River and Jersey Palisades to the west.

The house was built by Roger Morris, who was an aid to George Washington. Built in the Georgian Federal style, the Morris-Jumel house has a two-story portico with a fanlight supported by Doric columns, with the door and fanlight window design repeated on the second floor. The house has what is believed to be the first-ever octagonal room at the rear of the house. Built of brick, the façade is of wooden boards that simulate stone with quoins in the corners. The hipped roof and balustrade on the widow's walk add decorative details to the classic architecture.

Subsequent ownership of the house passed through a number of hands. In 1810, the structure was restored to its original purpose as a country house by the French emigrant Stephen Jumel and his wife, Eliza. The Jumels renovated the house in the fashionable Federal style and added new doorways and stained glass to the façade and furnished much of the house in the French Empire style. Many of those objects, including a bed said to have belonged to the Emperor Napoleon, remain in the museum house.

Stephen Jumel died in 1832, and Eliza, then one of the wealthiest women in New York, later married the former vice president, Aaron Burr. Their marriage lasted only two years. Eliza retained ownership of the property until her death in 1865. After a twenty-year court battle finally settled by the U.S. Supreme Court, the property was divided and sold. The structure survived, although on a smaller plot of land, and had a number of owners until it was acquired by the City of New York in 1903 for its historical value.

The first floor includes a parlor in which Eliza Jumel married Aaron Burr in 1833. The basement houses a typical kitchen of the Colonial period with the original hearth and a beehive oven and a collection of early American cooking utensils. Through its architecture and collection of decorative arts objects, each room tells part of the story of the colorful history of the Morris-Jumel Mansion.

The house is open 10:00 a.m. to 4:00 p.m. every day except Monday and Tuesday, when it is open by appointment only. The museum is closed on the following holidays: New Year's Day, Memorial Day, Independence Day, Labor Day, Thanksgiving Day, and Christmas Day.

There is a nominal admission fee. Guided tours for walk-in visitors are available only on Saturdays at noon. Due to limited capacity, group tours must be scheduled in advance.

NATIONAL ACADEMY OF DESIGN

1083 Fifth Avenue at 89th Street
PHONE: (212) 369-4880
www.nationalacademy.org
E-MAIL: info@nationalacademy.org

THE NATIONAL ACADEMY OF DESIGN was founded in 1825 by leading artists of the day, including Samuel F. B. Morse (1791–1872), Asher B. Durand (1796–1886), and Thomas Cole (1801–1848). Its mission was to promote art in America through exhibition and education, and to achieve that end, the Academy established a school and a juried annual exhibition of contemporary art. Since its inception, the academy has selectively elected members whose accomplishments and achievements rank them among the best American artists.

It was not until 1865 that the previously itinerant academy was located to a permanent home where it could house its school, its exhibitions, and its collection. The academy remained in a Venetian Renaissance-style building until that space was sold in 1900. The academy moved to its current location, the five-story former home of the philanthropist and scholar Archer Milton Huntington and his wife, the sculptor Anna Hyatt Huntington (1870–1955), in 1942. In 1913, Huntington purchased the property and commissioned the architect and interior designer Ogden Codman Jr. (1863–1951) to enlarge and remodel the home into the Beaux-Arts style mansion that was eventually donated to the academy. Considered a preeminent tastemaker in his day, Codman, who coauthored *The Decoration of Houses* (1897) with Edith Wharton, added, among other details, the stunning domed circular stairwell.

The tradition of requiring inductees to donate to the academy a representative work has allowed the museum to amass a comprehensive collection that reflects many of the high points of American art history. Although the academy has been criticized for being too academic and not cutting-edge enough for an organization that supports contemporary art with its annual exhibitions, its membership still reads like a "who's who" of American artists.

Some of the highlights of the collection include Anna Hyatt Huntington's elegant bronze sculpture **DIANA** (1922), which graces the rotunda; the Hudson River School painter Frederic Edwin Church's (1826–1900) panoramic and luminous **SCENE ON THE MAGDALENE** (1854); William Merritt Chase's (1849–1916) moody **YOUNG GIRL (OR) AN IDLE MOMENT (OR) AT HER EASE** (1890) that recalls and recasts in shades of red James McNeill Whistler's (1834–1903) famous rendering of his mother from 1871; the sculptor Louise Bourgeois's (b. 1911) **UNTITLED (GERMINAL)** (1967), a bronze bowl of delicate, phallic forms; and the Photorealist Chuck Close's (b. 1940) **SELF-PORTRAIT** (1988), which reflects the grid technique for which he is well known.

In addition to exhibiting some of its immense permanent collection on a rotating basis and hosting juried annual exhibitions, the National Academy also presents important temporary exhibitions of American art throughout the year.

The National Academy is open Wednesday and Thursday 12:00 to 5:00 p.m.; Friday through Sunday 11:00 a.m. to 6:00 p.m. The museum is closed Monday and Tuesday. Admission fees apply.

■ NEUE GALERIE NEW YORK, 1914

1048 Fifth Avenue (at 86th Street)
ARCHITECT: John Merven Carrère (1858–1911)
    and Thomas Hastings (1860–1929)
PHONE: (212) 628-6200
WEB SITE: www.neuegalerie.org
E-MAIL: museum@neuegalerie.org

NEUE GALERIE NEW YORK, which houses one of the finest collections of twentieth-century German and Austrian art, opened in 2001 in an extraordinary remodeled former Fifth Avenue mansion originally built in 1914 by the renowned Beaux-Arts-style architects John Merven Carrère and

Thomas Hastings, who were also responsible for the **NEW YORK PUBLIC LIBRARY**, the **FRICK COLLECTION** (see p. 14) building, the Standard Oil building, and the Cathedral of St. John the Divine.

German Expressionism, the Vienna Secession, the Bauhaus, and the Wiener Werkstäte are well represented at the museum, allowing the viewer to better understand the close, symbiotic relationship between the fine and decorative arts that artists of several of these twentieth-century movements

According to press reports, Klimt's Adele Bloch-Bauer I *(1907) was sold in 2006 for US $135 million to Ronald Lauder's Neue Galerie; that price was a record for any painting.*

explored and emphasized. The collection of the Neue Galerie is divided into two sections. The second floor of the museum houses works of fine art and decorative art from early twentieth-century Austria, including paintings; and the third floor exhibits various German works from the same era, including art movements such as Der Blaue Reiter (The Blue Rider), Die Brücke (The Bridge), and the Bauhaus, The Neue Galerie has fine examples of work from artists Max Beckmann (1884–1950), Ernst Ludwig Kirchner (1880–1938), Egon Schiele (1890–1918), László Moholy-Nagy (1895–1946), and designer-architect Josef Hoffmann (1870-1956), among others.

The jewel of the collection is Gustav Klimt's (1862–1918) **ADELE BLOCH-BAUER I** (1907). In a work that reflects Klimt's signature "Golden Style," the painter characteristically combines oil paints with gold and silver to create shimmering, decorative mosaic patterns that merge with the figure of Adele to become at once background and subject. In this painting, Klimt, the foremost painter of the Vienna Secession, the Austrian Art Nouveau movement, offers a penetrating portrait of a woman whose intelligence and sensuality are intermingled in ways that parallel the complexities of the painting as a whole.

The Neue Galerie is open Saturday, Sunday, and Monday 11:00 a.m. to 6:00 p.m.; Friday 11:00 a.m. to 9:00 p.m. It is closed Tuesday and Wednesday. Admission fees apply; audio tours are available with admission. Free guided tours are offered with admission on Saturdays and Sundays at 2:00 p.m. Parking is available in a commercial garage on 86th Street across from the Galerie.

◼ NEW-YORK HISTORICAL SOCIETY

170 Central Park West (between 76th and 77th Streets)
PHONE: (212) 873-3400
WEB SITE: www.nyhistory.org
E-MAIL: webmaster@nyhistory.org

THE NEW-YORK HISTORICAL SOCIETY was founded in 1804 and houses a wide-ranging collection of art, artifacts, and various documents, newspapers, and manuscripts that help reflect four centuries of American history and culture, with a special emphasis on New York City and State.

The collection displays extraordinarily strong examples of landscape painting by the Hudson River School painters, not the least of which is the monumental five-painting cycle, **THE COURSE OF EMPIRE** (1834–36), by Thomas Cole (1801–48). Cole was perhaps the foremost of the Hudson

A watercolor from John James Audubon's Birds of America

River School painters who sought to capture the beauty of the American landscape in the early to mid-nineteenth century. The almost operatic series serves in some respects as a cautionary tale with regard to an ideology of manifest destiny. Though the first use of the phrase "manifest destiny" post-dates *The Course of Empire* by about ten years, the notion of civilization marching forward and the belief that it was America's destiny to expand and grow stronger had a long history. For example, Benjamin Franklin wrote in 1789, "America, an immense territory, favored by nature with all advantages of climate, soil, great navigable rivers and lakes, must become a great country, populous and mighty; and will, in a less time than is generally conceived, be able to shake off shackles that may be imposed on her and perhaps place them on the imposers."

Cole's series celebrates the unspoiled American landscape, beginning with THE SAVAGE STATE and THE PASTORAL OR ARCADIAN STATE. At the same time, Cole visualizes the extraordinary possibilities of the process of civilization and expansion in THE CONSUMMATION OF EMPIRE. However, the series crescendos and culminates with DESTRUCTION AND DESOLATION, warning of the cyclical character of nature and of history.

THE COURSE OF EMPIRE was donated to the society along with a number of other notable works in the collection of Luman Reed, an important early-nineteenth-century patron. In his lifetime, Reed expressed an interest in sharing his collection with the public, opening his personal gallery, housed on the top floor of his Greenwich Street mansion, to the city once a week. The society has tried to recapture what must have been a remarkable semipublic/semiprivate, nineteenth-century viewing experience by establishing the Luman Reed Gallery on its second floor, where Cole's COURSE OF EMPIRE can be viewed along with works by other significant nineteenth-century American artists.

The society also owns the 431 known original watercolors that were the preparatory works for John James Audubon's (1785–1851) masterpiece, BIRDS OF AMERICA, which was engraved and published between 1827 and 1838. Audubon, who was also an ornithologist, naturalist, and hunter, set out to study and depict the birds of North America in extraordinary detail, in works that are as remarkable for their scientific contributions as they are for their artistic ones.

Other highlights at the New-York Historical Society include Eastman

Johnson's (1824–1906) **NEGRO LIFE IN THE SOUTH (OLD KENTUCKY HOME)** (1857), an important nineteenth-century genre picture, which presents a consideration of black life and slavery. Johnson sensitively offers a multifigure domestic scene, depicting several black figures, all with noticeably different skin tones from one another, perhaps to address the complicated question of miscegenation. Though the title suggests that the painting's domestic scene is set against the backdrop of a ramshackle house somewhere in the South, it is generally agreed that Johnson was actually responding to conditions he witnessed in his own city of Washington, D.C., where Southern congressmen, for example, were known to bring their slaves during their tenure in the city.

The New-York Historical Society also houses important, sometimes historic examples of furniture and decorative arts. Highlights include George Washington's inaugural armchair and Valley Forge camp bed, and a chair (1779) made for Queen Marie-Antoinette's private chambers in Versailles and later purchased by the American ambassador to France.

Among the Society's decorative art jewels is one of the world's most comprehensive and important collections of **TIFFANY LAMPS**, a collection of 132 pieces donated by Dr. Egon Neustadt. Louis Comfort Tiffany (1848–1933) was known for his extraordinary, multicolored, nature-inspired glassworks, which include lamps, stained glass windows, and other decorative objects that reflect the influence of the Art Nouveau movement in America.

Neustadt was one of the foremost collectors of works by the Tiffany Studios. Neustadt demonstrated his encyclopedic knowledge of Tiffany in his book, *The Lamps of Tiffany* (1970). The numerous works remaining in his collection after his gift to the New York Historical Society became part of the **NEUSTADT COLLECTION OF TIFFANY GLASS** when Neustadt died in 1984. The collection includes lamps, windows, metalwork, and a unique group of pieces of flat and pressed glass used to create the windows, mosaics, and lamps for which Tiffany is so well known. Parts of the Neustadt Collection of Tiffany Glass are always on display in the Neustadt Gallery at the **QUEENS MUSEUM OF ART**. The Queens Museum is located at Flushing Meadows Corona Park, Queens. It is open Wednesday to Friday, 10 a.m. to 5 p.m.; Saturday and Sunday 12 to 5 p.m. Admission fees apply. For more information, call (718) 592-9700.

The New-York Historical Society is open Tuesday to Saturday from 10:00 a.m. to 6:00 p.m.; Sunday 11:00 a.m. to 5:45 p.m. Admission fees generally apply; however on Fridays from 6:00 to 8:00 p.m., the museum can be accessed for free. Docent-led tours are offered twice daily and are free with admission. Check the Web site for times. The museum's collection of more than 60,000 works can also be viewed online at emuseum.nyhistory.org.

Public parking garages are located at 203 West 77th Street, 207 West 76th Street and 201 West 75th Street, all between Broadway and Amsterdam Avenue.

WHITNEY MUSEUM OF AMERICAN ART, 1966
945 Madison Avenue at 75th Street
ARCHITECT: Marcel Breuer (1902–1981)
PHONE: (212) 570-3600 or (212) 570-3676;
  or tickets: 1-877-WHITNEY
WEB SITE: www.whitney.org

THE WHITNEY MUSEUM houses one of the world's foremost collections of twentieth-century American art—approximately 12,000 works encompassing painting, sculpture, multimedia, drawings, prints, and photography. The history of the museum began in 1918 as the Whitney Studio Club—an exhibition space on West 8th Street founded by artist, patron, and collector Gertrude Vanderbilt Whitney (1875–1942). She was the eldest surviving daughter of Cornelius Vanderbilt II and a great-granddaughter of Commodore Cornelius Vanderbilt; she married the wealthy Harry Payne Whitney. The museum's second home was on West 54th Street. By 1929, Whitney, a passionate collector of modern art, had amassed nearly 700 works of contemporary American art, which she offered to **THE METROPOLITAN MUSEUM OF ART**. The gift was rejected and Whitney instead founded her own museum—the Whitney Museum of American Art—in 1931.

At the time of the opening, Whitney acquired more work to provide a more thorough overview of American art in the early decades of the century. She favored independent artists, particularly those associated with realism and American Scene paintings such as Robert Henri (1865–1929), John Sloan (1871–1951), George Luks (1867–1933), Everett Shinn (1876–1953), Edward

Hopper (1882–1967), John Steuart Curry (1897–1946), and Thomas Hart Benton (1889–1975). Her collection also had a significant representation of modernist artists, including Stuart Davis (1894–1964), Charles Demuth (1883–1935), Charles Sheeler (1883–1965), Max Weber (1881–1961), and others.

Although Whitney generously funded acquisitions over the next twenty years, the collection was also built through acquiring work of contemporary artists, particularly out of their annual exhibitions, and more recently, the Biennial, as it continues to do to this day. Although the Whitney's acquisition budget was always rather modest, the museum makes the most of its resources by purchasing the work of living artists, particularly those whose reputations have yet to be established.

Edward Hopper and Reginald Marsh (1898–1954) began showing at the Whitney Studio Club in the 1920s and both continued to exhibit at the museum. In appreciation of the Whitney's enduring support of their art, Josephine Nivison Hopper and Felicia Marsh, the artists' widows, made substantial bequests of their husbands' works to the museum. Today, the Whitney holds the world's largest collection of Hopper's art—more than 2,500 oils and works on paper, including two of his iconic images, **EARLY SUNDAY MORNING** (1930) and **RAILROAD SUNSET** (1929). The museum's Marsh collection numbers nearly 200 works in all media, among them a number of the artist's best-known paintngs, such as **WHY NOT USE THE "L"?** (1930) and **TWENTY CENT MOVIE** (1936).

The Whitney Museum also has the largest body of work by Alexander Calder (1898–1976) in any museum, including his popular **CIRCUS** (c. 1926–31) as well as his large-scale mobiles and stabiles. Other in-depth concentrations include major holdings by Marsden Hartley (1877–1943), Georgia O'Keeffe (1887–1986), Charles Burchfield (1893–1967), Gaston Lachaise (1882–1935), Louise Nevelson (1899–1988), and Agnes Martin (1912–2004).

Other highlights of the permanent collection include Ashcan painters William Glackens's **HAMMERSTEIN'S ROOF GARDEN** (1902) and Robert Henri's **PORTRAIT OF GERTRUDE VANDERBILT WHITNEY** (1915–16) and **LAUGHING CHILD** (1907). Two Precisionist masterpieces—Charles Demuth's **MY EGYPT** (1927) and Charles Sheeler's **RIVER ROUGE** (1932) are also in the permanent collection: **MY EGYPT** is a view of a grain elevator in Demuth's hometown of Lancaster, Pennsylvania and **RIVER ROUGE** is derived from a commission Demuth received from the Ford Motor Plant in River Rouge, Michigan. On the cusp between representation and abstraction, the Precisionists streamlined form and celebrated the abstract and severe and spare forms of geometry seen in machines and the industrial world.

Other masterpieces of American art include: Stuart Davis, **EGGBEATER NO. 1**, (1927), one of a breakthrough series of works in American abstraction; George Tooker's masterwork **THE SUBWAY** (1950), which is a definitive statement of urban anxiety and despair; and Max Weber's **CHINESE RESTAURANT** (1915), an early example of American Cubism. Weber was one of the earliest of the Americans to bring back ideas about European modernism to this country. The **PASSION OF SACCO AND VANZETTI** by Social Realist Ben Shahn (1898–1969) is his most well-known painting. Executed in tempera, the composition depicts the funeral of the two immigrants who were accused of murder and sentenced to death after a dubious and scandalous trial. A three-panel marble and enamel mosaic was commissioned by Syracuse University in 1967 and Shahn again chose to represent this theme. Other unforgettable works include Jasper Johns (b. 1930), **THREE FLAGS** (1958), one of his signature encaustic flag images. Also a work of an enormously compelling nature is Edward Kienholz's (1927–1994) **THE WAIT**, (1964–65), which is a room-size tableau, powerfully addressing the theme of old age and death in a harsh and biting moral and social commentary.

Besides the Whitney Museum permanent collection, the building itself is a work of art. Designed by Bauhaus-trained, Hungarian-born architect Marcel Breuer, the 1966 building is a fine example of Brutalism. Its inverse-stepped ziggurat-like structure sheathed in granite with an open forecourt and the use of precast concrete are defining traits of this style of architecture. Brutalist buildings usually

The Whitney Museum of Art, designed by Marcel Breuer (1966), is a fine example of mid-century Brutalism.

exhibit repetitive geometric or block forms that reveal the texture of wooden forms used to shape the material, which is most often poured concrete. The Whitney Museum building has achieved recognition as one of New York's unique and identifiable buildings, mirroring the museum's history and dedication to art of the American avant-garde.

The museum is closed Monday and Tuesday. It is open Wednesday, Thursday, Saturday, and Sunday, 11:00 a.m. to 6:00 p.m., and Friday from 1:00 p.m. to 9:00 p.m. Admission is charged, though it is free to members and children under twelve.

MIDTOWN

AMERICA TODAY MURAL (1930–32)
AXA Equitable Building Lobby
787 Seventh Avenue at 51st Street
ARCHITECT: Thomas Hart Benton (1889–1975)

THOMAS HART BENTON'S monumental **AMERICA TODAY** mural, originally executed for the New School for Social Research, was Benton's first complete mural painted after making several trips across the country to study and sketch the people, places, and industries that made up modern American life.

Taking a vignette approach to painting the industrialized America he had studied, he created panels entitled **CITY ACTIVITIES WITH DANCE HALL; CITY ACTIVITIES WITH SUBWAY; CITY BUILDING; COAL; STEEL; CHANGING WEST; MIDWEST; DEEP SOUTH; INSTRUMENTS OF POWER**; and **OUTREACHING HANDS**. These almost operatic panels reflect Benton's characteristic figural distortions and exaggerations, which manage to be both modern, like his subjects, and partially indebted to historical precedents, like El Greco's (1541–1614) mannerist paintings.

To deal with the problem of organization in such an epic mural series, Benton created Art Deco moldings to separate his scenes. The geometric and even decorative qualities of the moldings offer a nod to more abstract, modernist art. Benton's insistence on their variations and irregularities echo the heightened energies and rhythms of the scenes within the murals.

Benton's mural is but one of several fine examples of modern art on view within the public spaces of the Equitable Building. The Minimalist Sol LeWitt's (1928–2007) **WALL DRAWING: BANDS OF LINES IN FOUR COLORS AND FOUR DIRECTIONS SEPARATED BY GRAY BANDS** (1984–85) is a group of six murals that were part of LeWitt's larger series of wall drawings, about which he once said, "I wanted to do a work of art as two-dimensional as possible." The wall is always integral to the works in this series. In LeWitt's words, "Different kinds of walls make for different kinds of drawings." LeWitt painted several such "drawings" on walls throughout New York City, including at the Jewish Museum, the Whitney Museum, the Museum of Modern Art, the Embassy Suites Hotel at Battery Park City, the New School University, and Christie's.

Also on view at the Equitable Building are murals by two giants of the Pop Art movement: Roy Lichtenstein's (1923–1997) pun-filled **MURAL WITH BLUE BRUSHSTROKE** (1984–85) and James Rosenquist's (b. 1933) **NASTURTIUM SALAD** (1984), which displays his signature crosshatch technique.

■ CHANIN BUILDING, 1929
122 East 42nd Street
ARCHITECT: Sloan & Robertson

BUILT BY IRWIN CHANIN (1891–1988) a builder and trained architect who worked closely with Sloan & Robertson on the design, the Chanin Building is one of the finest and most exuberantly decorated Art Deco buildings in New York. The building reflects the luxurious use of materials such as bronze, Belgian marble, and terra-cotta, with elaborate detailing inspired by French Art Deco.

It is a fifty-six-floor, steel-frame structure with soaring vertical emphasis that is composed of a limestone base and a buff brick exterior that is accented with stepped buttresses. The corners of the building are highlighted with finlike protrusions—a typical Deco motif. The building has a setback in accordance with zoning laws established in 1916, and from the street, decorative elements such as a bronze band that depicts the theory of evolution from primitive life forms to the development of birds are visible, as well as a terra-cotta frieze of stylized plant forms by the Deco artist René

Paul Chambellan (1893–1955), who specialized in architectural sculpture and was popular in the 1920s.

It is the two lobbies that are the building's most extraordinary features. Designer Jacques Delamarre, who worked with Chanin on the decoration, was inspired by the luxurious and more highly decorative French Art Deco style. There is the use of marble for architectural details. Elaborate metalwork designs can be seen in the grills, screens, mailboxes, and elevator doors, which derive from Cubism and Futurism. A series of metal bas-reliefs in the lobby outline intellectual and physical pursuits in stylized cubist figures. Deco motifs such as rays, coils, zigzags, chevrons, and thunderbolts abound and are combined with curvilinear forms that leave little surface area left undecorated. The lobby is a sight not to be missed for Art Deco enthusiasts.

■ **CHAPEL OF THE GOOD SHEPHERD, 1977**
Saint Peter's Church
619 Lexington Avenue at 54th Street
Louise Nevelson (1899–1988)
PHONE: (212) 935-2200
WEB SITE: www.saintpeters.org
E-MAIL: Administrator@saintpeters.org

LOUISE NEVELSON'S five-walled chapel, which is a mere 28 by 21 feet, offers visitors an intimate spiritual and contemplative experience. Nevelson's extraordinary white sculptural program presents abstract interpretations of traditional Christian subjects, including the Trinity, the Cross of the Resurrection, and the Cross of the Good Shepherd.

One of the most celebrated sculptors of the twentieth century, Nevelson used ordinary, discarded materials to assemble sculptures that she painted monochromatically, often using either black, white, or gold. In the Chapel of the Good Shepherd, Nevelson significantly chooses to work in white. Her white sculptures against a backdrop of white walls, frosted white windows, and bleached ash floors and pews emphasize light, creating a meditative space that recalls the New Testament scripture, "God is light, and in him no darkness at all." Still, despite the fact that her abstract sculptural program relates to Christian subjects, Nevelson, who was Jewish, strived to move beyond religious differences and to create a transcendent spiritual experience.

Manhattan boasts other noteworthy examples of Nevelson's work, including **SHADOWS AND FLAGS** (1977) in the Louise Nevelson Plaza in Legion Memorial Square at Maiden Lane and William and Liberty Streets. In a city landscape punctuated by skyscrapers and pedestrians, Nevelson's six black sculptures that accentuate verticality speak to the urban experience and bring to mind Nevelson's own admission: "New York represents the whole of my conscious life . . . many of my works are real reflections of the city."

The Nevelson Chapel is open 8:00 a.m. to 9:00 p.m. every day. In the summer months, call ahead for closing schedules, particularly for evening visits. Worship services are held on weekdays at 12:15 p.m., Wednesdays at 6:00 p.m., Sundays at 8:45 a.m. and 1:30 p.m. (The 1:30 mass is in Spanish.) The general public may attend the services.

CHRYSLER BUILDING, 1930

405 Lexington Avenue at 42nd Street
ARCHITECT: William Van Alen (1883–1954)

THE CHRYSLER BUILDING is an iconic building by William Van Alen whose Art Deco design epitomizes the machine age. This building was one of the first to have stainless steel overlaying a vast portion of its exterior. The seventy-story building with a stepped, arched tower augmented by the extended spire briefly won the competition for the title of world's tallest building, until it was surpassed in height by the **EMPIRE STATE BUILDING** in 1931. It still reigns as the world's largest brick building.

The Art Deco style of the structure incorporates many different types of design motifs, such as sunbursts, basket weave, chevron, and zigzags, but the forms are all based on geometric shapes. The exterior body of the building is composed of white and dark gray brick, and these decorative details can be seen from the street.

Ground was broken for the building in 1928 and construction was completed in 1930. Van Alen designed the structure on speculation and

Walter P. Chrysler assumed the lease and exerted influence on the results, including the request for a distinctive tower and automotive symbols. On the corners of the thirty-first floor are decorative replicas of Chrysler radiator caps. The corner stainless steel eagle gargoyles that grace the setbacks of the sixty-first floor are taken from the 1929 Chrysler hood ornament. There is a frieze of decorative elements that derive from hubcaps and mudguards on the setback at the tower base, and other decorative details taken from automobile designs are incorporated into the exterior.

The building's sleek stepped forms narrow and culminate in its graceful spire. Black Belgian granite arches over the entrance lead into an exceptionally elegant lobby. Red Moroccan marble walls complement the yellow Siena marble floor, and decorative motifs abound in the lobby. The elevators are composed of steel, aluminum, onyx, and exotic wood. There is a ceiling mural in the lobby by Edward Trumbull (1884–1968) entitled **TRANSPORT AND HUMAN ENDEAVOR** that celebrates advances in modern technology.

The most exceptional feature of the structure is its crowning tower. It is created from seven terraced radiating arches clad in stainless steel with linear ribs that glint and refract light, calling attention to the structure from a considerable distance.

■ **EMPIRE STATE BUILDING, 1931**
350 Fifth Avenue between 33rd and 34th Streets
ARCHITECT: William F. Lamb (1883–1952),
    and Shreve, Lamb, and Harmon
PHONE: (212) 736-3100
WEB SITE: www.esbnyc.com

THE EMPIRE STATE BUILDING was the tallest building in the world at the time of its completion in 1931, surpassing the previous record held by the **CHRYSLER BUILDING;** it remained the tallest in the world until the completion of the World Trade Center in 1972. One hundred and three floors, the building is 1,454 feet to the top of the lightning rod. William F. Lamb was the chief designer of the structure, which was inspired by the form of a pencil. A steel frame with stone cladding, the design is a stripped-down Art Deco style that makes effective use of setbacks, which also emphasize the verticality of the tower.

William Lamb, an architect at the firm Shreve, Lamb and Harmon, was chosen to design the Empire State Building. His design was influenced by the perpendicular style of another architect, Eliel Saarinen, whose 1922 second-place competition entry presages the style of the Empire State Building in its scale, modest decoration, and soaring lines. The base of the building is five stories above street level, the entrance is four stories high, and the lobby is three floors high. There are large setbacks on the fifth floor and from there the building soars without a break to the eighty-sixth floor. The various setbacks give the building a sense of balance and monumentality.

While the plan for the building was conceived by General Motors vice president John Raskob during the 1920s, work on the structure started in March of 1930, after the stock market crash, and though its construction was completed, much of its office space went unrented for some time. The building was not profitable until 1950. It is made of Indiana limestone and granite with aluminum-lined mullions and there are 6,500 windows, with spandrels sandblasted to blend their tone to that of the windows. This created the visual effect of vertical striping on the façade. The windows and spandrels are also flush with the limestone facing—an aesthetic and economic decision. There were many time-saving measures implemented in the construction of the building, which was completed in record time—in one year and forty-five days.

Some standout Art Deco features of the building are the modernistic entrances on 33rd and 34th Streets that include stainless steel canopies, with the four-story streamlined motif rising above the canopies. From the center are geometric glass and aluminimun architectural adornments that evoke mullions in church stained glass windows.

Behind this, the interior lobby boasts two-story-high corridors around the elevator core. These are crossed by stainless steel and glass-enclosed bridges at the second-floor level. The lobby layout has all hallways leading to the elevators and is decorated with marble and aluminum detailing. The centerpiece of the lobby is an aluminum relief, three stories high, of the skyscraper without the antenna, which was not added until 1952 to make it taller. There are motifs of bridges and the industries that reference the construction of the building.

The building has eighty-five stories of commercial and office space and an indoor and outdoor observation deck on the 86th floor. The remaining sixteen stories are the Art Deco tower, topped by an observatory on the 102nd floor, which opened to the public in 1931.

Tickets for the 102nd-floor observatory are only sold upon arrival at the Empire State Building for an additional cost beyond the regular admission. The observatory is open daily 365 days a year from 8:00 a.m. to 2:00 a.m.; the last elevator goes up at 1:15 a.m.

■ FORD FOUNDATION, 1963–67

321 East 42nd and 320 East 43rd Streets
ARCHITECT: Kevin Roche (b. 1922), John Dinkeloo (1918–1981)
PHONE: (212) 573-5000

RECOGNIZED AS A NEW TYPE of urban space and one of the best buildings of the 1960s, the award-winning Ford Foundation was the first office building dedicating a major part of its space to a horticultural environment. Kevin Roche was the primary architect behind the design for this twelve-story, open space design, composed of granite walls with COR-TEN steel that encloses a major botanical garden with a variety of exotic plant species.

The building is in the second International Style, and it pioneered the type of open-space glazed atrium that later became a pervasive form for public building projects. The Ford Foundation building houses the country's largest philanthropic organization. The two highest floors close the square of the building and contain the executive office and dining areas, which look out onto the atrium garden. The building is not set back but extends out to the building line and its pinkish gray granite piers instill a sense of monumentality from the exterior. There are two entrances to the atrium, on 42nd and 43rd Streets, but once inside, the visitor is transported into another world.

Upon entering the space, enclosed on top by a patterned skylight, the visitor is transported to a lush tropical forest-like environment with trees, a running stream, lily ponds, orchids, shrubs, and all types of flora. The botanical space occupies one third of an acre and appears on a hill, as there is a one-story height differential between the topography of 42nd Street and that of 43rd Street. This public space is a true oasis amid the noise and traffic of midtown Manhattan.

The garden atrium is open to the public during normal office hours.

■ LEVER HOUSE, 1948–52
390 Park Avenue between 53rd and 54th Streets
ARCHITECT: Gordon Bunshaft (1909–1990)
   and Skidmore, Owings & Merrill

LEVER HOUSE marks the advent of a modern age of the corporate skyscraper with Bunshaft's design for the American headquarters of the British company Lever Brothers. In a departure from the masonry style, Bunshaft produced one of the earliest examples of a new type of office building with glass curtain walls and stainless steel sheathing that were distinguishing characteristics of the International Style.

The building's design consists of two basic rectangular forms. An exceptional feature of it is the base structure, which is a thin rectangular box on its side raised on stilts or pilotis above street level, which creates an open plaza and garden. Upon this base rectangular structure sits an upright rectangular tower. Stainless-steel columns support the base structure and the tower. The lobby is only under the tower portion of the site. Another unusual feature is the bank of elevators, which is enclosed in glass. The remainder of the ground-floor space is open and serves as an arcade, probably the city's widest. An open public space was an innovative concept at the time of its introduction.

This lower rectangle appears to float, as does the tower slab that rises from the north end of the platform. The lower structure originally contained a lounge and other employee facilities, including a cafeteria and roof terrace garden. The upper part of the building is twenty-four stories enclosed in blue-green tinted glass and which was designed for cost and maintenance efficiency. The structure achieves balance through its carefully defined proportions and its horizontal and vertical tension.

The building underwent major renovations after the departure of Lever Brothers in 1997 and its acquisitions by new owners. An Isamu Noguchi sculpture garden (designed by the sculptor) was part of the building's original design but was never realized until the renovation, which now includes a modified version of it. Since the completion of the Lever House renovation, the building's plaza and lobby have been used as a gallery for the Lever House Art Collection and contemporary art exhibitions.

Though the design superficially appears simple with pared-down aesthetic—upon consideration, it is actually sophisticated and complex. Lever House was among the first and most influential modern skyscrapers that established the archetypal metal-and-glass corporate architecture of the 1950s.

■ LINCOLN CENTER FOR THE PERFORMING ARTS

Metropolitan Opera House

New York State Theater

Damrosch Park

New York Public Library for the Performing Arts

Mitzi E. Newhouse Theater and Vivian Beaumont Theater

Avery Fisher Hall

Josie Robertson Plaza

Alice Tully Hall

The Juilliard School

Samuel B. & David Rose Building

The Walter Reade Theater

Frederick P. Rose Hall

Located between 62nd and 65th Streets and Columbus and
    Amsterdam Avenues

PHONE: (212) 875-5456

WEB SITE: www.lincolncenter.org

LINCOLN CENTER SITS ON sixteen acres and comprises buildings that house twelve organizations devoted to the performing arts. This enormous complex, the world's largest cultural center, built between 1962 and 1968, was realized by the fundraising and organizational efforts of a group of New York's civic leaders, led by John D. Rockefeller III.

The center was a significant byproduct of the urban revitalization masterminded by the extremely influential urban planner Robert Moses (1888–1981), who at one time held twelve separate titles as the head of various public authorities in New York, and whose mark on New York City is also apparent in the many projects that he either spearheaded or to which he contributed his expertise in some way, including numerous bridges, expressways, public housing projects, Shea Stadium, and the United Nations Headquarters.

A project on the scale of Lincoln Center required the participation of a number of architects, including Wallace Harrison (1895–1981), who was responsible for the master plan as well as the Metropolitan Opera House; Philip Johnson (1906–2005), New York State Theater; Pietro Belluschi (1899–1994), Juilliard School and Alice Tully Hall; Gordon Bunshaft (1909–1990), New York Public Library for the Performing Arts; and Eero Saarinen (1910–1961) and Associates, Vivian Beaumont Theater.

The open plan of the Lincoln Center campus allows easy movement for visitors within the complex. Although designed by different architects, the buildings are unified by their travertine exteriors and their simple, clean lines, unornamented façades, repetition of architectural elements, and continuous windows, reflecting the principles of the International Style in architecture that emerged in the 1930s.

The campus, however, has often been criticized as being isolated from the city as a whole, making it vulnerable to charges of elitism. Partly in response to criticism and partly for practical considerations, Lincoln Center has begun in recent years an extensive redevelopment and renovation project to modernize the various facilities, to provide expansion where necessary, and to be more open to the city.

In addition to being a cultural center devoted to presenting the performing arts, the Lincoln Center complex also functions as a museum of sorts, displaying in its buildings and outdoor spaces more than thirty examples of important twentieth-century art, including Henry Moore's (1898–1986) **THE RECLINING FIGURE** (1964), in the reflecting pool outside Vivian Beaumont and Mitzi E. Newhouse Theaters; Alexander Calder's (1898–1976) **LE GUICHET** or THE BOX OFFICE (1963), outside of the New York Public Library for the Performing Arts; and David Smith's (1906–1965) **ZIG IV** (1961), in the lobby of Avery Fisher Hall.

Perhaps the most well-known works of art at Lincoln Center are Marc Chagall's (1887–1985) two murals, **SOURCES OF MUSIC** and the **TRIUMPH OF MUSIC** (1966), located in the lobby of the Metropolitan Opera House, in many ways the focal point of Lincoln Center. Chagall's murals, which are each thirty-six-feet tall, are visible from the building's exterior, through its continuous arched windows.

The murals reflect the magical world that we are accustomed to seeing in Chagall's paintings. His joyful **SOURCES OF MUSIC** is full of musicians, dancers, and embracing couples who float above the skyline of New York of the 1960s against a mostly yellow background; in **THE TRIUMPH OF MUSIC**, Chagall's signature floating figures, here dominated by trumpeting angels, energetically swirl around in circles against a dominant red background.

Chagall's interest in the performing arts had a long history, and before the Metropolitan murals, he had also worked on sets and costumes for various ballets and plays, such as costumes and sets for the first performance of Mozart's *The Magic Flute* at the Met in 1967.

In addition to the Chagall murals, the interior design and ornamentation of the approximately 3,800-seat Metropolitan Opera House is noted for its winding double grand staircase, featuring three sculptures by Aristide Maillol (1861–1944), **SUMMER** (1910–11), **VENUS WITHOUT ARMS** (1920), and **KNEELING WOMAN: MONUMENT TO DEBUSSY** (1950–55); its immense and spectacular starburst Austrian crystal chandeliers, often referred to as "Sputniks," after the Russian space satellites; and its gold square proscenium, which measures an impressive 54 feet by 54 feet.

Within several of the center's buildings there are also a number of art galleries displaying changing exhibitions; among them are the Onslanger Gallery and the Vincent Astor Gallery, both at the New York Public Library for the Performing Arts, and the Cork Gallery at Avery Fisher Hall.

Lincoln Center offers daily, guided one-hour tours of the campus at 10:30 a.m., 12:30 p.m., 2:30 p.m., and 4:30 p.m. Call the Lincoln Center tour desk at (212) 875-5350 for reservations and information. Tour fees apply.

Self-service parking is available at the Lincoln Center Park and Lock Garage. To reserve parking in advance, call (212) 721-6500.

NEW YORK CITY

THE MORGAN LIBRARY AND MUSEUM

225 Madison Avenue at 36th Street
ARCHITECT: Charles Follen McKim (1847–1909)
and Renzo Piano (b. 1937)
PHONE: (212) 685-0008
WEB SITE: www.themorgan.org
E-MAIL: visitorservices@themorgan.org

TURN-OF-THE-TWENTIETH-CENTURY American financier John
Pierpont Morgan amassed an extraordinary collection of books, manuscripts,
works on paper, art, and artifacts. By 1902, the library had outgrown
Morgan's Madison Avenue residence, so he hired Charles Follen McKim to
design a building to house his collection. Work on the library was completed
in 1906.

McKim, who was part of the famed architectural firm of McKim, Mead,
and White, was one of the foremost architects of the classicizing Beaux-
Arts style in America. He envisioned an Italianate marble palazzo that paid
homage to the High Renaissance. The library's Tennessee pink marble façade
was based on two sixteenth-century Roman sources, the Nymphaeum of
the Villa Giulia and the entrance to the Villa Medici. It is rectangular with a
recessed portico and six Doric pilasters. The exterior's geometric repetitions
and symmetries are also accompanied by sculptural ornamentation carried
out by Andrew O'Connor (1874–1941); Adolph Weinman (1870–1952), a
student of Augustus Saint-Gaudens; and Edward Clark Potter (1857–1923),
who was also responsible for the famous lions on the terrace of the New
York Public Library.

The Renaissance-inspired interior, which consists of the rotunda and
the three rooms that radiate from it, is particularly ornate, in contrast to
the relative simplicity of the façade. The opulent mosaic panels, variegated
marble, lapis lazuli panels, and the paintings on the walls, ceiling, and apse
of the rotunda by Harry Siddons Mowbray (1858–1928), as well as the wall
paintings and decorative work within the library space, speak to Morgan's
great wealth.

Mowbray's wall paintings also quote from Renaissance precursors,
including Raphael (1483–1520) and Pinturricchio (1454–1513). In the

Rotunda, Mowbray's visual program declares the building's dedication to housing great works of literature and art. The pursuit of knowledge and art are celebrated in a series of rectangular panels above the spandrels (**THE ANNUNCIATION, THE CROWNING OF ART, THE TRIUMPH OF LIGHT OVER DARKNESS**, and **KNOWLEDGE TRANSMITTED**); female allegorical figures within the roundels also represent Religion, Philosophy, Science, and Art. Within the library itself, Mowbray alternated images of the "muses" with important thinkers and historical figures, including Dante, Socrates, Herodotus, Galileo, and Christopher Columbus.

Although McKim's building initially had been envisioned as a primarily private space, Morgan's son and heir opened the library and the museum to the public in 1924. Since being established as a public institution, the Morgan Library and Museum, which today occupies half a city block, has seen the addition of the Annex, Morgan's former residence on Madison and 37th Street, and a garden court meant to unite the buildings. Most recently, the acclaimed Italian architect Renzo Piano was commissioned to create three intimate pavilions of steel and glass that would unify the campus and make it appear more open and accessible.

Piano, also responsible for the new **NEW YORK TIMES BUILDING** at 620 Eighth Avenue (between 40th and 41st Streets) among other important projects, completed the expansion of the Morgan Library and Museum in 2006. From the exterior, Piano's new entrance to the museum appears to be a simple box of steel and glass. To fully appreciate Piano's achievement, one must enter the building to witness its ethereal lightness and openness and to grasp the architect's nuanced understanding of the relationship between space, surface, and natural light. The addition presents an interesting contrast to the intimate, darker, and more lavishly decorated spaces originally designed for Morgan's personal use by McKim.

The strengths of the museum's art collection lie primarily in its holdings of manuscripts and works on paper. Particularly notable among its important examples of Medieval and Renaissance illuminated manuscripts are the extraordinary gold and jewel-encrusted cover of the **LINDAU GOSPELS** (c. 880); the **REIMS GOSPEL BOOK** (c. 860), the only Medieval manuscript from the influential Reims painting school to be written in gold; the illuminator Jean Poyet's (active c. 1483–1503) **HOURS OF HENRY VIII**

(c. 1500), which exhibits Poyet's expertise in rendering perspective as well as his stunning handling of color; and the **FARNESE HOURS** (1546), by the illuminator Giulio Clovio (1498–1578), whom the Renaissance biographer Giorgio Vasari referred to as the "new, if smaller Michelangelo."

The museum also represents many of the great artists from the fourteenth to the twentieth centuries with its impressive collection of sketchbooks, albums, and thousands of drawings and other works on paper. Among its noteworthy holdings of works on paper are a number of drawings and etchings by Rembrandt van Rijn (1609–1669), including the highly detailed drypoint rendering of **CHRIST PRESENTED TO THE PEOPLE** (n.d.); William Blake's (1757–1827) imaginative watercolors for a series of illustrations for the Book of Job, including **WHEN THE MORNING STARS SANG TOGETHER** (1823); and Caspar David Friedrich's beautiful

(1774–1840) **MOONLIT LANDSCAPE** (before 1808), a watercolor with the moon cut out and replaced with a separate piece of unpainted paper in order to make it "transparent," or a work meant to be illuminated from behind.

The museum is open Tuesday through Thursday 10:30 a.m. to 5:00 p.m.; Friday 10:30 a.m. to 9:00 p.m.; Saturday: 10:00 a.m. to 6:00 p.m.; Sunday: 11:00 a.m. to 6:00 p.m. Admission fees apply. Free admission on Fridays 7:00 to 9:00 p.m. Free admission to McKim rooms Tuesdays 3:00 to 5:00 p.m. and Sundays 4:00 to 6:00 p.m. Public parking is available nearby.

Plate fourteen of William Blake's illustrations of the Book of Job titled When the Morning Stars Sang Together *(1823)*

MUSEUM OF MODERN ART

11 West 53 Street

ARCHITECTS: Edward Durell Stone (1902–1978),
  Philip Johnson (1906–2005), and Yoshi Taniguchi (b. 1937)

PHONE: (212) 708-9400

WEB SITE: www.moma.org

FOUNDED IN 1929 as the culmination of the vision of three women patrons of the arts who sought to challenge the more conservative practices of traditional museums, the Museum of Modern Art was established to exhibit and celebrate the contributions of modern artists. Its founding director, Alfred H. Barr, Jr., intended for MOMA to be the "the greatest museum of modern art in the world."

Indeed, MOMA houses some of the most iconic works of modern painting, sculpture, and design. Some, like Vincent van Gogh's (1853–90) **THE STARRY NIGHT** (1889), are among the most reproduced and familiar images in our visual culture. Others, like Pablo Picasso's (1881–1973) **LES DEMOISELLES D'AVIGNON** (1907), which introduces the fracturing of surfaces that prefigured the development of Cubism and which borrows from and validates primitive forms, function as watersheds in MOMA's comprehensive presentation of the trajectory of modern art.

Among the highlights of MOMA's midcentury masterpieces is Jackson Pollock's (1912–1956) **THE SHE-WOLF (1943)**, a work that demonstrates the influences of Surrealism and Pollock's interest in the primal and the primitive. She-Wolf's spatters portend Pollock's "drip" style, which is exemplified by MOMA's **ONE (NUMBER 31, 1950)** (1950). Willem de Kooning's (1904–1907) gestural, almost violently rendered **WOMAN, I** (1950–52) offers a counterpoint to Pollock's later work, demonstrating that the figure could continue to play a role in the development of abstraction.

MOMA's extraordinary sculpture collection includes Auguste Rodin's (1840–1917) **MONUMENT TO BALZAC** (1897–98), which expresses the intellectual energy, genius, and monumental presence of Balzac, who is enveloped in a robe the author often wore while working. In **UNIQUE FORMS OF CONTINUITY IN SPACE** (1913), the Futurist Umberto Boccioni (1882–1916) celebrates speed, a defining marker of modernity, in a dynamic work featuring a striding figure.

Minimalist Robert Morris's (b. 1931) **UNTITLED** (1969), composed of gray green vertical felt strips draped along the wall and floor, is one of the many works that demonstrates the increasingly fluid and ever-changing definition of sculpture in the twentieth century. Also noteworthy within MOMA's collection of objects made from nontraditional materials or mixed media is Meret Oppenheim's (1913–1985) **OBJECT (LE DÉJEUNER EN FOURRURE)** (1936), a teacup, saucer, and spoon made out of fur. There is perverse humor in the piece, as the fur, a soft and luxurious material, which may bring tactile pleasure, is repulsive if used in the way Oppenheim sarcastically suggests. There is also humor in Marcel Duchamp's (1887–1968) **BICYCLE WHEEL** (1951, after lost original of 1913), which challenges our understanding of what art is or should be, by attaching an ordinary bicycle wheel atop an everyday kitchen stool. *Bicycle Wheel* is one of Duchamp's famous readymades, which are composed of common objects slightly manipulated to defy expectations.

Vincent van Gogh's The Starry Night *(1889)*

MOMA also houses an important collection of photography, including the stunning and lyrical **MOONRISE, MAMARONECK, NEW YORK** (1904) by Edward Steichen (1879–1973); Man Ray's (1890–1976) technically innovative **RAYOGRAPH** (1922), a photogram, which is made on photographic paper without a camera; and Cindy Sherman's (b. 1954) **UNTITLED FILM STILL #21** (1978), one of a series of sixty-nine "film stills" that Sherman orchestrated to explore the pervasive and powerful role movies played in twentieth-century culture.

The collection also includes remarkable examples of modern design, including **RED BLUE CHAIR** (c. 1923) by Gerrit Rietveld (1888–1964), a piece that emphasizes simplicity and uses only primary colors and black. This practice reflects the influence of the De Stijl movement, whose most famous practitioner, Piet Mondrian (1872–1944), is represented at MOMA by **BROADWAY BOOGIE WOOGIE**, (1942–43). The undulating form of Frank Gehry's (b. 1929) **BUBBLES CHAISE LOUNGE** (1987), which is made of corrugated cardboard, offers a counterpoint to Rietveld's hard planes and angles. Gehry's chaise was designed to function as both artwork and potentially usable object and is made of inexpensive materials that allow Gehry to promote his interest in making good design affordable.

The MOMA exhibition spaces have undergone many transformations over the years. Most recently, MOMA hired the Japanese architect Yoshi Taniguchi (b. 1937) to oversee a building and renovation project that would expand the museum to 630,000 square feet and would integrate the various additions made to the building since its founding. Taniguchi's design of glass, aluminum, black granite, and green slate incorporates MOMA's architectural past by maintaining such elements as the 1939 façade, designed by Philip Goodwin (1885–1958) and Edward Durell Stone (1902–1978), as well as Philip Johnson's (1906–2005) sculpture garden, which has been restored and expanded.

Meret Oppenheim's Object (Le Déjeuner en fourrure) *(1936)*

In 2000, MOMA established a formal partnership with **P.S.1 CONTEMPORARY ART**

CENTER, which is located in Long Island City within a brick Romanesque Revival building that once functioned as a New York City public school. Founded in 1971, P.S. 1 is one of the oldest and most important venues for the exhibition of cutting-edge work and the promotion of discourse and ideas relating to contemporary art.

MOMA is open Saturday to Monday and Wednesday to Thursday, 10:30 a.m. to 5:30 p.m.; Fridays 10:30 a.m. to 8 p.m. MOMA is closed on Tuesdays. Admission fees apply. MOMA participates in the City Pass program that offers a discounted rate for a combined ticket to six top attractions in the area (American Museum of Natural History, Empire State Building, Guggenheim Museum, Metropolitan Museum of Art, Circle Line Sightseeing Cruises or Statue of Liberty).

Discounted parking is available at the nearby 1345 Garage (at 101–41 West 54th Street between the Avenue of the Americas and Seventh Avenue). Parking stubs must be validated at the Lobby Information Desk or Film Desk in the Museum Lobby.

P.S. 1 is located at 22–25 Jackson Avenue at the intersection of 46th Avenue, Long Island City. It is open Thursday to Monday, 12:00 to 6:00 p.m. Admission fees apply but are free with purchase of MOMA tickets. Call (718) 784-2084 for more information. WEB SITE: www.ps1.org.

■ **RADIO CITY MUSIC HALL**
1260 Avenue of the Americas
ARCHITECT: Edward Durell Stone (1902–1978) (architect)
   with Wallace Harrison (1895–1981)
ARCHITECT: Donald Deskey (1894–1989) (interior)
PHONE: (212) 307-7171
WEB SITE: www.radiocity.com

RADIO CITY MUSIC HALL, which has 6,200 seats, was the world largest theater at the time of its opening in 1932; it was conceived as the major entertainment center of **ROCKEFELLER CENTER** (see p. 69). The architect of the building was Edward Durrell Stone, who is best known for his design of the **MUSEUM OF MODERN ART** (see p. 63), and the interiors were done by the noted Art Deco designer Donald Deskey.

As part of John D. Rockefeller's grand gesture of optimism amid the

Great Depression, he developed Rockefeller Center, of which Radio City was a part. The site was originally designated to be a new Metropolitan Opera House, but its location on the "speakeasy belt" soon instigated a reinvention of the structure, which became known as "Radio City" music hall. The Radio Corporation of America became a commercial partner in the enterprise; their NBC radio station and RKO movie studios were producing popular programming, and they joined forces with entertainment entrepreneur S. L. Rothafel, known as "Roxy," to create this new venture.

The Great Stage of Radio City is one of the largest indoor stages in the world and is among the most impressive, yet it still maintains a feeling of intimacy. Its most distinguishing feature is the proscenium arch on the stage that suggests a sunburst with radiating arches, and a state-of-the-art hydraulic system from the 1930s that is still in operation today. It was built with many of the most progressive technical features of the day and is still considered to be one of the best-designed and equipped performance halls in the world.

Deskey's legacy was assured with his innovative interior plans for Radio City. His scheme included more than thirty separate interior spaces, including eight lounges and smoking rooms, each with its own motif. Of particular note are Deskey's own tobacco design wall covering in the second mezzanine men's lounge, and his design for the first mezzanine ladies' lounge—an icon of Art Deco chic. Also of note is the exotic flower motif done as an oil mural in the second mezzanine ladies' lounge by modern artist, Yasuo Kuniyoshi (1893–1953). The flowers are integrated into the placement of furniture and architecture, creating a total feminine environment. Other works by notable artists include an untitled mural by modernist Stuart Davis (1894–1964) of 1932, (reinstalled in 1999) in the men's lounge off the grand lounge; the low relief elevator door panels cast in stainless steel, bronze auditorium door plaques, and the six low-relief bronze plaques of vaudeville acts on the exterior entrance, all by sculptor René Paul Chambellan (1893–1955); and three monumental cast aluminum nude sculptures, which created a stir in their day: **GIRL AND GOOSE** (1932) by Robert Laurent (1890–1970) in the first mezzanine; **EVE** (1932) by Gwen Creighton Lux (1908–2001); and the most important of the three, **DANCING FIGURE** (1932), by modernist William Zorach (1887–1966), which is in the grand lounge.

Defined by elegance and glamour, the overall interior design was the result of an integrated concept that was all-encompassing and included collaborations with textile designers, mural artists, sculptors, and various craftsmen. Deskey's designs included the furniture and carpets, and he coordinated the railings, balustrades, signage, and decorative details that he felt complemented the theater's interior. He also incorporated a variety of materials, some of an unconventional nature, in his rejection of the typical over-embellished decoration of theaters in the day. Materials that can be found in the interior include: glass, aluminum, marble, gold foil, Bakelite, Permatex, cork, and chrome. His ideas defined modern Art Deco, with streamlined and geometric ornamentation that borrowed from the European modern aesthetic. To this day, the theater maintains its character and allure after undergoing a major renovation in 1999.

Tours of the theater are available and tickets are sold on a first-come, first-served basis, Monday through Saturday, 11:30 a.m. to 6:00 p.m. Daily and advance tour tickets are also sold through the box office and through other means. Telephone or check the Web site for additional information.

ROCKEFELLER CENTER, 1929–39
48th and 51st Streets between Fifth and Sixth Avenues
ARCHITECT: Raymond Hood (1881–1934) (with other architects,
including Wallace K. Harrison, Max Abramovitz, the firms of
Reinhard & Hormeister and Corbett, Harrison, & MacMurray)
PHONE: (212) 588-8601

ROCKEFELLER CENTER is a complex of nineteen commercial buildings covering twenty-two acres in mid-Manhattan. It was conceived by John D. Rockefeller, who underwrote the project after the onset of the Great Depression. A monumental undertaking, it was the largest private building project in modern history.

The initial plan included fourteen buildings in the Art Deco style, and construction on them extended from 1930 to 1939 under the supervision of the principal architect, Raymond Hood, who also collaborated with and led three architectural firms, with a team that included Wallace Harrison, who also designed the Metropolitan Opera House at **LINCOLN CENTER** and the **UNITED NATIONS** (see p. 74). Thirty Rockefeller Plaza was the largest building and the first to be constructed, and served as the centerpiece of the complex.

The center is a combination of two building complexes: the older and original fourteen Art Deco office buildings from the 1930s, and a set of four International Style towers built along the west side of Avenue of the Americas during the 1960s and 1970s (plus the Lehman Brothers Building). The Time-Life Building, the McGraw-Hill, and News Corporation/Fox News Channel headquarters are the newer additions to Rockefeller Center.

Rockefeller Center is also unique in the plan to integrate public art into the design program in such a major way. There are over one hundred works of art that have been incorporated into the plan throughout the entire complex. Sculptor Lee Lawrie (1877–1963) contributed the largest number of individual pieces—twelve—including the massive cast bronze Streamlined Moderne statue **ATLAS** (1937) that faces Fifth Avenue and the friezes over the main entrance at 630 Fifth Avenue. Atlas, a Titan and brother of Prometheus, is shown with muscles bulging after he is condemned to carry the weight of the world as his punishment for leading the Titans in a revolt against the gods. Lawrie's other most prominent work is a colorful limestone clock and Art Deco–style grille. The grille is subdivided into fifteen individual scenes that trace human evolution, entitled **THE STORY OF MANKIND** (1937), which can be seen over the entrance to 29 West 50th Street.

Along with the Atlas sculpture, **THE STORY OF MANKIND** was a collaboration with René Paul Chambellan (1894–1955) who modeled the statue and also contributed a number of works throughout Rockefeller Center, including sculptures for Channel Gardens, located in front of the Skating Rink off Fifth Avenue; a decorative cartouche over the main entrance; four panels in the spandrels of 620 Fifth Avenue on themes relating to Britain; and four panels on the spandrels of 610 Fifth Avenue relating to French history.

The single most recognizable work of art at the center is Paul Manship's (1885–1966) monumental gilded bronze sculpture **PROMETHEUS**, which presides over and appears to float above the skating rink in the sunken plaza in front of 30 Rockefeller Plaza—the central focal point of Rockefeller Center. The sculpture shows the mythological figure holding up the fire he stole from the Chariot of the Sun and introduced to man. Manship also executed two sculptures that flank the staircase connecting the promenade to the lower level of the plaza

A diverse array of other artists working in a variety of styles and materials are represented in Rockefeller Center, including Isamu Noguchi (1904–1988). An archetype of Art Deco styling with its dynamic Streamlined Moderne conception bisected by sector lines, his cast stainless steel sculpture **NEWS** (1940) is located above the main entrance to 50 Rockefeller Plaza. The building was formerly occupied by the Associated Press and the sculpture pays homage to the business of the prior tenant—news and communication. The sculpture was cast in nine separate pieces. After it was assembled and mounted, the artist hand finished the surface in his only effort in this unusual medium.

Swedish-born Carl Milles (1875–1955), who was director of the sculpture program at Cranbrook Academy in Michigan, produced one of his most important commissions for Rockefeller Center, **MAN AND NATURE** (1937), which is mounted high on the west wall of the main lobby of One Rockefeller Plaza. A three-part high-relief wood carving is inspired by lines from German poet Johann Gottfried Seume: "Where song is, pause and listen; evil people have no song." Milles carved the sculpture from Michigan pressed-pine planks, the largest of which is a man on horseback (representing mankind) who has stopped to listed to the silver bird in the tree. There are two flanking figures—an evil faun and a virtuous nymph. The sculptor wanted the bird in the sculpture to move and sing. With the help of engineers he fabricated a mechanism to make the bird move and flap its wings and move its beak; NBC engineers recorded a bird's song, which can sometimes be heard.

Gaston Lachaise (1882–1935), known for his sculptures of voluptuous female nudes, in this case worked in an atypically restrained style. He represented aspects of civilization in four stone bas-reliefs titled **GENIUS SEIZING THE LIGHT OF THE SUN, THE CONQUEST OF SPACE, GIFTS OF EARTH TO MANKIND**, and **THE SPIRIT OF PROGRESS**. The carvings, titled as a group **THE ASPECTS OF MANKIND** (1935), are located on the sixth-floor façade of 1250 Avenue of the Americas. He also executed two exceptionally fine (and large) limestone bas-relief panels above the entrance to 45 Rockefeller Plaza which commemorate the workers who built Rockefeller Center. Installed in 1935, the workmanship shows Lachaise's exceptional knowledge of anatomy and facility and range as a sculptor, who typically worked with different media, style, and subject matter.

Above the entrance to 620 Fifth Avenue, which was the British Empire Building, is the work of sculptor C. Paul Jennewein (1890–1978). He executed a large (eighteen-feet-high) cast bronze high relief panel with gilding of nine figures inscribed with the various commodities from provinces that provided major sources of income for Britain. Situated over the panel, **INDUSTRIES OF THE BRITISH EMPIRE** (1933) is a sculptural representation of the British Coat of Arms. At One Rockefeller Plaza over the main entrance, Jennewein also produced two bas-relief limestone carvings with gilding of two figures in a streamlined Deco style that represent **INDUSTRY** and **AGRICULTURE** (1937). Jennewein's classicized sculptural style made him a fitting choice for many architectural commissions.

In 1933, NBC hired noted photographer Margaret Bourke-White (1904–1971) to create the biggest photographic mural in America for the rotunda of their studios in Rockefeller Center, which was titled **TRAPPING THE MAGICAL WAVES OF SOUND**. The subject was broadcasting equipment and it was on display for about twenty years.

The Mexican painter Diego Rivera (1886–1957) was commissioned by Nelson Rockefeller in 1932 to paint a fresco for the lobby of the RCA Building. Rivera's communist political interests were reflected in his inclusion of a portrait of Lenin, which was found objectionable and was subsequently destroyed. In its place, the Catalan artist José María Sert (1876–1945) was commissioned to produce a mural, which is titled **AMERICAN PROGRESS** (1937). It is an allegorical scene of the development of America through its various achievements and contains the figures of Abraham Lincoln and Ralph Waldo Emerson. The vast mural wraps around the west wall of the main lobby over the information desk at 30 Rockefeller Center. Sert also completed seven other murals in the building between 1933 and 1941, all using a limited range of tones.

A later addition was a mural, **THE HISTORY OF TRANSPORTATION** (1946), by the famous illustrator Dean Cornwell (1892–1960), which spans three walls of the main lobby of 10 Rockefeller Plaza. Executed in a limited palette and a stylized montage manner, the three panels each depict a different aspect of the evolution of transportation, with the titles: **NIGHT FLIGHT**, **NEW WORLD UNITY**, and **DAY FLIGHT**.

The Time-Life Building, located at 1271 Avenue of the Americas (6th Avenue) in Rockefeller Center, opened in 1959. It was designed by the Rockefeller family's architect Wallace K. Harrison, of Harrison, Abramovitz, and Harris. It was the first expansion of Rockefeller Center west of the Avenue of the Americas. There are large murals by abstract artists Joseph Albers (1891–1965) and Fritz Glarner (1899–1972) in the lobby.

The forty-five-story tower of 1211 Avenue of the Americas occupies the southwest corner of Rockefeller Center and was completed in 1973. Abstract artist Robert Natkin (b. 1930) was commissioned to produce a twenty by 42-foot mural in 1991 for the renovation of the lobby. He produced a glowing and colorful image, which can be seen from the street.

Gilded figures representing the Industries of the British Empire *(1933) on the entrance to 620 Fifth Avenue by C. Paul Jennewein*

These are only a few highlights of the many works located in and around Rockefeller Center. For information on an art and architecture tour of Rockefeller Center, call (212) 664-3700.

Other Art Deco skyscrapers designed by Raymond Hood worthy of visiting include the stellar **AMERICAN RADIATOR BUILDING** (1923–24), located at 40 West 40th Street, off Avenue of the Americas; the **MCGRAW-HILL BUILDING** (1930), located at 330 West 42nd Street; and the **DAILY NEWS BUILDING**, also known as **THE NEWS BUILDING**, (1929–30), located at 220 E. 42nd Street.

SEAGRAM BUILDING, 1954–58

375 Park Avenue (between 52nd and 53rd Streets)
ARCHITECT: Ludwig Mies van der Rohe (1886–1969)
in collaboration with Philip Johnson (1906–2005)

GERMAN ARCHITECT Mies van der Rohe is considered the leading and most influential exponent of the style of glass-and-steel architecture of the mid-twentieth-century known as the International Style.

The Seagram Building is thirty-eight stories and in its unity, subtle refinement, and sense of proportion and scale, emphasizes its verticality. The building is positioned on sturdy two-story stilts that are recessed from the façade, creating a deep plaza space and the open portal to the lobby. It has an edifice of dull bronze and gray amber glass, which gives the structure a warm tone and is seen to best advantage in the late afternoon sun.

Van der Rohe strived toward an architecture with a minimal framework of structural order balanced against the implied freedom of free-flowing open space. His approach to buildings is "skin and bones" architecture and his rationality steered the creative process of design, and is known for his dictums, "less is more" and "God is in the details."

One of the most characteristic traits of the International style was to have an external expression of a building's structural elements. The Seagram building has a steel frame, as did most skyscrapers of the time, though on the exterior, the structure is suggested by his use of nonstructural bronzed I-beams, which emphasize the vertical rise of the building and surround the windows. Nonstructural glass walls are hung from the steel frame.

The construction of the Seagram Building was the most expensive skyscraper to date due to Mies's demand for high quality materials such as bronze and marble. The interior design scheme complemented the aesthetic of the exterior and together were intended as a cohesive entity for a unified aesthetic.

The Seagram Building, along with **LEVER HOUSE** (see p. 56), which is just across Park Avenue, set the architectural paradigm for commerical office buildings in the International Style in New York for several decades. The Seagram Building is essentially a box form set back from the street with an open plaza. The space in front of the building became the standard for other commercial buildings, which were modeled according to new zoning laws whose intention was to encourage developers to create public space.

The building was the first with floor-to-ceiling windows, and among the earliest with nonstructural curtain walls, which became the archetype of modern skyscrapers. Van der Rohe asserted that the Seagram Building was his American effort that met the exacting standards of his European designs.

Mies was also the architect of three privately owned residential buildings in nearby Newark, New Jersey. Soon after completing the Seagram Building, he designed three towers near Branch Brook Park, which is north of downtown Newark. Two of the buildings, called the Pavilion Apartments, face each other across a lawn, and the third, called the Colonnade, is a long rectangle that overlooks Branch Brook Park. The Pavilion and Colonnade Apartments (1958) opened in 1960 and were intended to bring middle-income families to the area.

■ ST. PATRICK'S CATHEDRAL, 1858–78

460 Madison Avenue (Fifth Avenue between 50th and 51st Street)
ARCHITECT: James Renwick, Jr. (1818–1895) with William Rodrique
PHONE: (212) 753-2261
WEB SITE: www.saintpatrickscathedral.org

ST. PATRICK'S IS THE largest Gothic Revival cathedral in North America. Designed by noted American architect James Renwick, Jr., it is finely balanced in its proportions, details, and decoration. Together with its auxiliary buildings it comprises one entire city block between Fifth and Madison Avenues, and 50th and 51st streets. At the time of its construction the structure dominated this part of Manhattan, which was more removed from the heart of the city. The cornerstone was laid in 1858, but work on the cathedral was interrupted by the Civil War; construction resumed in 1865. The cathedral was completed in 1878 and dedicated the following year. The towers were added in 1881. Towers on the west façade were added in 1888, and an addition on the east, including a Lady Chapel, designed by Charles T. Mathews, began in 1901 and was completed in 1908.

The cathedral is in the typical Gothic form of a cross created by the nave and transept. Its exterior is more evocative of French and German Gothic architecture, while the interior is inspired by English Perpendicular style with the elaborate and decorated ribbed vaulting over the aisles, the window tracery, and graceful proportions. The nave is composed of white marble. Other notable features on the interior include the St. Michael and St. Louis altars, which were designed by Tiffany & Co. **THE STATIONS OF THE CROSS** won a prize for artistry at the World Columbian Exposition in Chicago in 1893.

The west vestibule is flanked by the towers with a gallery, and the nave has six bays with aisles and side chapels that are crossed by transepts with east and west aisles. The choir has a five-sided east apse with aisles and an ambulatory with chapels of various sizes; the largest is the Lady Chapel at the east end. There are beautiful decorative details, with the highlight being the stained glass windows, whose opulent darker reds and blues create a stirring atmosphere.

The cathedral is open daily from 6:30 a.m. to 8:45 p.m.

■ **UNITED NATIONS HEADQUARTERS**
First Avenue between 42nd Street and 48th Street
ARCHITECT: Wallace K. Harrison (1895–1981)
PHONE: (212) 963-8687
WEB SITE: www.un.org/tours/
E-MAIL: unitg@un.org

LOCATED ON EIGHTEEN ACRES on the East Side of Manhattan, the United Nations Headquarters was built between 1947 and 1953 and comprises four central buildings: the Secretariat Building, the General Assembly Building, the Conference Building, and the Dag Hammarskjöld Library. The complex was designed by an international team of eleven architects led by the U.S. architect Wallace K. Harrison, who was also responsible for the **METROPOLITAN OPERA HOUSE** and the master plan of **LINCOLN CENTER**.

The Secretariat Building (1950), a thirty-nine-story structure that features New York's earliest glass curtain wall, was the city's first International Style skyscraper based on plans by the renowned Swiss-born architect Le Corbusier (1887–1965). The building reflects the simplicity and repetition of geometric form central to the International Style and is composed of green glass, marble, and bands of metal detailing.

The English sculptor Barbara Hepworth's (1903–1975) twenty-one-foot bronze sculpture **SINGLE FORM** (1962–63) in memory of the statesman

Dag Hammarskjöld, the second Secretary-General of the U.N., who died in a plane crash in 1961, sits outside the Secretariat Building overlooking an ornamental pool. An organic shape with curved contours, the sculpture is pierced by a hole, as are many of Hepworth's works, which treat negative space as substantially as they do material form.

Another highlight of the U.N. art collection is Marc Chagall's (1887–1985) stained-glass mural located in the Public Lobby. Chagall and U.N. staff members donated the mural as a gift in memory of Hammarskjöld. Fifteen feet wide and twelve feet high, the memorial is a celebration and call for peace and love. It is full of the floating figures for which Chagall is known and features details such as a child being kissed by an angelic face emerging from a mass of flowers. The mural has both figurative and literal symphonic qualities, achieved in part with Chagall's incorporation of musical symbols to reference Beethoven's *Ninth Symphony*, a favorite of Hammarskjöld.

Mural in stained-glass by Marc Chagall that incorporates musical symbols from Beethoven's Ninth Symphony

Adjacent to the Secretariat is the five-story General Assembly Building with its extraordinary domed General Assembly Hall, which seats 1,800 people and is the largest room in the U.N complex. Within the hall are two large abstract murals designed by the French painter Fernand Léger (1881–1955). The works are nonrepresentational and organic, asserting universality over partisanship, qualities integral to the goals of the United Nations. Also in the General Assembly Building is The Foucault Pendulum (1955), a gold-plated sphere suspended seventy-five feet above the lobby, which offers visual proof of the rotation of the earth.

Located in the Visitor's Plaza, facing First Avenue at 45th Street, is a large bronze sculpture, **NON-VIOLENCE (THE KNOTTED GUN)** (1980) by Karl Fredrik Reutersward (b. 1934). Another of the complex's artworks calling for peace and the end of violence, the sculpture, which makes a dramatic and graphic statement, represents a forty-five-caliber revolver, the barrel of which is tied into a knot.

Next to the U.N. complex is a small park bordering the East River which also features works that address the function and spirit of the United Nations, including **LET US BEAT SWORDS INTO PLOWSHARES** by the Socialist Realist sculptor Evgeniy Vuchetich (1908–1974). Donated by the Soviet Union in 1957, the dynamic sculpture represents a man holding a hammer in one hand and, in the other, a sword that he is making into a plowshare. The work is an appeal for peace and a vision of the transformation of tools of destruction into creative vehicles that can benefit us all. The park also displays a piece of the Berlin Wall.

One of two murals by Fernand Léger (1952) featured in the U.N. General Assembly Hall

The U.N. offers daily guided tours that begin in the General Assembly Public Lobby. The tours are offered Monday through Friday 9:45 a.m. to 4:45 p.m. and last approximately forty-five minutes. Fees apply and tickets are limited and may be sold out early in the day, so plan ahead and call (212) 963-8687 for updated information. There are no parking facilities.

The U.N. displays changing exhibitions throughout the year in the U.N. Visitor's Lobby at East 46th Street and First Avenue. March through December, hours are 9:00 a.m. to 5:00 p.m., seven days a week. In January and February it is open only on weekdays. There are no admission fees to see the exhibits. For more information on the exhibition schedule, see www. un.org/events/UNART/.

DOWNTOWN

■ BAYARD-CONDICT BUILDING, 1897–99
65–69 Bleecker Street
between Broadway and Lafayette Streets
ARCHITECT: Louis H. Sullivan (1856–1924)

THE BAYARD-CONDICT BUILDING is the only New York example of Chicago architect Louis Sullivan's innovative and distinctive style. Leader of the Chicago School, he was one of the pioneers of the skyscraper, and this twelve-story, steel-frame loft building shows the synthesis of ornamentation with the modern style as it heralds the dawn of the modern office building; it was one of the first steel skeleton-frame skyscrapers in New York City. The edifice emphasizes the vertical elevation through the division of three bays, subdivided by six piers. Though the progenitor of a modern style, Sullivan was an advocate of organic decoration, seen in florid details visible at the street level and at the top crown moldings and the cornices. The building façade is composed with Sullivan's preferred material—white terra cotta. In comparison to other early New York skyscrapers, Sullivan's Chicago Style offers a very different aesthetic, with stronger ties to historical Romanesque, Gothic, and Renaissance details, making it completely original and unique.

An advocate of the principle "form follows function," Sullivan divided his office buildings into three components: the street level contains storefronts devoted to services; the mid section is devoted to offices; and the top section houses the mechanical operations of the structure. The original street-level storefronts were recreated in 2003.

Cast iron was initially used only for decorative details; however, it became an important material in constructing façades between 1840 and 1880. Economical, strong and flexible, cast iron was adaptable for elaborate decoration and could also be painted. An American architectural innovation, it was cheaper to use for façades than materials such as stone or brick. Classical French and Italian architectural designs often served as inspiration for these façades. In the neighboring streets, many such examples can be seen.

When visiting the Bayard Building, it is also worthwhile surveying the surrounding Soho area, which boasts the greatest number of cast iron structures in the world. There are about two hundred and fifty cast iron buildings in the city, with the greatest number concentrated in Soho.

BLUE BUILDING
105 Norfolk Street
ARCHITECT: Bernard Tschumi (b. 1944)

WHEN MOST RESIDENTS of the Lower East Side first learned about NYC-based architect Bernard Tschumi's Blue Building from reading the advertisement on the construction site, the general reaction among them was mixed. Some felt the building was extremely sleek and feared that its presence would lead to the area turning into another expensive neighborhood. Others feel less positive about the choice of color, even going so far as to say that it looks like "one of those big toilet bowl cubes that turn toilet water blue."

Tschumi's work in general has been criticized for subjugating the human to the intellectual. But the critical criteria that one must take into consideration when viewing the Blue Building—his second building in New York (Columbia University's Alfred Lerner Hall, 1999, is his first) and his first residential structure ever—are complex. The neighborhood, and NYC in general, will always need more affordable housing, and since the economic meltdown of '08 this may conceivably be one of the last glass boxes to be built in the area (it opened in 2007). Yet most see this seventeen-story condominium positively in comparison to most luxury residential towers of recent design.

Tschumi's crystaline structure of pixilated blue glass bends over a lower commercial building next door to accommodate the maximum amount of floor space imposed by zoning laws. Its cheery, mottled blue surface picks up the random patchwork of the area's hodgepodge of commercial and domestic (tenement) structures. Squeezed into a quarter of Old New York, the Blue Building's eccentricity reminds the viewer of its individuality with beautiful color and form, qualities lacking in most domestic architecture built during the same period in Chelsea.

CITY HALL, 1802–1811
City Hall Park
ARCHITECTS: Joseph François Mangin (French, 1764–1818),
    and John McComb Jr. (1763–1853)
PHONE: call 311; from out of town: (212) NEW-YORK
WEB SITE: www.nyc.gov/html/artcom/html/tours/city_hall.shtml

NEW YORK CITY HALL is among the finest civic buildings representing the American Federal style of architecture; it is also the oldest American city hall still functioning for its original purpose. City Hall is exceptional for its balance, elegance, and refinement of proportions. It is interesting that the design is attributed to a collaboration between two architects from different backgrounds.

New York City Hall is actually the third structure that housed city government. The first city hall was built in the seventeenth century by the Dutch and was on Pearl Street. The second dates to 1700 and was located on Wall and Nassau Street; it was later renamed **FEDERAL HALL** when New York was established as the nation's capital after the Revolutionary War. In 1802, a competition was held for the commission of the present structure after a site was chosen on the northernmost limits of the city, now City Hall Park in Lower Manhattan.

The first prize for the commission was jointly awarded to John McComb Jr. and to Frenchman Joseph François Mangin. McComb was a builder architect and his father had worked on the old City Hall. He was a native of New York and had previously designed **CASTLE CLINTON** in

Battery Park. Mangin studied architecture in France before relocating to New York where he served as city surveyor in 1795 and published an official map of the city in 1803. Mangin had also served as the architect of St. Patrick's Old Cathedral on Mulberry Street.

The new City Hall design was decried as being too extravagant. In response, a design was implemented that reduced the size of the building and used brownstone to face the rear exterior of the building (which was less expensive than the marble used on the other three sides) to lower costs. With building delays, City Hall was finally dedicated in 1811 and opened in 1812.

The design of City Hall is an homage to Internationalism. The individual roles played by joint competition winners McComb and Mangin is still much disputed. The design is indebted to both English and French architectural traditions, though more notable is the influence of the English architect Sir William Chambers (1726–1796), whose book on architecture McComb had studied and had in his own library. There is much more documentation emphasizing McComb's greater input than there is referencing Mangin, and it was McComb who was solely involved in the construction of the building, seeing it through to completion.

City Hall is a three-story structure whose entrance faces downtown, which was the populated part of the city in that era. There is a formal staircase entrance capped by a one-story portico that marks the entryway to the building. The roof of the portico is surrounded by a balustrade that encloses a balcony that runs the length of five large rounded windows outside the Governor's Room. A cupola, topped by a statue of Justice, is a reconstruction from 1917, after the second of two fires. Above that rises an attic story with squared windows.

The French influences can be most seen in the decorative details, such as the low portico without a pediment, large arched windows, recessed panels with delicate ornamental swags, the raised attic story above the central story, and the more decorative Ionic- and Corinthian-styled columns and pilasters.

All the exterior surfaces were severely compromised over time and the building was refaced between 1954 and 1956 with Alabama limestone and a Missouri granite base, finally resulting in a uniform exterior.

The Governor's Room, completed in 1915–16, serves as a museum and reception room celebrating the civic history of New York and America; included is a collection of over one hundred paintings from the late eighteenth through the twentieth centuries. Among them is the 1805 portrait of Alexander Hamilton by American painter John Trumbull that was the basis for the face on the ten-dollar bill. The collection also encompasses historic furnishings, including examples by Charles Honoré Lannuier (1779–1819), and other notable artifacts, such as George Washington's desk.

The architectural style of the interior is largely American-Georgian, as is its overall design, consisting of a central pavilion with two projecting wings. The rotunda is a soaring space with a grand marble stairway rising up to the second floor where ten fluted Corinthian columns support the coffered dome.

Tours are offered free of charge and are available for groups on Mondays, Wednesdays, and Fridays at 10:00 a.m., and for individuals on Thursdays at 10:00 a.m. To make a reservation, visit the Web site, call 311, or (212) NEW-YORK outside of New York City.

At Broadway in City Hall Park is an important sculpture, **NATHAN HALE** (1890), by American sculptor Frederick MacMonnies (1863–1937). It depicts the twenty-one-year-old patriot in 1776 following the utterance of his famous quote as he is about to put to be death by the British.

Other notable buildings in Manhattan by John McComb worth visiting are **CASTLE CLINTON NATIONAL MONUMENT (AND GARDEN)** (1808–11), located in nearby Battery Park in Lower Manhattan. The structure was originally known as West Battery and served as a fort in defense of New York City from the British up to the War of 1812. Renamed Castle Garden, it subsequently served a number of different functions, including that of a promenade, beer garden/restaurant, exhibition hall, opera house, theater, and aquarium. It was designed as an open-air structure and was eventually roofed over to accommodate these activities. For more information visit: http://www.nps.gov/cacl/.

Another design by McComb was a residence for the statesman Alexander Hamilton known as **HAMILTON GRANGE**. The home is currently being relocated to St. Nicholas Park in Upper Manhattan and is temporarily closed to the public while undergoing a major renovation. For more information visit: www.nps.gov/hagr/.

NEW YORK CITY

■ **FEDERAL HALL (ORIGINALLY THE U.S. CUSTOM HOUSE), 1833–42**
28 Wall Street (at Nassau Street)
Ithiel Town (1784–1844)
    and Alexander Jackson Davis (1803–1892)
PHONE: (212) 826-6888
WEB SITE: http://www.nps.gov/feha/

DESIGNED BY ITHIEL TOWN and Alexander Jackson Davis when they were partners in the firm Town & Davis, the exterior of Federal Hall is the finest example of Greek Revival architecture in Manhattan. Originally the United States Custom House, the edifice is stately and monumental in its proportions, with eight large Doric columns supporting the portico with an architrave of sixteen triglyphs that in turn supports the pediment and pays homage to the Greek Parthenon.

The original design included a rooftop dome and cupola, but after the foundation was laid, it was determined that the interior columns would not support the structure, and so the dome was eliminated. Other modifications in the construction of the building were said to pain Davis, who felt the original design had been compromised. The building is made of marble quarried in Westchester County and is sited in a way to accommodate the elevation in grade from Pine to Wall Street.

The site on which Federal Hall sits was originally that of New York's second city hall, which became the seat of congress when New York was the nation's capital. It was in fact the place where George Washington took the oath of office as America's first president. That structure was subsequently demolished and plans for this building as the Customs House commenced. When that space was outgrown in 1862, the building functioned as the U.S. Sub-Treasury. In 1955, the National Park Service took over the building and it was designated a memorial museum in celebration of Washington and his inauguration. Noted American figurative sculptor John Quincy Adams Ward executed a statue of **WASHINGTON** (1883) on the building steps on what is believed to be the approximate location at the original building where Washington took the oath.

The interior includes a Neoclassical rotunda which is a stunning design by John Frazee. The interior also exhibits elegant Neoclassical decorative details with Corinthian columns and iron railings with female figures and vine motifs.

Federal Hall is open Monday to Friday 9:00 a.m. to 5:00 p.m. and is closed on all national holidays. Open weekends and holidays in July and August. Admission is free.

Another notable Neoclassical façade design attributed to Davis and worthy of a visit is **LAGRANGE TERRACE (COLONNADE ROW)**, built in 1833 and located at 428–434 Lafayette Street. Nine grand row houses with marble façades and two-story colonnades with Corinthian columns originally ran from 418–434 Lafayette Street. They were built for the privileged mercantile class; John Jacob Astor, William Makepeace Thackeray, Washington Irving, and Cornelius Vanderbilt were among those who lived there. There is some dispute whether the design was by Davis, though it is believed he had some involvement.

FLATIRON BUILDING (ORIGINALLY THE FULLER BUILDING), 1902

ARCHITECT: Daniel H. Burnham (1846–1912)
Fifth Avenue and Broadway at 22nd and 23rd Streets

ONE OF THE MOST DISTINCTIVE build-ings in the city, the Flatiron Building was designed by Chicago architect Daniel Burnham; it became recognized for its unique triangular form, in-spired by its site at the convergence of Broadway and Fifth Avenue at Madison Square. The build-ing was at the northernmost end of the fashionable shopping district of the early twentieth century, known as Ladies' Mile. In its day, the twenty-one-story building's height of 300 feet was considered to be disquieting, despite its all-steel frame. The Flatiron Building was among the earliest sky-scrapers to employ the innovation of the steel frame.

The building was commissioned by the Fuller Construction Company, but soon became known as the Flatiron Building because its shape summons up the form of a clothes iron. An early skyscraper, the building's heavy walls are composed of rusticated limestone, and the façades boast Italian Renaissance ornamentation executed in white terra cotta, recalling a palazzo and makng it unlike the typical modern skyscraper. Burnham was the lead designer of the 1893 World Columbian Exposition (Chicago World's Fair) and was responsible for altering the concept of civic architecture. He designed other buildings in New York, including a building for the Wanamaker's department store at Eighth Avenue and Broadway in 1903, a Gimbels's store at Sixth Avenue and 33rd Street in 1909, and the Old Fire Companies Building at 80 Maiden Lane in 1912.

The Flatiron Building has become one of the signature profiles of the New York skyline and has inspired many works of art, most notably Pictorialist photographer Edward Steichen's evocative 1905 night view.

40 BOND

40 Bond Street, near Lafayette Street
ARCHITECT: Jacques Herzog (b. 1950)
and Pierre de Meuron (b. 1950)

THE SWISS ARCHITECTURE FIRM Herzog and de Meuron, named after the firm's founders and senior partners, Jacques Herzog and Pierre de Meuron, is best known for its design of the new home of London's Tate Museum of Modern Art, which was placed in the converted Bankside Power Station. Called "one of the most admired architecture firms in the world" by the *New York Times*, the company was the winner of the Pritzker Prize, the highest honor given in architecture. When 40 Bond was commissioned and announced to the public by developer Ian Shrager (former nightclub owner turned hotelier) in early 2006, expectations were high for this luxury condominium. All of the multimillion-dollar units were sold before the building was close to completion. Its façade—a grid of glass and shiny stainless steel—is an homage to the surrounding area's nineteenth-century cast-iron buildings (the rear façade has a grid of copper). The interior consists of twenty-seven units, including five triplexes entered at ground level; above these units are twenty-two loftlike domiciles, each with eleven-foot ceilings.

Some critics assert that the building design is already looking dated—the *New York Times* stated that the "façade feels slick and mannered" and that the elaborate gate at the front of the building "is an embarrassing effort to tap into a bygone underground scene." Nevertheless, 40 Bond was one of the city's first serious residential projects by an internationally known firm, and it remains part of the eclectic fabric of downtown New York. Next up by Herzog and Meuron, a 57-story, teetering stack of asymmetrical condominium glass cubes at 56 Leondard Street in Tribeca (2010 opening).

GRACE CHURCH, 1843–46
802 Broadway at 10th Street
ARCHITECT: James Renwick Jr. (1818–1895)
PHONE: (212) 254-2000
WEB SITE: www.gracechurchnyc.org

AT THE AGE OF TWENTY-FIVE, James Renwick Jr., who was to become one of the most important architects of his time, received his first major architectural commission by winning a design competition for Grace Church in New York City. An architectural masterpiece of the early American Gothic Revival, Grace Church was built on land purchased from Henry Brevoort, who was an uncle of Renwick's. The church is sited so that when looking from downtown up Broadway as the avenue curves, the view concludes with the church tower. This Episcopal parish was among the most prestigious in New York, catering to elite society.

Its design is distinctive for its prominent transepts and typically Gothic lacy ornamental details. Aspects of the design also closely mirror elements of the English Perpendicular Style, a type of Gothic detailing that exhibits crenellated parapets, high pinnacles, elongated thinner piers, jointed groin vaults, and large peaked windows. There are details that depart from the English styling, including the curvilinear tracery, which is more typically French Gothic, so the result is an eclectic mélange of Gothic-style details.

Renwick insisted that the church be constructed of white marble, adding enormous expense to the project; the steeple, originally made of wood, was replaced with marble in 1883.

The focal point of the chancel and nave is an English stained-glass window of 1878 by Clayton and Bell, whose theme is "Te Deum," depicting prophets, apostles, and marytrs in praise of Christ. Other decorations include the reredos with mosaic figures of the evangelists Matthew, Mark, Luke, and John beside Christ. This and the altar were designed by Renwick and were fabricated by Ellin & Kitson in 1878. The choir was added in 1903 after the chancel was lengthened an additional fifteen feet in a renovation designed by Heins and La Farge, after Renwick's death in 1895.

Just north of the church, the rectory (1846–47) is another Renwick masterpiece and can be seen behind the cast iron fence and green lawn. In 1880–81 he also designed Grace House, which connects the church and the rectory, and echoes the earlier design of the church.

William Renwick, nephew of the architect, redesigned the chantry exterior and added an outdoor pulpit in 1910 after the acquisition of the land now known as Huntington Close.

■ IAC BUILDING, 2007
555 W. 18th Street
ARCHITECT: Frank Gehry (b. 1929)
PHONE: (212) 314-7300
E-MAIL: info@iac.com

FRANK GEHRY'S TEN-FLOOR IAC Building in Chelsea houses the Internet company IAC, a business conglomerate that operates more than sixty brands; the two-tiered structure features an arresting composition of vaguely rectangular forms that billow outward at their bases and curve to one side as if shaped by a strong wind. The silvery building utilizes angled concrete and glass to achieve an unusual softness, despite its dimensions, making the blockier structures around it appear squat and dense. The construction is the first in which a glass curtain wall underwent cold-warping, with the glass panels being bent on site to create the distinctive roundness of the outer windows.

The impressive exterior design is equaled by the building's interior layout, where a custom-built "open office" facilitates increased interaction among employees. With a full 100 percent of its workspaces bathed in natural light, the gloom of a dimly lit maze of cubicles is effectively banished. A sixth-floor wraparound terrace allows employees to escape the monotony of the indoors altogether, offering conference tables, wireless Internet, and electricity in an outdoor setting.

Though the façade may be the main attraction, be sure to head inside to the ground-floor lobby to see the world's largest high-resolution video walls.

■ JEFFERSON MARKET COURTHOUSE (NOW NEW YORK PUBLIC LIBRARY BRANCH), 1874–77

425 Sixth Avenue (near 10th Street)
ARCHITECT: Calvert Vaux (1824–1895)
    and Frederick Clarke Withers (1828–1901)
PHONE: (212) 243-4334
E-MAIL: jefferson_market@nypl.org
WEB SITE: www.nypl.org/branch/local/man/jmr.cfm

THIS CASTLELIKE DESIGN with its tower, pinnacles, turrets, gables, and Venetian Gothic elements is one of the most eccentric and distinctive buildings in New York for its asymmetrical form; it remains one of the most exceptional examples of High Victorian Gothic architecture.

Jefferson Market was originally a courthouse and police station, and the main clock tower served as a fire watch. The infamous trial of Harry Thaw for the assassination of architect Stanford White took place in the courthouse.

The building reflects an inclination toward British Victorian architec-ture and the input of British architect Frederick Clarke Withers. The building overlay is red and black brick, with yellow Ohio sandstone trim and granite belts, creating a polychromatic effect. With elaborate ornamentation and sculptural details, including gargoyles and finials, few surfaces are left unarticulated. The designs are both geometric and organic, including an elaborately ornamental corner drinking fountain with water, plant, and animal decoration. A sculptural pediment depicts the trial scene from *The Merchant of Venice*. Arched Gothic trefoil and lancet windows and architectural elements embellish the exterior.

Jefferson Market was vacant from 1958 until it was remodeled and opened in 1967 as a branch of the New York Public Library. The conservation of this building was one of the early landmark preservation efforts and was spearheaded by the Greenwich Village community.

■ THE LITTLE SINGER BUILDING (NOW THE PAUL BUILDING), 1902
561 Broadway between Prince and Spring Streets
ARCHITECT: Ernest Flagg (1857–1947)

ONE OF NEW YORK'S early steel-and-glass-façade skyscrapers, it foreshadows the glass-curtain-wall design seen in post–World War II skyscrapers, and is one of Ernest Flagg's most inventive designs. The Little Singer Building has twelve stories with an elegant façade of three bays; a wide central bay is crowned by an arched spandrel on the lowest band and another crowning the top floor. The building has a steel frame that is encased in brick with floor to ceiling windows and narrow balconies. There is much detailed decoration in red terra cotta and wrought iron tracery surrounding the windows. The top tier of the building also maintains similar design flourishes and has a decorated roof cornice. The building is situated amid Soho's notable cast iron district. Notable for its strength, versatility, and practicality, cast iron was an innovation used in many mid-nineteenth-century buildings, particularly those built for commercial purposes.

The Little Singer Building is actually an L shape and has a smaller entrance at 88 Prince Street. The structure was meant to hold offices and factory space of the Singer Manufacturing Company. Flagg's major Singer Tower, which was the headquarters of the company, was completed in 1908 at Broadway and Liberty Street and was the tallest building in New York at the time; it was unfortunately destroyed in 1968. The Little Singer Building is one of Flagg's major extant endeavors; another notable New York example of his work is the **SCRIBNER STORE** (1832) at 597 Fifth Avenue, completed in 1914, which reflects similar design elements.

MERCHANT'S HOUSE MUSEUM

29 East 4th Street
PHONE: (212) 777-1089
WEB SITE: www.merchantshouse.com
E-MAIL: nyc1832@merchantshouse.org

TUCKED AWAY ON A site just a few doors from Washington Square, the Merchant's House Museum stands as New York's only surviving merchant family home from the mid-nineteenth century. Completed in 1832, the red brick and white marble row house is architecturally significant for the late-Federal exterior and Greek Revival interiors. Moreover, the collections preserved within the house are arguably the greater treasure, as well as a key to interpreting the domestic life of a wealthy New York merchant family. Three floors and eight period rooms feature the belongings of the family that lived there for almost a century. Seabury Tredwell, a prosperous New York merchant, acquired the house in 1835. After the death of his last surviving daughter in 1933, the Merchant's House and its contents—furnishings, clothing, and personal items—were carefully preserved as a record of domestic life during the time New York expanded from a colonial seaport to the thriving center of American commerce.

Museum visitors learn what life was really like in mid-nineteenth-century New York. They get an intimate look at the kitchens and family dining room, as well as the formal Greek Revival parlors with their black and gold mantelpieces, mahogany pocket doors, and detailed plaster ceiling medallions and ornamentation. Reflecting the prevailing taste of the day, these architectural elements create an ideal setting for furniture from New York's finest cabinetmakers (including Duncan Phyfe (1768–1868) and Joseph Meeks (1771–1868)), opulent decorative accessories such as Argand oil lamps with crystal prisms, silver candlesticks, and oil paintings that the Tredwells acquired over the years. The bedroom story and garden are also on view.

In addition to offering self-guided tours with docents on site to answer questions, the Merchant's House Museum presents ongoing exhibitions, such as *Called by the Bell—What Life Was Really Like for a Mid-Nineteenth-Century Servant*, as well as highlights of the permanent collection and rotating displays that include gowns and accessories worn by Tredwell's wife and daughters. Themed tours, such as "Life at Home in Nineteenth-Century New York City" and "Where Pinkies Find their Purpose" (which includes afternoon tea) are also available.

The museum is open from 12:00 to 5:00 p.m. Thursday through Monday. Closed Tuesday, Wednesday, and the following holidays: Easter Sunday, July 4, Thanksgiving Day, and Christmas Day. Group and school tours available by advance reservation. Admission fees apply.

◼ NATIONAL MUSEUM OF THE AMERICAN INDIAN

The George Gustav Heye Center
Alexander Hamilton U.S. Custom House
One Bowling Green
PHONE: (212) 514-3700
WEB SITE: http://americanindian.si.edu
E-MAIL: NMAIcollections@si.edu

THE GEORGE GUSTAV HEYE CENTER of the National Museum of the American Indian opened in 1994 and occupies part of the historic (ALEXANDER HAMILTON) U.S. CUSTOM HOUSE (see p. 102) adjacent to the northeast corner of Battery Park in Lower Manhattan. It is a branch of the Smithsonian's National Museum of the American Indian, which also has facilities in Washington, D.C. and Maryland. The museum houses thousands of extraordinary works made by Native Americans across North and South America, including a diverse range of objects such as wood and stone carvings, masks, pottery and baskets, painted hides, and much more, as well as works on paper and canvas. In addition to displaying its permanent collection and hosting temporary exhibitions of the works of both historical and contemporary Native American artists, the museum also sponsors music and dance performances, films, and other programs that explore the history, culture, and contributions of the Native people of the Americas.

The museum's collection of art and artifacts was assembled primarily by George Gustav Heye, a wealthy New Yorker who made his fortune in the petroleum industry and later in investment banking in the early twentieth century. Heye's interest in Native American art and artifacts began when he purchased his first artifact, a Navajo deerskin shirt, while working in Arizona. Heye would soon amass the largest private collection of Native American objects in the world. In 1922, the Heye Foundation's Museum of the American Indian opened to the public at 155th Street and Broadway. That location was closed in 1994, when the Smithsonian opened the National Museum of the American Indian with Heye's collection as its cornerstone in the Customs House location.

The exceptional objects in the collection are drawn from across the Americas, and include stone carvings and masks from the Northwest Coast of North America; baskets and pottery from the Southwest; objects from the Great Lakes region that date to the eighteenth century; a collection of objects from the southeastern United States amassed by the amateur archaeologist C. B. Moore; beautifully painted hides from the North American Plains; and Navajo weavings. Also represented are works by native people of the Caribbean, Mexico, Central and South America; ceramics from Costa Rica, central Mexico, and Peru; Olmec and Mayan carved jade; textiles and gold from the Andes; and elaborate Amazonian featherwork. The National Museum of the American Indian is devoted to not only displaying these works for their fine aesthetic qualities but also to contextualizing them to better ask and begin to answer larger cultural questions.

The museum is open 10:00 a.m. to 5:00 p.m. daily; Thursdays until 8:00 p.m. Admission is free.

THE NEW SCHOOL FOR SOCIAL RESEARCH, 1930
Joseph Urban (1872–1933)
A CALL FOR REVOLUTION AND UNIVERSAL BROTHERHOOD, 1930–31
66 West 12th Street
José Clementé Orozco (1927–1934)
WEB SITE: www.newschool.edu

THE NEW SCHOOL COMMISSIONED the Austrian architect Joseph Urban to design a building that would communicate the school's dedication to serving as a center of modern thought, culture, and art. The façade of the school reflects the modernist influences of the International Style, with its geometric repetitions and rhythms, such as those established by alternating white horizontal brick stripes against a dark background in patterns that echo the horizontal arrangement of rows of rectangular windows.

Urban, who arrived in the United States in 1911 and earned a reputation as an important set designer for the Metropolitan Opera and the Ziegfeld Follies in New York, also designed the **JOHN L. TISHMAN AUDITORIUM** at the New School. A striking, egg-shaped space that features an arched proscenium and a layered ceiling painted in nine shades of gray, the auditorium is an Art Deco masterpiece that may have been a model for **RADIO CITY MUSIC HALL**.

On the seventh floor of Urban's building is a five-fresco mural cycle by the famed Mexican Muralist José Clemente Orozco. Orozco, along with Diego Rivera (1886–1957) and David Alfaro Siqueiros (1896–1974), was one of the "Big Three" of what is sometimes referred to as the Mexican Muralist Renaissance, a state-sponsored public painting program begun in the 1920s to bring art that celebrated Mexico's past to the masses.

For the New School, Orozco painted **A CALL FOR REVOLUTION AND UNIVERSAL BROTHERHOOD** (1930–31), which offers a Marxist vision of peace and equality. It is the only mural by the Mexican Muralists in New York City that is still intact and in its original location; the others have either been destroyed or moved.

Just outside the mural room the viewer is greeted by the first fresco, **THE ALLEGORY OF SCIENCE, LABOR AND ART**, which asserts the equality of all men by picturing intellectual and physical labor involved in a symbiotic relationship with one another. Orozco also celebrates the laborer and heroicizes physicality by depicting the scientist and artist as active, raising their muscled arms to work just like their brothers on construction sites or in the fields.

Across from the entrance on the south wall is **THE FRATERNITY OF ALL MEN: THE TABLE OF UNIVERSAL BROTHERHOOD**, a coming together of men of various races, ethnicities, and classes at a single table, perhaps awaiting a meal and serious conversation, a scenario that may be a nod to the space's original function as a dining room at the New School.

On the north wall is **HOMECOMING OF THE WORKER OF A NEW DAY**, where Orozco anticipates another meal, with a table set with food and books for intellectual and physical sustenance. In the final two walls, historical figures like Gandhi, Stalin, and Lenin feature prominently in scenes that explore themes of oppression and hope through revolution.

Because the Orozco room is still used for meetings and conferences by the New School, it is not always accessible. It is, however, available and free to the general public by appointment. Please call (212) 229-5803, Ext. 2370, to make appointments. Appointments are not accepted for weekends or holidays. The Tishman Auditorium is of course used for events and performances. Contact the school to check on its availability.

It is worth noting that there are other important examples of work by Joseph Urban and José Clemente Orozco in New York City. Urban designed the much more theatrical **INTERNATIONAL MAGAZINE BUILDING** at 951–969 Eighth Avenue (now the Hearst Magazine Building) for publisher William Randolph Hearst in 1926–27. Urban's original building, which is capped by fluted columns that rise higher than the building itself, was even more dramatically topped off by a forty-six-story glass tower by the British architect Norman Foster (b. 1935) in 2006. Foster's **HEARST TOWER**, located at 57th Street and Eighth Avenue, has been certified by the United States Green Building Council and has been declared by one critic as "the most beautiful skyscraper to go up in New York since 1967."

Orozco's **DIVE BOMBER AND TANK** (1940), a six-panel "moveable" fresco, can be viewed at the **MUSEUM OF MODERN ART**. The panels, which Orozco painted in public view over a period of five weeks, can be arranged in any order and depict body parts and weaponry in a chilling vision of war and its consequences.

■ NEW MUSEUM OF CONTEMPORARY ART, 2002–07

235 Bowery
ARCHITECT: Kazuyo Sejima (b. 1956)
   and Ryue Nashizawa (b. 1966)
PHONE: (212) 219-1222
WEB SITE: www.newmuseum.org
E-MAIL: info@new museum.org

THE NEW MUSEUM'S NEW HOME, designed by the Tokyo-based architectural firm SANAA (Kazuyo Sejima and Ryue Nishizawa), with Gensla, New York, serving as executive architect, is a seven-story, 60,000-square-foot stack of shiny metal boxes. The museum's international board took a year searching for a new locale for the museum, away from its previous site on Prince Street, deep in consumer-driven SoHo; the mid-block Bowery location of this aluminum-clad wedding cake places it amid single-room-occupancy hotels and cooking-supply stores. The museum's lobby, a simple but ingenious expanse of wall-to-ceiling clear glass, places art squarely in the face of passers-by while also making the viewer keenly aware of the world outside its borders.

The stack of boxes that makes up the museum has also given SANAA the ability to create several large skylights that work in tandem with artificial lighting to give each gallery a softer light, depending on the weather conditions of the moment. Each gallery is large, raw, and simple, with concrete floors and exposed steel I-beams—and the top of the museum offers a 3,000-square-foot multipurpose space, offering views over the tenements of the Lower East Side and past the downtown towers to Brooklyn.

Set amidst a neighborhood that once was home to artists and a now waning bohemia, the museum's tower sits in a New York quarter from which those very inhabitants are now being displaced. Yet New York has always persisted with the positive aspects of change and growth in its neighborhoods. There has not been another tower by an architectural firm or architect in recent years in the city that has been this successful in creating a relationship with the city outside its doors.

Open Wednesday 12:00 to 6:00 p.m.; Thursday and Friday 12:00 to 10:00 p.m.; Saturday and Sunday 12:00 to 6:00 p.m. Closed Monday and Tuesday; the seventh-floor "Sky Room" with panoramic views is open on weekends only. CIT Free Thursday Evenings (from 7:00 to 10:00 p.m.).

RUBIN MUSEUM OF ART

150 West 17th Street
PHONE: (212) 620-5000
WEB SITE: www.rmanyc.com
E-MAIL: info@rmanyc.com

THE RUBIN MUSEUM OF ART offers a comprehensive collection of Himalayan paintings, sculptures, and textiles, dating from the twelfth through the twentieth centuries. The Himalayan mountain range is more than a 1,000 miles long, separating India from the Asian plateau, and the modern countries that are considered part of the geographic area addressed by the Rubin are Pakistan, India (including the province of Sikkim), Bangladesh, Nepal, Bhutan, and China (including the Tibetan Autonomous Region).

The museum, which opened in 2004, is housed in what was the Barneys department store in Manhattan's Chelsea neighborhood. Although extensively renovated, details from the original building were maintained, including French designer and interior architect Andrée Putman's (b. 1925) gorgeous steel-and-marble staircase that spirals through the seven-story gallery tower.

The museum has a particularly strong collection of painted textiles from the abstract **VAJRAVALI MANDALA** (c. 1440), which depict four of the forty-two mandalas of a Tibetan ritual text from the eleventh century. A mandala, often translated as "circle-circumference" or "completion," is used for contemplation or meditation to gain wisdom and compassion and generally is depicted as a tightly balanced, geometric composition within which deities reside. The Rubin also displays less abstract textiles with figuration and narrative such as the extraordinary **BUDDHA AMITABHA IN HIS PURE LAND** (nineteenth century), a brightly colored cloth from central Tibet, which features a glorious vision of paradise.

NEW YORK CITY

The collection's sculptural masterworks include the **VAJRADHARA, THE PRIMORDIAL BUDDHA** (fourteenth century), from Nepal, whose serenity and gentleness emerge from his lavishly decorated and gilt trappings. Similarly, the gilt and painted copper **BUDDHA SHAKYAMUNI** (thirteenth century) serves as a model of meditative calm and spirituality.

The museum is open Monday and Thursday, 11:00 a.m. to 5:00 p.m.; Wednesdays 11:00 a.m. to 7:00 p.m.; Fridays 11:00 a.m. to 10:00 p.m.; Saturday and Sunday 11:00 a.m. to 6:00 p.m.; closed Tuesdays. Admission fees apply, except on Fridays from 7:00 to 10:00 p.m., when the gallery is open free of charge. There is a parking garage at 17th Street and Avenue of the Americas and garages along 17th Street toward Union Square.

For those interested in continuing an exploration of Tibetan art, the **JACQUES MARCHAIS MUSEUM OF TIBETAN ART** in Staten Island displays art of the region within a more intimate setting designed to resemble a Tibetan temple. Located at 338 Lighthouse Avenue, Staten Island. (718) 987-3500. WEB SITE: www.tibetanmuseum.org. E-MAIL: info@tibetanmuseum.org.

STATUE OF LIBERTY, 1886
National Park Service
Statue of Liberty National Monument
Liberty Island
ARCHITECT: Frédéric Auguste Bartholdi (1834–1904)
PHONE: (212) 363-8343
WEB SITE: www.nps.gov/stli

THE STATUE OF LIBERTY was the culmination of plans set forth by the French government to commemorate the Centennial of the United States with a gift that would celebrate the ideal of liberty central to its founding.

The sculptor Frédéric Bartholdi was inspired by classical sculpture and by his understanding of Libertas, the Roman goddess of liberty. Additionally, Bartholdi's "Lady Liberty," whose right foot is raised as if in forward movement, recalls Eugène Delacroix's (1798–1863) *Liberty Leading the People* of 1830 and other representations of Marianne, an allegorical figure who represents liberty and is a symbol of the French Republic. Instead of a flag, which is a common attribute of Marianne, Bartholdi's Liberty holds a torch to guide the way and to welcome to America all those who would seek refuge from tyranny or oppression. Liberty also wears a crown of seven spikes to represent the seven seas and the seven continents, and she holds a tablet upon which the date July 4, 1776, is inscribed to honor the birth of the nation. Bartholdi initially envisioned that the statue would also literally function as a lighthouse, its torch lighting the way for those who sailed in the nearby waters. And, indeed, from 1886 to 1902, a lighthouse keeper was in charge of the operation of its electric light, which could be seen from about twent-four miles away. The torch was originally made of stained glass so that it could be lit from within. However, because of damage sustained by the statue in 1916 as a result of a sabotage-related explosion in the harbor carried out by German spies after the start of World War I, the glass was eventually removed and the torch was coated in gold leaf.

Because of the sheer size and technical and financial logistics of the project, the Statue was not completed and dedicated until ten years after the original goal of the Centennial. Even before being erected in New York Harbor, Bartholdi's achievement had captured the attention of both France and the United States through various exhibitions, including the presentation of the right arm and torch at the Centennial Exposition in Philadelphia and of the head at the Paris Exposition of 1878. Also, both countries participated in numerous fundraising endeavors, such as the sale of miniatures made possible when Bartholdi secured a U.S. patent of the statue. Performances like the staging at Paris's famed Opera of *Liberty Enlightening the World (La liberté éclairant le monde)* by the composer Charles Gounod not only helped fundraising efforts but also assured Liberty's fame well before her official unveiling in 1886 by President Grover Cleveland.

The statue is 151 feet tall, and, together with its pedestal and foundation, it soars to 305 feet. Its technical achievements alone are impressive and required Bartholdi to collaborate with, among others, Alexandre Gustav Eiffel (1832–1923), the engineer best known for the Eiffel Tower. Eiffel designed the armature for the statue's pure copper sheeting, creating an enormous iron pylon and a secondary steel framework for the statue's copper "skin." The pedestal, for which it was agreed the Americans would be responsible, was carried out by the American architect Richard Morris Hunt (1827–1895).

Hours are adjusted seasonally. Call (212) 363-3200 for current schedule information. There is technically no fee to enter the Statue of Liberty or Ellis

Island. However, visitors must have a "Monument Access Pass," which is available with the purchase of a ferry pass from Statue Cruises. It is strongly advised that you plan ahead and purchase Reserve Tickets, selecting the "Monument Pass" option, especially during high traffic periods like weekends and holidays, because there is a limit to how many visitors will be permitted each day. For more information on Statue Cruises go to www.statuecruises.com or call (877) 523-9849.

The Statue of Liberty participates in the City Pass program, which offers a discounted rate for a combined ticket to six top attractions in the area (American Museum of Natural History, Empire State Building, Museum of Modern Art, Metropolitan Museum of Art, Guggenheim Museum, Circle Line Sightseeing Cruises or Statue of Liberty).

Visitors must pass through security screenings comparable to passing through airport security checkpoints. Allow ample time for this process in planning your visit.

■ TRINITY CHURCH, 1846
89 Broadway
ARCHITECT: Richard Upjohn (1802–1878)
PHONE: (212) 602-0700
WEB SITE: www.trinitywallstreet.org

■ ST. PAUL'S CHAPEL, 1766
209 Broadway and Church Street
ARCHITECT: Andrew Gaultier (master craftsman)
PHONE: (212) 233-4164
WEB SITE: www.saintpaulschapel.org

FOUNDED BY CHARTER of King William III of England in 1697, the Parish of Trinity Church has been an important one in New York City. There have been three Trinity Church buildings at Broadway and Wall Street; the first Trinity Church building, a modest rectangular structure with a gambrel roof and small porch, was constructed in 1698. The present structure, designed by Richard Upjohn, was consecrated in 1846 and is an excellent architectural example of the Gothic Revival. When it was constructed, the church spire was a beacon of Lower Manhattan and could be seen from a distance from the New York harbor.

Upjohn was an English cabinetmaker who immigrated to the United States and became a leader of the American Gothic Revival. The basilica plan church is built in the Perpendicular Gothic Style, which was the vogue in fourteenth-century England. Many aspects of the church recall medieval precursors, including the stained glass windows. The church is built of brownstone, which was a local material that became popular around the time of the church construction.

The ornate bronze doors pay homage to the Baptistry in Florence, Italy. They were a gift of William Waldorf Astor as a memorial to his father, John Jacob Astor III, who had been a longtime active member of Trinity until his death in 1890. The architect Richard Morris Hunt (1828–1895) received the commission for the doors. He held an open competition to select the sculptors who would depict the expulsion of Adam and Eve from the Garden of Eden. Karl Bitter (1867–1915) won first place and executed the doors to the main entrance. His competition panel can be seen at the lower left. Charles Henry Niehaus (1855–1935) and J. Massey Rhind (1860–1936) were the runners-up and did the north and south church doors.

Trinity's churchyard predates the original church and was a Dutch burial ground. The original burial ground at Trinity Church includes the graves and memorials of many historic figures, including Alexander Hamilton, William Bradford, Robert Fulton, and Albert Gallatin. The churchyard of St. Paul's Chapel, at Broadway and Fulton, also has many historic tombstones.

ST. PAUL'S CHAPEL

COMPLETED IN 1766, St. Paul's Chapel is New York's oldest public building in continuous use and is one of the finest examples of American Georgian architecture. The chapel belongs to the Parish of Trinity Church and was built on land granted by Queen Anne of Great Britain.

Andrew Gaultier served as master craftsman, and James Crommelin Lawrence and Thomas McBean were possibly involved in various capacities in erecting this Episcopal chapel in the Georgian Classical style, which resembles James Gibbs's St. Martin-in-the-Fields in London, on which it is closely modeled. It is constructed of Manhattan mica-schist with brownstone quoins; all of its woodwork, woodcarving, and door hinges were done by hand.

George Washington worshiped at St. Paul's Chapel on his Inauguration Day on April 30, 1789. Washington also attended services at St. Paul's during the two years that New York served as the capital of the country. He had his own pew designed by Pierre L'Enfant, the designer of the city of Washington, D.C.

The chapel survived the Great New York City Fire of 1776 when a quarter of New York City burned following the British capture of the city in the Battle of Long Island in the Revolutionary War. St. Paul's is the only surviving church of the Revolutionary era in New York.

The chapel interior is elegant and spare. It stands in contrast to the interiors of grand style of European medieval cathedrals, such as Trinity Church, and instead has pale colors, a flat ceiling, and glass chandeliers that appear more akin to residential interiors. On the Broadway side of the chapel's exterior is an oak statue of the church's namesake, St. Paul, carved in a primitive style.

■ **(ALEXANDER HAMILTON) U.S. CUSTOM HOUSE, 1901–07**
ARCHITECT: Cass Gilbert (1859–1934)
■ **U.S. CUSTOM HOUSE MURALS, 1937**
One Bowling Green
ARCHITECT: Reginald Marsh (1898–1854)

A DESIGN COMPETITION was held in 1899 for the U.S. Custom House planned for the site where New York was founded by Dutch settlers. The competition was won by St. Paul architect Cass Gilbert, who later executed the famous **WOOLWORTH BUILDING** in New York in 1913 (see p. 104). The Custom House is one of New York's grandest examples of Beaux-Arts architecture and is adorned by notable works of painting and sculpture. The rotunda is one of the most majestic open public spaces.

The façade is appointed with four major sculptures by Daniel Chester French (1850–1931): the Four Continents, symbolized by a female figure, from left to right: **ASIA**, **AMERICA**, **EUROPE**, and **AFRICA**. There is a high-relief cartouche that crowns the attic façade by Karl Bitter (1867–1915). But the most important jewel, aside from the building itself, is the Treasury Relief

Art Project (WPA) mural commissions that decorate the rotunda interior by Social Realist Reginald Marsh, completed in 1937. Painted in *fresco seco* (on dry plaster), the eight large panels chronicle port activity in New York and the arrival in the city of three ocean liners: *The Washington* (American); *The Queen Mary* (British); and the *Normandie* (French). There are eight smaller panels in grisaille that depict famous explorers. It is among New York's most notable mural cycles, and the artist remarked upon receiving the commission:

> I feel very proud that the honor to paint these walls has fallen to me. It's a man-sized job, with many problems—all those curves, etc... Here is a chance to paint contemporary shipping with a rich and real power neither like the storytelling or propagandist painting, which everybody does. I have in the past painted dozens of watercolors around N.Y. harbor, and would like to get at it with some of this knowledge.

The lavish building has a Roman dome, and is an ideal of Beaux-Arts design. It has a first floor, topped on the second level with imposing Corinthian columns, which is capped by two narrow attic stories. With grandeur, the building incorporates elaborate and formal design elements; the sculpture, painting, and decoration by well-known artists are integral to the architectural conception of the building.

WASHINGTON SQUARE ARCH, 1892
Washington Square Park and Fifth Avenue
ARCHITECT: Stanford White (1853–1906)

DESIGNED BY THE gilded age's most prominent architect, Stanford White, Washington Square is defined by the monumental arch that stands at the north end of the park at the beginning of Lower Fifth Avenue.

In celebration of the centennial in 1889 of George Washington's inauguration as the first president of the United States, a large temporary plaster and wood memorial arch designed by

White was constructed over Fifth Avenue north of the park for the festivities. For the celebration, it was festooned with papier-mâché wreaths and garlands of flowers, and lit with hundreds of newly invented incandescent lights. It proved to be so popular that White was commissioned to create a permanent marble arch, which he designed in homage to Roman triumphal arches. White modeled the arch after the Arc de Triomphe in Paris. There

Woolworth Building, with surrounding buildings, c. 1913

is decorative sculpture as part of the architecture: winged figures by the noted American sculptor Frederick MacMonnies (1863–1937) are additions to the arch; in 1918 two statues of George Washington were added to the north side. The sculptures depict Washington as a warrior and in peacetime: **WASHINGTON IN WAR** (1916) by Herman A. MacNeil (1866–1947) is on the East Pier; and **WASHINGTON IN PEACE** (1918) by A. Stirling Calder (1870–1945) is on the West Pier. The arch was completed in 1892 and was dedicated in 1895.

Washington Square Park is built over a former cemetery that was closed in 1825. The remains of more than 20,000 people rest under the square. The area, however, became a fashionable residential district by 1830. A row of houses, built of red brick in Greek Revival style, became known as "The Row." The entrances are flanked by Ionic and Doric columns and have marble balustrades. By the end of the nineteenth century, the north side continued to attract rich and leading citizens, while the south side was populated with immigrants living in tenement houses.

In 1849, work on the area began to create the first true park on the site. As of 1971, cars were no longer allowed passage under the arch as they once were. The protected row of Greek Revival–style houses on the north side of the park remains intact. The square has become a centerpiece to New York University, whose campus surrounds much of the park, and the arch has become one of the most prominent landmarks of Greenwich Village.

■ WOOLWORTH BUILDING, 1911–13
233 Broadway between Barclay Street and Park Place
ARCHITECT: Cass Gilbert (1859–1934)

CASS GILBERT'S ARCHITECTURAL MASTERPIECE, the Neo-Gothic Woolworth Building, was called a "Cathedral of Commerce" because of its homage to European Gothic cathedrals. The pioneering skyscraper of fifty-seven stories opened in 1913 to a whirl of media hype as the tallest building in the world; it remained the tallest until 1930. Frank W. Woolworth of the five-and-dime empire commissioned the building in 1910; he paid $13.5 million in cash for the building and wanted a structure inspired by the Houses of Parliament in London that was taller than the Metropolitan Life Tower.

The building is a sturdy tower that rises flush from the twenty-four-story setback and then is topped by Gothic cap and spire. With the skyscraper still a relatively new innovation, Gilbert and engineers Gunvald Aus and Kort Berle designed an extra-sturdy structure. With a steel frame on massive caissons and decoration masking its reinforced design, the building was said to be able to withstand winds of 200 miles per hour. The lower floors are composed of limestone and have portal arches. The extensive Gothicized decorative carving on the façade and the tower is white terra cotta and has additional Gothic details such as buttresses and gargoyles.

The lobby is one of the most ornate in the city and was designed by Heineicke and Bowen—a firm known for its interiors. The lobby includes a barrel-vaulted ceiling with a Byzantine-style mosaic and a stained glass dome over the marble staircase. Elaborate bronze mailboxes incorporate the letter "W" into the design and have shields with caducei that symbolize Mercury, the god of commerce. The splendor of the elevator banks is worthy of a church choir and altar. There are also lobby sculptures of Woolworth counting his dimes and the architect Gilbert cradling the model of the buildings. Murals on either side of the mezzanine-level hallway depict the allegories of Labor and Commerce

Greek marble used in the lobby and Vermont marble for the lobby floors are among the expensive materials and contribute to the unparalleled splendor seen in this architectural jewels of the early twentieth century.

THE BOROUGHS

BROOKLYN

BROOKLYN BRIDGE, 1883
ARCHITECT: John Augustus Roebling (1806-1869)

ONE OF THE OLDEST suspension bridges in America at the time of its completion in 1883, the Brooklyn Bridge was the largest suspension bridge in the world. In 1840 John Roebling, a bridge designer and the owner of a wire and rope company in Trenton, New Jersey, patented a way of spinning wire rope, a watershed development in bridge design. This advance won him bridge commissions, including the Niagara Falls Suspension Bridge (1841–55) and the Cincinnati Bridge (1856–67), which were precursors to the Brooklyn Bridge

As early as 1855, Roebling conceived of building a suspension bridge from Manhattan to Brooklyn over the East River from Fulton Street using steel-wire cables and stays. It took some years to garner enthusiasm for the project, but construction on the bridge began in January 1870. Roebling died as the result of an injury while surveying for the bridge. His son, Washington Roebling, continued his father's work and was greatly assisted by his wife, Emily Warren Roebling, who became versed in bridge engineering and saw the project through. She was also the first person to cross the bridge upon its opening in 1883.

The aerodynamics of bridge design were not fully understood and Roebling also designed the bridge to hold considerably more weight than was needed. That, along with the open truss structure that is less impacted by winds, accounts for the fact that the Brooklyn Bridge survived and could

Brooklyn Bridge

continue to function well into the future, surpassing other bridges of its era. The vast span and towers of the bridge necessitated the building of foundations seventy-eight feet below the water level. The span of the river is 1,596 feet and the total length of the bridge is 5,989 feet.

The sturdy twin granite and limestone masonry towers in the Gothic style with double peaked arches create the signature majestic look of the bridge. At the time of construction, their height was rivaled only by **TRINITY CHURCH** (see p. 100) in Lower Manhattan. The sweeping harplike cable supports combined with the wide expanse give the bridge a look of particular elegance and grace. Upon completion, the Brooklyn Bridge was called "The Eighth Wonder of the World."

The bridge is accessible by vehicle from FDR Drive, Park Row, Chambers/Centre Streets, and Pearl/Frankfort Streets and on the Brooklyn side there are entrances at Tillary/Adams Street, Sands/Pearl Streets, and Exit 28B of the eastbound Brooklyn-Queens Expressway.

Pedestrian access on the Manhattan side is available from Centre Street or the south staircase of the Brooklyn Bridge–City Hall IRT subway station. Pedestrian access on the Brooklyn side is at Tillary and Adams Streets or a staircase on Prospect Street between Cadman Plaza East and West. There is a wide pedestrian walkway in the center of the bridge elevated above the traffic lanes.

■ THE BROOKLYN MUSEUM, 1897

200 Eastern Parkway
ARCHITECT: McKim, Mead, and White
PHONE: (718) 638-5000
WEB SITE: www.brooklynmuseum.org
E-MAIL: information@brooklynmuseum.org

THE BROOKLYN MUSEUM OF ART is housed in a 560,000-square-foot building designed by the renowned architectural firm of McKim, Mead, and White, whose original plans for an enormous Beaux-Arts style building were only partially realized. Had the museum been built according to the first designs, it would have become the largest art museum in the world. Of particular architectural interest is the Beaux-Arts Court, with its extraordinary skylight and immense roof that spans more than two acres. The museum building has been extensively expanded and renovated since it first opened to the public in 1897, and today it houses one of the finest and most comprehensive collections of art; among its highlights are its American, European, Egyptian, African, and Islamic holdings.

Among the extraordinary paintings in the American collection are early portraits, including Gilbert Stuart's (1755–1828) **GEORGE WASHINGTON** (1796). Painted in the so-called Grand Manner style, it captures the noble character and importance of Washington, whose military accomplishments, presidency, and contribution to winning independence are referenced by symbolic details such as his sword and a copy of the U.S. Constitution. The Museum's Hudson River School landscape holdings include such breathtaking works as Albert Bierstadt's (1830–1902) sublime **A STORM IN THE ROCKY MOUNTAINS, MT. ROSALIE** (1866), a panoramic vista of dramatic mountain peaks, valleys, and ominous clouds and weather effects. American genre painting, which captured slices of ordinary life, became increasingly popular in the nineteenth century, and one of Brooklyn's most interesting genre paintings is Lilly Martin Spencer's (1822–1902) **KISS ME AND YOU'LL KISS THE 'LASSES** (1856). Spencer, who was a rare woman artist who financially supported her husband and children by painting primarily domestic scenes, here depicts a woman with a broad grin and an inviting gaze working within a kitchen space. John Singer Sargent's (1856–1925) **AN OUT-OF-DOORS STUDY (PAUL HELLEU SKETCHING WITH HIS WIFE)** (1889), painted in the artists' colony in the Cotswolds, England, is at once a portrait of a colleague and his wife painting *en plein air* and a self-referential record of his own working method in paintings of this type, reflecting the influences of Impressionist techniques and themes on his development.

Highlights of Brooklyn's collection of twentieth-century and contemporary American art include Georgia O'Keeffe's (1887–1986) **BROOKLYN BRIDGE** (1948), which reduces the iconic structure to the bridge's two Gothic arches and its cables. The streamlined painting is emphatically modern with its emphasis on industrial and geometric form, while its composition and the Gothic architecture it references recall the stained glass windows of historic cathedrals. Stuart Davis's (1894–1964) **THE MELLOW PAD** (1945–51) reflects the layering of flat shapes, bright colors, and graphics that are characteristic of Davis's often joyous and energized works, suggesting the influences of jazz, the American urban landscape and its billboards and signs, as well as artistic movements like Cubism.

Located within the museum's Elizabeth A. Sackler Center for Feminist Art is Judy Chicago's (b. 1939) **THE DINNER PARTY** (1974–79), perhaps the boldest and most monumental installation that was a product of the rise of the feminist art movement of the 1970s. The massive banquet table is triangular in form, measuring forty-eight feet on each side, to suggest equality. The table is divided into thirty-nine place settings, each uniquely designed to reflect the accomplishments of the honored guests—notable women throughout history, including primordial goddesses, queens such as Hatshepsut, the female pharaoh, writers like Emily Dickinson, activists like Sojourner Truth, and artists like Georgia O'Keeffe. On the "Heritage Floor" at the center of the room and upon which the triangular table sits are inscribed the names of 999 mythical and historical women on hand-cast porcelain tiles. The names and the project itself attempts to counteract and expose the marginalization and erasure of the names and accomplishments of countless women throughout history. In Chicago's words, **THE DINNER PARTY** asks "how many women had struggled into prominence or been able to make their ideas known."

The museum's holdings in American sculpture are exceptional and include one of the six versions of Hiram Powers's (1805–1873) Neoclassical **GREEK SLAVE** (1869), another version of which can be seen at the **NEWARK MUSEUM**. Shocking for its unprecedented nudity and celebrated for its ideal beauty, Greek Slave ranked among the most well-known works of the period. Beaux-Arts bronze sculpture is also well-represented by Augustus Saint-Gaudens (1848–1907), whose detailed bronze **BUST OF ABRAHAM LINCOLN** (1922) depicts Lincoln deep in thought, and Frederick MacMonnies (1863–1937), whose marble **BACCHANTE** (1894) appears to be exuberantly leaping into the viewer's space.

The museum's sculpture garden is dedicated to preserving the public sculptural history of New York by recovering and presenting turn-of-the-century architectural sculpture and ornament from buildings demolished throughout the metropolitan area. The museum building itself was elaborated with the sculptural work of Daniel Chester French (1850–1931), who was responsible for the sculptural program of the pediment and for the massive and classical female allegorical figures, **BROOKLYN** (1915) and **MANHATTAN** (1915).

The European collection comprises excellent work from the Medieval period to the present. Among the most noteworthy European paintings in the museum is Edgar Degas's (1834–1917) **MADEMOISELLE FIOCRE IN THE BALLET "LA SOURCE"** (c. 1867–68), a large work that at first glance has its roots in traditional history and narrative painting; however, upon closer inspection, details such as the cast-off ballet shoes and slouched-over women lost in their own thoughts reflect the Degas who was throughout his career preoccupied with picturing the behind-the-scenes, quiet, more intimate moments that occurred backstage at ballets or operas. Degas's Impressionist colleague Berthe Morisot's (1841–1895) beautiful portrait **MADAME BOURSIER AND HER DAUGHTER** (1873) demonstrates Morisot's exceptional application of quick brushstrokes and her keen understanding of color. Among the best sculptural works in the European galleries is Jean-Baptiste Carpeaux's (1827–1875) **A NEGRESS** (1868), an expressive bust of a struggling woman whose torso is bound with ropes and who allegorically represents Africa and the institution of slavery. The bust's inscription reads *"Pourquoi naître esclave"* (Why born a slave?).

The Brooklyn Museum's collection of ancient Egyptian art is extraordinary and one of the largest in the United States. Among the well-known objects in the collection is the abstracted **FEMALE FIGURINE** or **BIRD LADY** (c. 3650–3300 B.C.), a painted terracotta figure made in the pre-Dynastic period, before the development of writing. Given its age, little is known about the purpose of this graceful figure, though it has been posited based on evidence from similar figures depicted on vessels from the period that she may have been a goddess. **THE WILBOUR PLAQUE** (c. 1353–36 B.C.) is a limestone slab that was used as an instructive model for sculptors; the hole at the top indicates that it may have been hung from a wall of a workshop for easier viewing and study. It features King Akhenaten and his wife, Nefertiti, and is rendered in the elegant style of the Amarna period, with the elongated head and neck of the figures carved in low relief by a lovely serpentine line that gently outlines the form, features, and accessories of the king and queen.

The African Art collection is the largest in an American museum and includes more than 5,000 objects from more than a hundred different cultures. The collection includes figurative sculpture, Berber jewelry, masks, beadwork, processional crosses, and works by contemporary African artists. Among the most extraordinary African works at the museum is **FIGURE OF A HORNBLOWER** (1500–50) from the Royal Court of Benin, a figure composed of a copper alloy and designed to sit on an ancestral altar to pay tribute to the culture's deceased kings. One of only ten such figures that are known to have survived, the hornblower has garments and a hat that are covered with beautiful geometric and floral patterns. The **FIGURE OF A MOTHER HOLDING A CHILD (LUPINGU LUA LUIMPE)**, a nineteenth-century wood and copper alloy sculpture from the Democratic Republic of the Congo, celebrates motherhood and also serves as a protective figure to bring health and safety during pregnancy and childbirth; the elongated mother's lower body extends into a point, making it possible to be planted into a pot that would have contained natural materials thought to have protective powers.

The museum's Islamic holdings span several centuries and regions, with particular strengths in Persian art, including miniatures, oil paintings, calligraphy, ceramics, lacquerwork, carpets, textiles, and costumes, constituting one of the most renowned collections of Persian art outside of Iran. A high point of the Persian collection's particularly exceptional group of works from the Qajar dynasty (1785–1925) is the richly painted **PORTRAIT OF PRINCE YAHYA** (c. 1835–36), attributed to Muhammad Hasan (active 1808–1840) and most likely designed to fit into an architectural niche. The prince's stylized face is truly beautiful and almost androgynous, with its porcelain skin and reddish cheeks that contrast dramatically with his thick black hair and eyebrows. The artist delights in suggesting the status and importance of the prince by representing his material wealth in such details as the jewels, the beautiful carpet on which he kneels, and his bold, red, and elaborate clothing. The Museum's Islamic collection also represents works from other regions with objects such as Ottoman Turkish carpets, textiles, and manuscripts and North African and Turkoman textiles, costumes, and jewelry.

The Brooklyn Museum is open Wednesday to Friday 10:00 a.m. to 5:00 p.m.; Saturday 11:00 a.m. to 6:00 p.m. (hours are generally extended to 11:00 p.m. on the first Saturday of each month, where from 5:00 to

11:00 p.m. they feature free art and entertainment); Sunday 11:00 a.m. to 6:00 p.m.; closed Mondays and Tuesdays. Admission with a suggested donation. Downloadable audio tour podcasts are available of the Museum's Web site. Limited paid parking is available off Washington Avenue at the rear of the museum.

The Brooklyn Museum is part of a larger system of parks and gardens that includes **PROSPECT PARK** and the **BROOKLYN BOTANIC GARDEN**, also partly designed by McKim, Mead, and White. Located on a fifty-two-acre site southeast of the museum, the garden, built between 1912 and 1917, was deliberately aligned with the museum so that the Cherry Esplanade is located on an axis directly behind the museum. The Brooklyn Botanic Garden is a truly extraordinary space devoted to nature and to exhibiting countless plants, trees, flowers, and brilliant landscape designs. Its numerous gardens include the first Japanese garden to be completed within an American public garden.

The garden has seasonal hours and is generally open Tuesday to Friday, March through October, from 8:00 a.m. to 6:00 p.m.; weekends and holidays, 10:00 a.m. to 6:00 p.m.; November through February, hours are 8:00 a.m. to 4:30 p.m., Tuesday to Friday; weekends and holidays, 10:00 a.m. to 4:30 p.m.; closed Mondays. Admission fees apply; combination art and garden tickets that offer admission both to the Museum and the Botanic Garden are available. Free guided tours are offered at 1:00 p.m. on weekends. 1000 Washington Avenue; PHONE: (718) 623-7200; WEB SITE: www.bbg.org

■ **GRAND ARMY PLAZA AND PROSPECT PARK**
ARCHITECT: John H. Duncan (1855-1929)
■ **PROSPECT PARK (1860s)**
Eastern Parkway and Flatbush Avenue
Frederick Law Olmsted (1822-1903) and Calvert Vaux (1824-1895)
PHONE: (718) 965-8951
WEB SITE: www.prospectpark.org
E-MAIL: info@prospectpark.org

LOCATED IN THE HEART of Brooklyn, Prospect Park is a 585-acre natural retreat designed by the celebrated landscape architects Frederick Law Olmsted and Calvert Vaux, who were also responsible for **CENTRAL**

PARK. Inspired by the English pastoral style, Olmsted and Vaux designed an extraordinary space that offered viewers a range of sights and experiences, from the picturesque to the sublime, and created a haven from the increasing pace and the heightened stimulation of modern city life. Among the park's highlights are the deliberately undefined grassy slopes of Long Meadow; **LITCHFIELD VILLA** (1857); **LEFFERTS HISTORIC HOUSE** (c. 1783); the **BOATHOUSE** (1905); the **TENNIS HOUSE** (1910); numerous water features including the sixty-acre lake; and the last remaining natural forest in Brooklyn.

The park's main entrance, **GRAND ARMY PLAZA**, is an eleven-acre oval plaza formed at the intersection of Flatbush Avenue, Eastern Parkway, Prospect Park West, and other streets. The plaza is anchored by a large triumphal arch inspired by such classic examples as the Roman Arch of Titus (after A.D. 81) or the Parisian Arc de Triomphe (1806). John H. Duncan, most famous for designing **GRANT'S TOMB** (see p. 16), was responsible for the **SOLDIERS AND SAILORS MEMORIAL ARCH** (1892), a tribute to the heroes of the Civil War, which serves as both a grand entrance and a line of demarcation, separating the urban space of the city from the oasis within the park.

Sculptural elements were later added by Frederick MacMonnies (1863–1937), who sculpted, among other pieces, **THE QUADRIGA** (1896), a chariot driven by an allegorical figure representing the United States that sits atop the arch. Such horse-drawn chariot groupings, based on the chariots of the gods in classical mythology, are commonly found capping off triumphal arches or other classically inspired structures.

Thomas Eakins (1844–1916) and William O'Donovan (1844–1920) also participated in the project, designing bronze equestrian relief panels featuring Abraham Lincoln and Ulysses S. Grant in the inner archway. The entrance was further enhanced by the acclaimed architect Stanford White (1853–1906), who added four eagle-topped Neoclassical columns, the paired granite pavilions, and the low wall with carved bronze urns.

The plaza also features fountains, including **BAILEY FOUNTAIN** (1932), with sculptures of the ferocious god of the sea, Neptune, along with male and female nudes representing Wisdom and Felicity, all sculpted by Eugene Francis Savage (1883–1978).

In addition to the tremendous landscape designs of Law and Olmstead,

Prospect Park also features several significant architectural and historical points of interest; these include **LITCHFIELD VILLA** (1857), built by the famous architect Alexander Jackson Davis (1803–1892), who also designed the Gothic Revival mansion **LYNDHURST** (see p. 144) in Tarrytown. The asymmetrical Italianate Litchfield Villa is a grand mansion with a variety of towers, bays, and porches, originally built for a railroad pioneer and real

The Soldiers and Sailors Memorial Arch at Grand Army Plaza

estate developer who was forced to surrender the property to the city when Prospect Park was built. The three-story villa features a dramatic Grand Hall, a circular reception area capped by a skylit dome and surrounded by a second-floor gallery. The house's interesting decorative elements include a multicolored tiled floor, columns resembling bamboo stalks, column capitals in the form of corn cobs and wheat stalks, and an elaborate ceiling mural.

LEFFERTS HISTORIC HOUSE, one of only a few surviving farmhouses from Brooklyn's Dutch Settlement period, was built in 1783 and today features period rooms and demonstration gardens and fields that recreate for the visitor daily life in the Brooklyn of the 1820s.

In 1905, Olmstead's and Vaux's original **BOATHOUSE** was replaced with the current Beaux-Arts-style building designed by Frank J. Helmle (1868–1939) and Ulrich Huberty (1876–1910), who also designed the **TENNIS HOUSE** (1910) on the Long Meadow. Inspired in part by a sixteenth-century Venetian library, the Boathouse features a white matte-glazed terra cotta façade with Tuscan columns and capped with a balustrade.

The Tennis House's Neoclassical colonnaded façade recalls ancient Greek temple designs and features a raised pavilion surrounded by columns and topped with arches and a red tile roof. The park once featured about 300 lawn tennis courts along the Long Meadow, and the Tennis House was a shelter and locker room for those who participated in the recreational pursuit.

Litchfield Villa, located at 95 Prospect Park West, near 5th Street, and currently used as administrative office space, has been undergoing extensive renovations over the last several years, but the Grand Hall and parts of the gallery are open to the general public Monday through Friday, 9:00 a.m. to 5:00 p.m. Admission is free.

Lefferts Historic House is located at the Children's Corner, inside the Park's Willink Entrance, at the intersection of Flatbush and Ocean Avenues and Empire Boulevard. Check the Web site for seasonal hours, but generally the house is open Thursday through Sunday and holidays, 12:00 to 5:00 p.m., April through November; it is open until 6:00 p.m. in July and August; and December through March, it is open weekends and school holidays, 12:00 to 4:00 p.m. Admission is free.

The Boathouse, which features the Prospect Park Audubon Center and the Park's Visitor Center, is located just inside the Lincoln Road and Ocean Avenue entrance. The hours of the Boathouse and the Audubon Center change seasonally, though it is generally open 12:00 to 5:00 p.m. Thursday through Sunday, from April to November; December through March, it is open on weekends and school holidays, 12:00 to 4:00 p.m. Check the Web site or call for more up-to-date information. Admission is free.

A herald figure from The Quadriga *(1896) atop the Grand Army Plaza Arch, by Frederick MacMonnies*

The Tennis House, located on the edge of the Long Meadow, is most easily reached from the 15th, 9th, and 3rd Street entrances.

To find out about seasonal events held at the park or for more information, see the Web site or call the events hotline at (718) 965-8999. Free parking is available by Wollman Rink, accessed either through the Parkside and Oceanside avenues or the Lincoln Road and Ocean Avenue entrances.

THE BRONX

■ BARTOW-PELL MANSION MUSEUM, 1836–42
895 Shore Road, Pelham Bay Park
The Bronx
PHONE: (718) 885-1461
WEB SITE: www.bartowpellmansionmuseum.org
E-MAIL: info@bpmm.org

THE HISTORIC BARTOW-PELL HOUSE, a Greek Revival stone mansion, was built between 1836 and 1842 for the Robert Bartow family. The land, which originally spanned some 9,000 acres, was first purchased in 1654 from the Siwanoy Indians by Thomas Pell, an English doctor.

The estate, which today includes the mansion, formal terraces, herb and perennial gardens, the Pell family burial grounds, and a carriage house, was sold to the city in 1888 and lay in disrepair until it was restored by efforts led by the International Garden Club, which commissioned the architectural firm of Delano and Aldrich to oversee the restoration beginning in 1914. The house and gardens, which recreate for the visitor stylish mid-nineteenth-century country life in the Pelham Bay area, opened to the public in 1946.

The house's period antiques and furnishings include extremely fine examples of Neoclassical American Empire and Gothic Revival furniture. One of the most stunning pieces in the house is the canopied **LANNUIER BED**, by the French-American early-nineteenth-century cabinetmaker Charles Honoré Lannuier (1779–1819). It is the only documented Launnuier bed that has its original crown.

Architectural highlights include the elegant, freestanding elliptical staircase that winds its way from the entrance hall through the upper floors and the Orangery or the Conservatory, which was redesigned by Delano and Aldrich, and is encompassed by beautiful Colonial Revival fan windows and architectural moldings.

The lovely grounds include Delano and Aldrich's Terrace Garden, a rectangular walled garden composed of descending terraces and divided into four quadrants by flagstone walks and steps. Neoclassical in style and influenced by British landscape design, the garden includes a water feature in the lowest terrace, where a square garden pool and fountain are bordered by seasonal planting beds and walks. The grounds also include a Carriage House, used as a barn and stable by the Bartow family, that reflects the mansion's architecture and construction.

The Bartow-Pell Mansion is open Wednesday, Saturday, and Sunday 12:00 to 4:00 p.m.; the Carriage House is open seasonally, April through October. Admission fees apply to visit the house. The gardens and grounds,

Bartow-Pell Mansion Museum

which also include hiking trails that allow visitors to view water and marshlands and the remains of a dock used by the Bartow family, are part of Pelham Bay Park. The garden and grounds, open 8:30 p.m. until dusk, are open daily and are free to the public.

HALL OF FAME FOR GREAT AMERICANS, 1901 GOULD MEMORIAL LIBRARY, 1899

Bronx Community College
University Avenue at 181st Street
The Bronx
PHONE: (718) 289-5100 or (718) 289-5161
ARCHITECT: Stanford White (1853–1906)
WEB SITE: www.bcc.cuny.edu/hallofFame

ONE OF THE BEST-KEPT SECRETS of the Metropolitan area is this architectural jewel—the Gould Memorial Library and Hall of Fame for Great Americans designed by the premier architect of the Gilded Age, Stanford White. Comparable to Columbia University's Low Library, which was designed by Charles McKim, White's colleague in their firm, McKim, Mead, and White, the Gould Memorial Library originally belonged to the Bronx campus of New York University.

Designed in the Neoclassical style with a great coffered dome, the library pays homage to the Pantheon in Rome. The library is in the form a Greek cross with the dome crowning the circular reading room. Sixteen Corinthian columns made of green Irish marble line the rotunda and statues of the Greek Muses line the balcony. There are also stained-glass windows by Tiffany in the vestibules and the mezzanine level of the rotunda.

The Hall of Fame, conceived as a Neoclassical promenade in an arc shape, is situated on the highest point in Manhattan and provides a panorama across the Harlem River to the Cloisters in Fort Tryon Park and the Palisades. Built of limestone and granite, it has a vaulted tile ceiling and was conceived to honor notable individuals. To be eligible for nomination, a person must have been American or a naturalized citizen (since 1914), been dead for twenty-five years (since 1922; from 1900 through 1920, a nominee had to be dead only ten years); and must have made a major contribution to the economic, political, or cultural life of the nation. Nominees were elected by a simple majority vote, except from 1925 through 1940, when a three-fifths majority was required, and in 1976 when a point system replaced the majority vote

The structure is an open-air colonnade with space for 102 bronze portrait busts that also have bronze plaques with the name, date, and achievements of the individuals. The first twenty-nine plaques were executed by Tiffany Studios.

There are ninety-eight bronze busts that line the colonnade, many executed by America's most distinguished sculptors, including Daniel Chester French, James Earle Fraser, and Frederick MacMonnies. Among those citizens who have been honored are authors, educators, architects, artists, statesman, musicians, scientists, philanthropists, and explorers, among others, such as: George Washington, Abraham Lincoln, Samuel F. B. Morse, Ben Franklin, Walt Whitman, Thomas Jefferson, Ralph Waldo Emerson, Nathaniel Hawthorne, Harriet Beecher Stowe, Gilbert Stuart, John Quincy Adams, Oliver Wendell Holmes, Edgar Allan Poe, Andrew Jackson,

Hall of Fame for Great Americans

James Fenimore Cooper, Alexander Hamilton, Daniel Boone, Patrick Henry, Augustus St. Gaudens, James McNeill Whistler, Stephen Foster, Booker T. Washington, Woodrow Wilson, Susan B. Anthony, and Theodore Roosevelt, among many others.

White also designed the adjoining buildings—the Hall of Languages (1894) and Philosophy Hall (1912).

The Hall of Fame is open to the public for tours daily between the hours of 10:00 a.m. and 5:00 p.m. Admission is free.

QUEENS

THE ISAMU NOGUCHI FOUNDATION AND GARDEN MUSEUM

32–37 Vernon Boulevard
Long Island City
PHONE: (718) 204-7088
WEB SITE: http://noguchi.org
E-MAIL: info@noguchi.org

FOUNDED BY THE JAPANESE-AMERICAN sculptor Isamu Noguchi (1904–1988) in 1985 to display his own work, the Noguchi Museum offers a tranquil oasis from the city. Designed to encourage an intimate relationship of quiet contemplation between visitors and Noguchi's sculpture and design, the museum occupies a renovated factory located across the street from Noguchi's Long Island City studio, where he had worked since the early 1960s.

The son of a Japanese father and an American mother, Noguchi established a museum that, like his work, reflects his personal biography, synthesizing and exploring sometimes opposing energies and traditions. The galleries, the Japanese-inspired sculpture garden, and the works within both spaces, reflect a merging of Eastern and Western sensibilities.

The museum offers a comprehensive view of Noguchi's diverse career and talents, exhibiting his mostly abstract sculpture made of a range of materials, alongside his famous **AKARI** light sculptures, architectural models, set designs for artists like the great dancer and choreographer Martha Graham, drawings, and furniture and interior designs.

Noguchi was inspired to create his first Akari light sculptures—light fixtures made of mulberry paper and bamboo—after a visit to Japan, where he observed the hanging paper lanterns illuminating night fishing on the Nagara River. About this new direction in his art, Noguchi said "Paper and bamboo fitted in with my feeling for the quality and sensibility of light. Its very lightness questions materiality, and is consonant with our appreciation today of the less thingness of things, the less encumbered perceptions. The name *akari*, which I coined, means in Japanese 'light as illumination.' It also suggests lightness as opposed to weight."

The museum also displays some of Noguchi's furniture designs, including an iconic **COFFEE TABLE** (1948) which was first designed in 1939, then later distributed by Herman Miller Inc., a leader in modern furniture design and manufacturing. Made of a glass top and two adjoining walnut pieces, the Coffee Table was inspired by Noguchi's interlocking biomorphic sculpture.

The museum is open Wednesday to Friday 10:00 a.m. to 5:00 p.m.; Saturday and Sunday 11:00 a.m. to 6:00 p.m. Admission fees apply. Free gallery talks are held at 2 p.m. Wednesday through Sunday. The Noguchi Museum entrance is located at 9-01 33rd Road (at Vernon Boulevard). Parking is often available on the streets around the museum.

TWA TERMINAL, 1956–62
Kennedy Airport
Jamaica, Queens
ARCHITECT: Eero Saarinen (1910–1961)
PHONE: (718) 244-4444

THE TWA TERMINAL at Kennedy Airport is one of the iconic structures of modern architecture of the twentieth century. Its futurist look and soaring, birdlike abstract form were suggestive of the rapidly evolving new aesthetic philosophy—one that placed the onus of expression on the architect. In winning the contract for this building, the Detroit-based architect Eero Saarinen designed the terminal, or flight center as it was first called, defining a new aesthetic vocabulary for architecture that emphasized the spatial relationships, both interior and exterior, that result from the design of the forms.

Finnish-born architect Saarinen (son of the Finnish architect Eliel Saarinen) created architecture dependent on engineering and used an invisible skeleton of steel that supports the sweeping sculptural concrete roof and decorative curvilinear forms. With a structure that suggests soaring flight and the drama of flight and travel, the terminal design suggests cool continental sophistication in its modern approach that capitalizes on wide sweeping vistas and interior spaces.

Other innovations were wide glass windows that slant out towards the runway; round carpeted tubes that passengers pass through; and progressive technology with centralized ticketing and security, closed circuit television, central public address system, baggage weigh-in stations and carousels, and electronic display for flight departures and arrivals. The curves, decorative elements, and individual design components based on a unifying concept result in a total designed environment dedicated to air travel.

Closed since TWA ceased operations in 2001, the terminal reopened as JetBlue's terminal in 2008, though the trumpet-shaped departure lounge and flight wings are no longer part of the structure.

NEW YORK STATE

NASSAU COUNTY MUSEUM OF ART
One Museum Drive
Roslyn Harbor
PHONE: (516) 484-9337
WEB SITE: www.naussaumuseum.com

LOCATED TWENTY MILES EAST of New York City in Roslyn Harbor on Long Island, the Nassau County Museum of Art is housed in the historic Georgian mansion purchased in 1919 by the wealthy industrialist Henry Clay Frick, cofounder of U.S. Steel Corporation, who purchased the property for his son, Childs. Much of the museum's land originally belonged to the poet, preservationist, and editor of the *New York Evening Post*, William Cullen Bryant, who was closely connected to the Hudson River School of landscape painting. When a large portion of the land was next sold in 1893, the new owner sought out the well-known architect and interior decorator Ogden Codman Jr. (1863–1951) to design a new home, Clayton, on a highpoint of the property overlooking Hempstead Harbor. When the Fricks purchased Clayton, they commissioned the British architect and decorator Charles Carrick Allom (1865–1947) to redesign the façade and portions of the interior.

Four years after Frick's death in 1965, Nassau County purchased the estate in order to convert it into the Nassau County Museum of Art. The museum's permanent collection of about 600 works focuses primarily on nineteenth- and twentieth-century American and European artists such as Edouard Vuillard (1868–1940), Pierre Bonnard (1867–1947), Auguste Rodin (1840–1917), Georges Braque (1882–1963), Roy Lichtenstein (1923–1997), Larry Rivers (1923–2002), Robert Rauschenberg (1925–2008), and George Segal (1924–2000).

The large and impressive grounds include lovely gardens and walkways redesigned in 1925 by Marian Cruger Coffin (1876–1951), one of the first women to be formally trained in landscape architecture. Coffin, who received her degree from the Massachusetts Institute of Technology in 1904, considered Clayton to be among her finest designs.

The 145 acres of the estate today function as an extension of the museum, as its "museum without walls" displays more than fifty sculptures by such artists as Fernando Botero (b. 1932), Alexander Calder (1898–1976), Tony Smith (1912–1980), and Richard Serra (b. 1939), some of which are part of the museum's permanent collection and others of which are on long-term loans from The Metropolitan Museum of Art and the Museum of Modern Art, among others.

Also located on the Nassau County Museum's grounds is the **TEE RIDDER MINIATURES MUSEUM**, which displays a unique collection of miniature houses complete with such delicately made items as a tiny reproduction of an eighteenth-century harpsichord with an oil painting inside the lid and a French grand salon illuminated by a three-inch electrified glass chandelier.

The Nassau County Museum of Art is open Tuesday through Sunday 11:00 a.m. to 4:45 p.m. The Tee Ridder Miniatures Museum is open Tuesday through Sunday 12:00 to 4:30 p.m. Admission fees apply. Parking is available for a small fee.

CEDARMERE, William Cullen Bryant's home, is also nearby and open to visitors. In addition to the house, originally built by a Quaker farmer in 1787, the property includes a Gothic mill, a pond spanned by a rustic stone bridge, and a small formal garden. While at Cedarmere, Bryant made several changes to the existing house, which featured an eighteenth-century façade. Bryant hired Calvert Vaux (1824–1895), who along with Frederick Law Olmsted was responsible for Central Park, to make some design alterations to the property. Because of Bryant's antislavery activism, Cedarmere is part of the New York State Underground Railroad Heritage

Trail. It is located on Bryant Avenue (just north of Northern Boulevard). The house is open Saturday and Sunday 1:00 p.m. to 5:00 p.m., April through November. Call (516) 571-8130 for more information. Admission is free.

◼ OLD WESTBURY GARDENS, 1906
71 Old Westbury Road
Old Westbury
PHONE: (516) 333-0048
WEB SITE: www.oldwestburygardens.org

IF THE VISION of a golden afternoon passed at an Edwardian country house stirs your imagination, then exploring Old Westbury Gardens is the perfect destination. The London connoisseur and designer George A. Crawley (1864–1926) conceived the Old Westbury estate for the American financier John S. Phipps (1874–1958) and his English bride, Margarita Grace Phipps (1876–1957). After its completion in 1906, Westbury House served as the Phipps family residence for more than fifty years. Surrounding the Charles II–style mansion is a park of over 160 acres with eighty-eight acres of formal gardens, tree-lined walks, grand allées, ponds, statuary, and architectural follies. The house and its contents, the gardens, and museum programs offer activities that visitors of diverse interests enjoy.

As heirs to the U.S. Steel and Grace Shipping fortunes, John S. Phipps and Margarita Grace Phipps expected nothing less from their designers than a stately home commensurate with their status. On one hand, Crawley provided his clients with surroundings of Baroque splendor that reminded Mrs. Phipps of her childhood home in England. On the other, Crawley's American associate, the architect Grosvenor Attenbury (1869-1956) oversaw the practical aspects of building the 20-room mansion. The collaboration resulted in a magnificent example of the early twentieth-century American Country estate.

After her parents' deaths, Peggie Phipps Boegner opened Old Westbury to the public. Since 1959, visitors passing through the exquisite wrought iron gates created by Robert Bakewell (1682–1752) in the early eighteenth century have entered a Grande Allee of tall European linden trees that forms the road into the property and builds anticipation for the spectacular landscape ahead. The English gardens feature primrose and lilac walks, a two-acre walled garden that many consider "the jewel of the place," and a thatched cottage and three log cabins–playhouses for the four Phipps children. Visible from the house, the spring-fed West Pond creates a tranquil landscape filled with wildlife. Beyond the pond is a reflecting pool flanked by boxwoods that were 100 years old when they were transplanted from Virginia in 1931. Throughout the garden copious plantings feature historic varieties, new hybrids, and experimental plants.

The huge fireplace in the entry hall of Westbury House still greets museum visitors with the same feeling of warmth and welcome that it must have conveyed to the Phipps family and friends during their occupancy. After passing beyond the entry, visitors walk into richly appointed rooms such as the White Drawing Room, the wood-paneled dining room, the Red Ballroom, and the Second Floor Hall. English furniture and decorative arts, sculpture, and paintings by artists including Sir Joshua Reynolds (1723–1792), Thomas Gainsborough (1727–1788), Sir Henry Raeburn (1756–1823), John Singer Sargent (1856–1925), and John Constable (1776–1837) complement the grand rooms.

Old Westbury House and Gardens are open every day except Tuesdays from April 26th to October 31st from 10:00 a.m. until 5:00 p.m., with the last vehicle allowed on to the property at 4:00 p.m. Check the Web site for openings at other times for special programs such as indoor and outdoor classical concerts and the annual Holiday Celebration in December. The Picnic Pops Concert Series takes place out-of-doors on summer evenings. Other museum programs and events include botanical arts and gardening classes, slide lectures, Scottish games, and family entertainments. Guests are invited to tour the house and gardens at their leisure. Volunteers provide tours of the house on the hour and half hour, and of the gardens at 11:00 a.m. and 2:00 p.m. Group tours of fifteen or more may be arranged by calling (516) 333-0048, ext. 310. Admission fees apply.

PARRISH ART MUSEUM, 1897

25 Job's Lane
Southampton
PHONE: (631) 283-2118
WEB SITE: www.parrishart.org
E-MAIL: info@parrishart.org

THE PARRISH ART MUSEUM, once known as the Art Museum at Southampton, was established in 1897 by Samuel Longstreth Parrish, a lawyer and important art collector, who built the museum to accommodate his collection of Italian Renaissance art and reproductions of Classical sculpture. In the 1950s, the president of the museum's board, Mrs. Robert Malcolm Littlejohn, decided to expand the museum's collection and to shift its focus to collecting and displaying the works of American artists, particularly those who had worked on the East End of Long Island. Littlejohn donated her personal collection of paintings by William Merritt Chase (1849–1916), Childe Hassam (1859–1935), Thomas Moran (1837–1926), and other artists, which serve as the core of the museum's American collection.

The Parrish Art Museum houses the largest public collection of paintings and works on paper by the American Impressionist William Merritt Chase. Chase spent his summers on the East End of Long Island and became the Shinnecock Hills Summer School of Art's first and most prominent teacher. The Chase holdings also include important archival materials and photographs relating to his life and artistic endeavors.

Chase's **THE BLUE KIMONO (GIRL IN BLUE KIMONO)** (c. 1888) is a stunning example of his pre-Impressionist works, which display his mastery of portraiture and his interest in decoration and *Japonisme*. Chase was particularly fond of painting women in decorative, domestic settings, where the women functioned in part as decorative objects within a larger scene.

THE BAYBERRY BUSH (c. 1895), one of Chase's many extraordinary pictures painted at Shinnecock, reflects his mature, Impressionist period, where he became interested in plein-air landscape painting. Despite the shift in his practice toward painting landscapes out of doors, Chase always maintained his interest in the decorative and the domestic. Here, three little girls pop out of the field in their colorful hats and clothing, perhaps functioning as personifications of flowers, while in the background the image of a house reaffirms the domestic nature of this particular landscape.

Fairfield Porter (1907–1975), an important twentieth-century American Realist and art critic, lived and worked in Southhampton from 1949 until his death in 1979. Because of Porter's relationship to the area, the Parrish received some 250 of his works and archival materials from his estate, including **ANNE** (1965). Anne, one of several portraits of his wife that Porter painted, exemplifies his modernist approach to painting the figure, with its formal simplifications and the use of areas of bright, unmodulated color.

The Parrish Art Museum recently hired the famed Swiss architectural firm of Herzog & de Meuron, who were responsible for the Tate Modern and 40 Bond Street in New York City (see p. 86), to design a new 64,000-square-foot building in Water Mill, on Long Island's East End. The building that will link together individual pavilions has been designed to evoke a series of art colonies, recalling the history of art practice on Long Island. The project is scheduled to be completed in 2010.

The museum is open Mondays and Thursday to Saturday 11:00 a.m. to 5:00 p.m. and on Sundays from 1:00 to 5:00 p.m. Closed Tuesdays and Wednesdays. Admission fees apply. Parking is available in the municipal lot to the rear of the museum.

William Merritt Chase's The Blue Kimono (Girl in Blue Kimono) *(1888)*

POLLOCK-KRASNER HOUSE AND STUDY CENTER

830 Fireplace Rd.
East Hampton
PHONE: (631) 324-4929
WEB SITE: http://naples.cc.sunysb.edu/CAS/pkhouse.nsf

IN 1946, Jackson Pollock (1912–1956), one of the most innovative artists of the twentieth century and the leader of the Abstract Expressionist movement, settled with his wife, the painter Lee Krasner (1908–1984), in this house overlooking Accabonac Creek in The Springs, a small rural community just four miles north of East Hampton. Pollock purchased the property and the house, which was built in 1879 for the family of a fisherman, with a loan from the philanthropist and art patron Peggy Guggenheim.

Pollock transformed the property's barn into the studio where he would create many of the drip paintings for which he is most famous. He worked in this studio from 1946 until his death in an alcohol-related automobile accident, which occurred about a mile from the home in 1956.

In the barn studio, visitors can essentially walk in Pollock's footsteps, as they tread, wearing special slippers, across the paint-splattered studio floor. Process and movement was central to Pollock's work, and the studio floor reflects for the viewer Pollock's very physical enterprise in much the same way as his monumental canvases do. Pollock said of his process, "On the floor I am more at ease. I feel nearer, more a part of the painting, since this way I can walk around it, work from the four sides and literally be in the painting."

Also on view at the Pollock-Krasner House and Studio, which is only open for six months each year, are prints by both painters and their working materials. The site also maintains a Study Center, which houses important archival materials and also hosts changing exhibitions.

Open Thursday, Friday, and Saturday, May 1 through October 31. Call to arrange prepaid tours. Admission fees apply.

UPSTATE NEW YORK

BOSCOBEL, 1808
1601 Route 9D
Garrison
PHONE: (845) 265-3638
WEB SITE: www.boscobel.org
E-MAIL: info@boscobel.org

NO PARTICULAR ARCHITECT has been identified as the designer of Boscobel, although the mansion is considered one of the finest examples of Federal domestic architecture in America in the style of English architect Robert Adam (1728–1792). It is the family home of States Morris Dyckman, a Loyalist during the American Revolution who served as a clerk for the British Army's Quartermaster Department in New York. The residence was originally built in the town of Montrose, fifteen miles south of its present location, in a site that overlooked the Hudson River from Haverstraw Bay. Nearly destroyed in the 1950s, the building was saved and relocated to its present site in Garrison.

The exceptional elegance of the house exterior is due to its slender proportions. It is made light and airy though its extensive use of windows and fine detailing on the façade, such as the carved wooden swags of drapery with bowknots and tassels placed between the slender columns on the second floor balcony under the pediment. The delicate attenuated proportions of this fine Neoclassical home are exceptional for the period.

The mansion also contains an extensive collection of decorative arts from the holdings of the Dyckman family, which includes: English china, silver, part of his library, and furniture in the period room settings. There is also a significant collection of furniture by noted New York cabinetmakers of the Federal period. Highlights from the permanent collection include a Duncan Phyfe (1768–1854) secretary bookcase of c. 1810–29; a c. 1800–08 chest of drawers by Michael Allison (1773–1855), a painting of Narcissus by Benjamin West (1758–1820) from 1808.

The mansion is open every day except Tuesdays, Thanksgiving, and Christmas from April through December from 9:30 a.m. to 5 p.m. The last tour begins at 4:15 p.m. The house and grounds close at 4 p.m. in November and December and the last tour begins at 3:15 p.m. The museum and grounds are closed from January through March. Group tours available by reservation. There is an admission fee except for children under the age of six.

■ CARAMOOR, 1939

149 Girdle Ridge Road
Katonah
ARCHITECTS: Christian Rosberg and Walter Kosen
PHONE: (914) 232-5035
WEB SITE: www.caramoor.org
E-MAIL: info@caramoor.org

LOCATED IN WESTCHESTER COUNTY, the Caramoor estate features an extraordinary mansion and gardens built by the Wall Street financier Walter Rosen and his wife, Lucie Bigelow Rosen. The home, which recalls a Mediterranean villa, was designed by the architect Christian Rosborg, in collaboration with Walter Rosen, and built between 1929 and 1939. The mansion, which was used as the Rosen's summer home, is an incredible showcase for the family's collection, which includes entire rooms that were imported from European palaces and mansions.

Today, twenty of the Rosen house's fifty rooms are available to the public, and they display incredible examples of fine and decorative European and Asian art, including tapestries, sculpture, paintings, textiles, furniture, stained glass, Urbino Maiolica, a fine jade collection, and exquisite wall coverings such as the hand-painted eighteenth-century Chinese wallpaper in the Reception Room and the Dining Room.

Highlights of the Rosen mansion include the seventeenth-century Burgundian Library, with its incredible vaulted, periwinkle blue ceiling decorated with biblical wall paintings; the Cabinet Room and its once extremely fashionable lacquered panels, created for the Palazzo Riccasoli in Turin in the mid-eighteenth century, which is among only a handful of such lacquered rooms that have survived; and the Dining Room's eight-fold Chinese screen, featuring forty carved jade panels depicting the Taoist paradise known as the Hills of Immortality.

A tribute to the Rosen's devotion to music, the Music Room's elaborate decorations and furnishings include a painting by Lucas Cranach (1472–1533), tin-enameled terra cotta reliefs from the workshop of Andrea della Robbia (1437–1528), sixteenth-century tapestries, wrought iron, stained glass, carved pilasters, and a first-rate collection of Urbino Maiolica, among other treasures.

The mansion's exceptional collection of furniture also includes a gilded bed that once belonged to Pope Urban VIII, a suite of eighteenth-century furniture from a Venetian dressmaker's shop, and red lacquered chairs designed by the English cabinetmaker Giles Grendey (1693–1780) for the Duke of Infantado's castle of Lazcano near San Sebastian, among other artifacts.

The estate spans some eight acres and features beautiful gardens, including a Spanish Courtyard cloistered by twelfth-century Byzantine columns; a Butterfly Garden, based on a design by the Renaissance architect Filippo Brunelleschi (1377–1446); the Venetian Circle framed by seventeenth-century Swiss gates that are topped by two Pegasus sculptures by the American sculptor Malvina Hoffman (1887–1966); a Tapestry Hedge which features seventeenth-century Italian sculptures; the Woodland Garden; the Sunken Garden; the Renaissance Gardens; and the Theater Garden.

The enchanting gardens have served as a setting for important musical performances and festivals open to the public since 1945. The mansion's Music Room is also a performance site. Check the Web site for performance schedules and pricing.

Guided tours of the mansion are offered Wednesday through Sunday from 1:00 to 4:00 p.m. (last tour at 3:00 p.m.). On Saturdays during the summer music festival season, the house is open from 1:00 to 5:00 p.m. (last tour at 4:00 p.m.). Admission fees apply.

■ **DIA: BEACON**
3 Beekman Street
Beacon
PHONE: (845) 440-0100
WEB SITE: www.diaart.org

DIA: BEACON OPENED its site on the Hudson River to the public in spring of 2003.

The Dia Art Foundation is a nonprofit institution founded in 1974 and is known for its commitment to showcasing, preserving, and supporting works by some of the most prominent artists of the 1960s and 1970s, with a special emphasis on Conceptualism and Minimalism. The Dia collection was founded by Philippa de Menil and Heiner Friedrich, who began collecting in the 1970s; they sought out and collected works by selected contemporary artists that posed exhibition challenges and could not be readily accommodated by more conventional exhibition spaces due to the nature or scale of the artworks. Among the original artists collected were: Joseph Beuys (1921–1986), John Chamberlain (b. 1927), Walter De Maria (b. 1935), Dan Flavin (1933–1996), Donald Judd (1828–1994), Blinky Palermo (1943–1977), Cy Twombly (b. 1928), and Andy Warhol (1929–1987), among others.

With the establishment of the Beacon exhibition space, the collection also acquired other artists of the same generation as those Dia historically supported. These artists are also now represented in depth in the collection: Bernd (1931–2007) and Hilla Becher (b. 1934), Louise Bourgeois (b. 1911), Michael Heizer (b. 1944), Robert Irwin (b. 1928), On Kawara (b. 1933), Sol LeWitt (1928–2007), Agnes Martin (1912–2004), Bruce Nauman (b. 1941), Robert Ryman (b. 1930), Gerhard Richter (b. 1932), Richard Serra (b. 1939), Robert Smithson (1938–1973), and Lawrence Weiner (b. 1942).

Dia: Beacon is housed in a former Nabisco factory building of over 300 thousand square feet. Built in 1929 out of steel, concrete, and glass and designed by a Nabisco staff architect, the building's modernist look and monumental scale make it a natural setting to exhibit the large-scale contemporary art installations for which Dia is known. More recently, the building was used as a printing factory and was owned by the International Paper Corporation, which donated the compound to the Dia Art Foundation.

NEW YORK STATE

Dia: Beacon is part of the Dia Art Foundation and is currently its primary exhibition space for the collection.

Each artist's work is collected in depth and exhibitions of the collection are presented on a rotating basis. The selected artist's work is displayed in a dedicated gallery or galleries; in many cases these presentations were created in collaboration with the artists themselves.

Dia collaborated with American artist Robert Irwin and architectural firm OpenOffice to formulate the plan for the museum building and its exterior setting. Irwin's master plan includes gardens for the exterior and a parking lot with a grove of flowering fruit trees. Dia: Beacon is situated on thirty-one acres on the banks of the Hudson River.

The museum is open for summer hours from Thursday to Monday 11:00 a.m. to 6:00 p.m. and is closed Tuesday and Wednesday. Winter hours are Friday to Monday 11:00 a.m. to 4:00 p.m. Call the museum or visit the Web site for the hours, which are subject to change. There is an admission charge, but members and children under the age of twelve are free.

■ DONALD M. KENDALL SCULPTURE GARDEN
PepsiCo World Headquarters
700 Anderson Hill Road
Purchase
PHONE: (914) 253-2000

THE DONALD M. KENDALL SCULPTURE GARDEN is located on the grounds of the PepsiCo Headquarters, across the street from the **NEUBERGER MUSEUM OF ART** in Westchester County. The PepsiCo headquarters building (1970) was designed by Edward Durrell Stone (1902–1978), who was also responsible for Radio City Music Hall. Stone's son, E.D. Stone, Jr., oversaw the original landscape project, which at the time displayed eight sculptures. Today, forty-five extremely strong examples of mostly twentieth-century sculpture sit on the grounds, which were redesigned in the 1980s by the famed British landscape architect Russell Page (1906–1985), who created walks and intimate gardens in an effort to establish a rapport between nature and art.

Despite the connections between nature and sculpture that Page achieved, the works at PepsiCo are not meant to blend into their environment. Instead, many are dynamic pieces, like the large, bright red stabile by Alexander Calder (1898–1976). Calder's **HATS OFF** (1969) is a monumental work whose geometric components jut in various directions and serve as a bold contrast to the quiet and calm setting.

George Segal's (1924–2000) **THREE PEOPLE ON FOUR BENCHES** (1979) is both more integrated into the landscape and more subtly disconcerting than larger works like Calder's. The cast bronze figures that have been painted white occupy the visitor's space and reality. There is almost an unspoken invitation to sit with Segal's park goers. However, rather than offering company or camaraderie, these starkly white figures can be disconcerting because of their hyperrealism and their introspective, pensive, and disconnected demeanors.

The Surrealist and Dadaist Max Ernst's (1891–1976) largest freestanding sculpture, **CAPRICORN** (1948), has been set against the backdrop of one of the ground's wooded areas. The couple, a regally horned male figure who holds a scepter, a fish, and a half-dog form, and a towering female mermaid figure with a long neck and birdlike features, is a fantastic vision from perhaps a dream—or a nightmare.

Claes Oldenburg's (b. 1929) **GIANT TROWEL II** (1976) establishes a humorous relationship between object and its specific space. Oldenburg takes a simple garden implement, magnifies its proportions, and plunges it into the earth. In doing so, he reminds the viewer of the extraordinary efforts (of both man and machine) necessary to create a garden on the scale of the space within which this sculpture has been placed. To that point, Arnaldo Pomodoro's (b. 1926) **TRIAD** (1979), the largest sculpture in the collection, took two cranes and three days to install on the grounds. Composed of three towering columns of bronze that loom over visitors, *Triad's* surfaces appear to have been peeled or burnt away.

The Kendall Sculpture Garden also displays works by Auguste Rodin (1840–1917), Aristide Maillol (1861–1944), Henry Moore (1898–1986), Jean Dubuffet (1901–1985), Alberto Giacometti (1901–1966), Barbara Hepworth (1903–1975), Joan Miró (1893–1983), Louise Nevelson (1899–1988), Isamu Noguchi (1904–1988), and other giants of twentieth-century sculpture.

In addition to displaying such extraordinary sculptures, the 162 acres of the PepsiCo grounds also include a lake, a stream garden, lily ponds, iris and perennial gardens, two woodland gardens, and groves of birch, oak, and sequoia, among others.

The Donald M. Kendall Sculpture Garden is open 7:00 a.m. to 7:00 p.m. April to October and 7:00 a.m. to 4:30 p.m. November to March. Admission is free. Visitors can pick up a brochure and a map of the grounds at the Visitor Center.

THE HYDE COLLECTION

161 Warren Street
Glens Falls
PHONE: (518) 792-1761
WEB SITE: www.hydecollection.org
E-MAIL: info@hydecollection.org

HOUSED IN A STUCCO Florentine Renaissance-inspired villa built in 1912 in the Adirondack region for the art collectors Louis and Charlotte Hyde, the Hyde Collection boasts an exceptional group of works by Renaissance and Baroque masters, including Sandro Botticelli (1445–1510), El Greco (1541–1614), and Rembrandt von Rijn (1606–1699), as well as giants of nineteenth- and twentieth-century European and American art, including Jean Auguste Dominique Ingres (1780–1867), Albert Bierstadt (1830–1902), and Pablo Picasso (1881–1973), among others.

Although the collection continues to grow and the museum's physical structure has been expanded over the years to include newer galleries that make up a larger complex, Hyde House is still its centerpiece and viewing the remarkable collection amidst first-rate antique furnishings and decorative arts allows visitors to see the collection within the private context where it was first amassed and displayed.

Among the old master gems at the Hyde is Botticelli's THE ANNUNCIATION (early 1490s), a subject he favored, as seen in other extraordinary versions located at THE METROPOLITAN MUSEUM (see p. 28) in New York and at the Uffizi in Florence. As in The Metropolitan Museum's version, the Hyde's ANNUNCIATION celebrates and exhibits the Renaissance values of symmetry and balance and demonstrates Botticelli's interest and deftness at rendering architectural detail and perspective.

El Greco's **PORTRAIT OF SAINT JAMES THE LESS** (c. 1595) is a compelling image that communicates the thoughtful inner life of the apostle and displays the hallmarks of El Greco's style, including the expressive handling of paint and the elongation of the body and its component parts.

Rembrandt's **PORTRAIT OF CHRIST** (c. 1655–57) is a striking, humanizing image of Christ that suggests a certain gentleness and kindness while reflecting the artist's skill at contrasting light and dark. Christ's softened features and expression emerge from the darkness and are cast in a light that further softens them.

The Hyde's **PAOLO AND FRANCESCA** (c. 1855–60) by Ingres is a gorgeous painting featuring the kiss and embrace of the ill-fated lovers who are featured in Dante's *Inferno*. In a canvas that exhibits the artist's particular gift for painting various surfaces, textures, and colors in a highly finished manner, Ingres also captures the lovers' sensuality and suggests how the rapt couple is thoroughly engrossed in one another.

The Hyde Collection also has several important American works, including the exceptional Hudson River School landscape painting **YOSEMITE VALLEY** (c. 1865) by Albert Bierstadt. Bierstadt's panoramic painting of the valley is majestic and an homage to the vast wonders found in untouched areas of the American landscape.

BOY HOLDING A BLUE VASE (1905) is a lovely work from Picasso's Rose Period, where his muted color palette is dominated by rosy pink tones in a quiet, moody image of a pensive young man very carefully holding a vase. The blues of the vase and the small area of blue gray within the predominantly rose background hearken back to Picasso's earlier Blue Period, making this in part a transitional work that addresses the artist's stylistic concerns of the past and present.

The Hyde also has an extraordinary collection of works on paper, including the enigmatic drawing **STUDY OF THE MONA LISA** (c. 1503), attributed to Leonardo da Vinci (1452–1519) and thought to be a preparatory work for one of the most famous paintings in the history of art. Because of the fragility of the drawing, it is only on view in temporary exhibitions, for short periods, rather than available to the public year-round.

The Hyde Collection is open Tuesday to Saturday 10:00 a.m. to

5:00 p.m., Sunday 12:00 to 5:00 p.m., and is closed on Mondays. Admission is free, though there is a suggested donation. Docent-guided tours are offered daily between 1:00 and 4:00 p.m. Parking is available on Warren Street and behind the museum; handicapped parking is in front of Hyde House.

KYKUIT, THE ROCKEFELLER ESTATE, 1913

Visitor Center
381 North Broadway (Route 9)
Sleepy Hollow
PHONE: (914) 631-8200 (Monday through Friday);
(914) 631-3992 (Saturday and Sunday.)
WEB SITE: www.hudsonvalley.org
E-MAIL: info@hudsonvalley.org

OCCUPYING MORE THAN 2,000 ACRES, the hilltop grounds, forty-room mansion, and outbuildings of Kykuit served as home to four generations of the powerful Rockefeller family. Kykuit, a Dutch term for "lookout," is located on the highest point of the Pocantico Hills and overlooks the Hudson River near Sleepy Hollow and Tarrytown, about one hour north of New York City. Kykuit's architects, Chester Holmes Aldrich (1871–1940) and William Adams Delano (1874–1960), worked in the Beaux-Arts style, borrowing eclectically from Greek and Roman classical sources to create a four-story structure using locally quarried, rough-cut fieldstone and Indiana limestone.

Aldrich and Delano collaborated significantly with two other figures, Ogden Codman Jr. (1863–1951) and William Welles Bosworth (1869–1966). Codman, the influential tastemaker, architect, and interior decorator, was responsible for the interiors, including the beautifully detailed ornamental plaster throughout the house. Bosworth designed the outstanding gardens, though his input is also reflected in architectural details such as the ornate wrought-iron gates and fieldstone gateposts.

The mansion is home to a particularly strong collection of Chinese ceramics. The Ming dynasty (1368–1644) collection includes temple jars, garden seats, and several richly colored figures executed using the *fa hua* ("bound design") technique, where a raised line of slip separates the glaze colors, achieving an effect similar to cloisonné. Kykuit also displays works from the earlier Han Dynasty (206 B.C.– A.D. 220), among them the funerary Tang horses, camels, and guardian figures that were originally created to accompany the deceased to the afterworld. The Qing (Ch'ing) Dynasty (1644–1911) collection includes several beautiful, highly detailed vases in the monochromatic *famille verte* (green), *famille jaune* (yellow), and *famille noire* (black) styles.

A collection of eighteenth-century Meissen birds are displayed in the dining room. And Kykuit also features a china room, created in the 1960s, to display its fine collection of English and Chinese dinner services, including the colorful Worcester Kylin pattern (1795) and the Stowe Service (1815), originally made for the Duke of Buckingham's Stowe House.

The mansion's collection of paintings includes mostly family portraits such as **JOHN D. ROCKEFELLER** (1917) by the master portrait painter John Singer Sargent (1856–1925). The bulk of Kykuit's remarkable collection of twentieth-century painting and some of its modern sculpture is located in the unusual underground art galleries, which were once subterranean corridors and terraces. Among the highlights in these galleries are Andy Warhol's (1928–1987) portraits of **NELSON** (1967) and **HAPPY** (1968) Rockefeller and twelve (of a series of eighteen) tapestries after paintings by Pablo Picasso (1881–1973), all executed between 1958 and 1975 with the approval of the artist.

Bosworth's training and interest in the classical and Italian traditions are reflected by Kykuit's spectacular gardens. Among elements that draw from Italian sources are the terraces, the grand stairs, an enormous fountain with Carrara marble figures carved in Florence, and a grotto. The grotto, which lies at the end of the subterranean art gallery and beneath the garden's classical temple, is a magical place featuring carved sandstone masks and clusters of green, icicle-like lights by Tiffany Furnaces.

The grounds, which also include a classical teahouse with ceiling paintings after Raphael, a rose garden, and a Japanese garden and Japanese Teahouse, also serve as a stage for the display of important examples of twentieth-century sculpture, as well as fine replicas of Italian Renaissance sculptures.

Representative works by Picasso, Aristide Maillol (1861–1944), Jacques Lipchitz (1891–1973), Gaston Lachaise (1882–1935), Elie Nadelman (1882–1946), Henry Moore (1898–1986), Alexander Calder (1898–1976), David Smith (1906–1965), Tony Smith (1912–1980), Karel Appel (1921–2006) and many others have been carefully chosen and deliberately sited throughout the property with consideration to the connections between specific locations, the natural world more generally, and their relevant themes.

Lipchitz's **CHANT DES VOYELLES (SONG OF VOWELS)** (1931–32), which features two abstracted harpists and references an ancient Egyptian prayer said to subdue nature, sits at the center of the Orange Tree Terrace. Picasso's **THE BATHERS** (1956–57), a whimsical group of six bronze figures of varying sizes that reflect a layering of geometric shapes, is located at the edge of the tennis lawn. Moore's **KNIFE EDGE—TWO PIECE** (1965–66) brings to mind both the "knife edge" of a breastbone and rocky terrains, mountains, or cliffs. Appel's amusing and colorful **MOUSE ON A TABLE** (1971) has been appropriately placed in the Children's Garden.

The estate's outbuildings also include the Orangerie (1908), designed by Bosworth and inspired by the Orangerie at the Palace of Versailles, to protect the Rockefellers' collection of dwarf orange trees from the harsh winter elements; the Coach House, built to house the Rockefellers' impressive collection of carriages and automobiles; and Kykuit's recreational center, the Playhouse (1925–27), which features a half-timbered façade and slate roof that pay homage to the architecture of Normandy.

The nearby **UNION CHURCH** (1921) of Pocantico Hills, which was built in large part because of the patronage of the Rockefellers, is certainly worth including in a tour of Kykuit because of its exceptional stained glass windows by Henri Matisse (1869–1954) and Marc Chagall (1887–1985). In addition to the beautiful rose window (dedicated in 1956) by Matisse, the Rockefellers commissioned Chagall to create nine windows, one of which relates the biblical story of the **GOOD SAMARITAN** (dedicated 1965). Full of brilliant colors and Chagall's signature floating figures, the Good Samaritan window is an exuberant interpretation of the parable from the Gospel of Luke.

It is highly encouraged that Kykuit visitors purchase tickets in advance either online or by phone, (914) 631-9491. There are various tour options that range in duration from one to three hours. Check the Web site or call for specific hours and days; some tours are only offered on Saturdays and Sundays, though there are options for visitors interested in weekday tours. All tours begin at Philipsburg Manor and the Kykuit Visitor Center on Route 9 in Sleepy Hollow.

Union Church is open to visitors on most weekdays (except Tuesdays), April through December, 11:00 a.m. to 5:00 p.m.; Saturdays 10:00 a.m. to 5:00 p.m. and Sundays 2:00 to 5:00 p.m. For more information, call (914) 631-2069. Admission fees apply. Guided and self-guided tours available.

LOCUST GROVE, 1830
The Samuel Morse Historic Site
2683 South Road
Poughkeepsie
ARCHITECT: Alexander Jackson Davis
PHONE: (845) 454-4500
WEB SITE: www.lgny.org
E-MAIL: info@lgny.org

SAMUEL F.B. MORSE, renowned for inventing Morse Code and the telegraph, acquired the Poughkeepsie estate Locust Grove and moved there with his three children in 1847. His first wife had died in 1825 and he remarried in 1848. In 1851, he engaged the noted architect Alexander Jackson Davis (1803–1892) to remodel and enlarge the residence into an Italianate villa. He continued to make refinements to the landscape design during the course of his residence there until his death in 1872.

Locust Grove had three stages in its evolution; first built as a Georgian-style house in 1830, with the help of Davis it underwent a transformation to a Tuscan-style villa, with the north and south wings, porte cochere, and billiards room to the east and a four-story tower to the west that faces the river. Then, in 1901, the dining room was added.

In 1901, the remaining Morse family sold the estate to William and Martha Young, who moved to the house with their two children and a staff of twelve servants. The Young family preserved the estate and their art collection. Their daughter, Annette Innis Young, created a private foundation in 1975 to maintain the historic estate, its collections, and the 150 acres of gardens and grounds.

The mansion suggests the trappings of upscale Edwardian life with a fine collection of New York furniture in the Chippendale, Federal, and Empire styles that is complemented by eighteenth-century Dutch landscapes, nineteenth-century Hudson River School paintings, and twentieth-century prints and drawings, as well as European glass, English silver, and porcelain. The Morse Exhibit Gallery in the visitor center features works of art by Samuel Morse, including portraits, landscapes, and sculpture that demonstrate his commitment to art. Though renowned as an inventor, his first passion was for painting.

Other Alexander Jackson Davis houses in the Hudson Valley include **LYNDHURST** in Tarrytown (see p. 144) and **MONTGOMERY PLACE** in Annandale-on-Hudson, both Gothic Revival in style. Montgomery Place is a 434-acre property with lush plantings and scenic topography, including woodland trails and the cascading waterfalls of the Sawkill. The mansion interior is currently undergoing restoration and is currently not open to the public. Nearby **SPRINGSIDE**, the estate of Matthew Vassar, was landscaped by Downing, whose ideas were also transported to the landscape of Locust Grove.

Hours for the visitor center are daily from 10:00 a.m. to 5:00 p.m. year-round. The visitor center and the mansion are closed Thanksgiving, Christmas, New Year's Day, and Easter. Hours may be subject to change, so call or check the Web site for current information. Admission is charged for the mansion and visitor center gallery. Group tours are available year-round by appointment.

LYNDHURST, 1838; 1864–65

635 South Broadway
Tarrytown
ARCHITECT: Alexander Jackson Davis (1803–1892)
PHONE: (914) 631-4481
WEB SITE: www.lyndhurst.org
E-MAIL: Lyndhurst@nthp.org

LYNDHURST, DESIGNED BY the noted architect Alexander Jackson Davis, is one of the most majectic estates overlooking the Hudson River and is a masterpiece of domestic architecrue and the Gothic Revival. The house was originally conceived as a country villa on sixty-seven acres in 1838 for General William Paulding. It was named "Knoll" for its hilltop location, though its turrets and asymmetrical profile were atypical for the time period. Architect and owner shared a common love of the region and an interest in the natural setting. The structure in evidence today is the result of two different phases of construction.

Davis directed major enhancement of the residence between 1864 and 1865, doubling it in size for its second owner, the New York merchant George Merritt, who renamed it "Lyndhurst" in honor of the linden trees on the property. Jay Gould, business magnate of Western Union Telegraph, the New York Elevated Railway, and the Union Pacific Railroad, acquired the property in 1880 as a summer escape and held it until his death in 1884. The property was passed down in the family until it was given to the National Trust for Historic Preservation in 1961.

The nineteenth-century landscape of the estate boasts expansive lawns, varied greenery and trees, and unexpected vistas, which were designed by Ferdinand Mangold (1828–1905) to complement the house. Unusual design elements are among the defining traits of the mansion, and include parapets, corbels, gables, ribbed groin vaults, steeply pitched roofs, the veranda, Gothic peaked windows with tracery, and the unmatched asymmetrical bays, which somehow achieve balance. The design is an amalgam of castellated Tudor and cottage style elements that creates a romantic, picturesque result. Despite the disparate key motifs, there is a certain cohesive unity, held together by the repetition of design forms. The structure is a wonderful summation of many of Davis's influential design principles relating to country houses and villas.

The interiors are also of note. Jay Gould hired Herter Brothers to decorate the interior, which is accented by paintings from his art collection which includes works by Corot, Courbet, Bouguereau, and others. There is also a significant collection of decorative arts. Gould also added the Gothic-style greenhouse with its cast iron framework, designed by the firm of Lord and Burnham

The estate is open from mid-April to October daily, except Mondays and holidays. The hours are 10:00 a.m. to 5:00 p.m., with the last admission at 4:15 p.m.

From November to mid-April the estate is open weekends only from

10:00 a.m. to 4:00 p.m., with the last tour departing at 3:30 p.m. The last tour on Sundays during the month of December will be at 2:00 p.m. Tours of ten or more are available by advance reservation. Parking is available. Admission is charged, though children under six are admitted free. Lyndhurst is adjacent to Washington Irving's residence, **SUNNYSIDE** (see p. 155).

■ MANITOGA/THE RUSSEL WRIGHT DESIGN CENTER

584 Route 9D
Garrison
Russel Wright (1904–1976)
PHONE: (845) 424-3812
WEB SITE: www.russelwrightcenter.org
E-MAIL: info@russelwrightcenter.org

MANITOGA ENCOMPASSES the home, studio, designed landscape, archives and design center of Russel Wright, one of the foremost designers of the mid-twentieth century, most popularly recognized for his stylish tableware. Manitoga, meaning "Place of the Great Spirit" in the Native language of the Algonquin, is one of few twentieth-century landmark homesites open on the East Coast.

Examples of Russel Wright's homewares for Steubenville Pottery, USA (1950s)

Wright acquired the forty-seven-acre property in 1947 and lived there with his wife, Mary, until his death in 1976, during which time he reconceived every aspect of its design, laboring over more than four miles of rugged and hilly woodland paths that traverse the landscape. Wright considered Manitoga one of his most important design achievements for its uniqueness and as an experiment in total living. The historic property includes the home, Dragon Rock, which is dedicated to Wright's concept of "easier living"—a design idea he pioneered and promoted along with Mary.

Wright is widely acknowleged for his role in modernizing the concept of the American domestic environment with inexpensive, mass-produced lines of interior furnishings that were well-designed, affordable, and contemporary.

Tickets are required for all tours. The tour season is April to October; daily tours: Monday, Thursday, and Friday at 11:00 a.m.; Saturday and Sunday at 11:00 a.m. and 1:30 p.m. Tours are limited to ten people. Tickets can be purchased at: www.brownpapertickets.org, or call for information.

Group Tours are available by appointment only. Call (845) 424-3812 to arrange group tours. There is a 20-percent discount for National Trust Members. Visitors can view Dragon Rock from the View spot at the base of the Quarry Pond. The path leading around the pond is open only by appointment.

■ MAVERICK CONCERT HALL, 1916

Maverick Road
West Hurley
ARCHITECT: Hervey White (1866–1944)
PHONE: (845) 679-8217
WEB SITE: www.maverickconcerts.org
E-MAIL: maverickmuse@aol.com

THE MAVERICK CONCERT HALL was conceived according to the vision of Hervey White. Called his "music chapel," the structure was built by hand by White and volunteer artists and musicians in a unique vernacular style. The concert hall hosts the longest continuous summer chamber music series in America.

White was a writer, dissident, social reformer, socialist, and financier, as well as a writer and poet who possessed a unique blend of traits and ideals. Born in Iowa to a poor family, he eventually attended Harvard University and graduated in 1894.

White had a long held interest in creating a utopian artist colony. First associated with the artist colony of Byrdcliffe in the Catskills, he eventually became disillusioned with it and struck out on his own in 1906. He acquired his own Catskill farm on which various structures built in a primitive style were eventually erected to accommodate a growing cadre of friends and intellectuals. The Maverick Art Colony evolved in this way, becoming a place in which artistic creativity flourished amid an unstructured environment.

In an effort to raise funds and keep the colony running, White created a Sunday concert series, which is still in existence. The concerts are housed in the rustic hall, which is a barnlike wooden structure open to the woods. It has four Gothic-arched doorways, and the façade is a mass of windows placed in a distinctive angled geometric pattern. The interior walls are tinted white and have log ribs; at the back of the stage, they too are angled in a geometric pattern. The roof is unpainted pine, and the hall is composed of rough unpainted pine boards that have weathered. One side of the roof is extended as an overhang, creating a large porch. Devoid of traditional references to any school or movement, the beauty, simplicity, and integrity of the Maverick Concert Hall are what distinguish this exceptional example of vernacular architecture.

■ MILLS MANSION, 1832/1895

Staatsburgh State Historic Site
Old Post Road
Staatsburgh
Mills-Norrie State Park
ARCHITECT: McKim, Mead, and White (1879–1910)
PHONE: (845) 889-8851
WEB SITE: www.staatsburgh.org

WHAT IS NOW THE Mills Mansion began as a large Greek Revival mansion built in 1832 by Morgan Lewis and his wife Gertrude Livingston. It was the second house built on the 1,600-acre site known as Staatsburgh. The residence came into the hands of Ruth Livingston Mills, who married the financier Ogden Mills and became prominent in high society. In 1895, the Mills commissioned the New York City architects McKim, Mead, and White to transform the home into a Neoclassical Beaux-Arts mansion with ornate exterior decoration that includes balustrades, pilasters, floral swags, and a highly reticulated pediment with monumental Corinthian columns that creates an imposing portico. The alteration more than doubled the number of rooms, resulting in sixty-five rooms and fourteen bathrooms.

Ornate and luxurious on the interior as well, the mansion has a fifty-foot-long dining room and a bedroom that is a replica of Marie Antoinette's in Versailles. The Mills used the residence from only September to January, and it served as the setting for many society parties and dinners. During other seasons, they had residences in New York, Paris, Newport, and California.

Ogden Mills's father had made a fortune in California selling supplies to miners during the Gold Rush and then was a cofounder of a bank. The union between the younger Mills and Ruth Livingston aligned the prominent Hudson River Valley Livingston family with new money of the Gilded Age. Ruth Livingston's ancestors included Morgan Lewis, third governor of New York and a general during the War of 1812, and his father Francis Lewis, a signer of the Declaration of Independence.

The mansion is open April 1 to October 31, Tuesday through Saturday 10:00 a.m. to 5:00 p.m., and Sunday 12:00 to 5:00 p.m.; January to March: Saturday and Sunday from 11:00 a.m. to 4:00 p.m.

The last tour starts one half hour before closing, and school and group tours are available year-round by appointment. Admission is charged, though children under twelve are free.

■ NEUBERGER MUSEUM OF ART, 1974

Purchase College, State University of New York
735 Anderson Hill Road
ARCHITECT: Philip Johnson (1906–2005)
PHONE: (914) 251-6100 (Monday through Friday)
or (914) 251-6117 (Saturday and Sunday)
WEB SITE: www.neuberger.org
E-MAIL: Neuberger@purchase.edu

LOCATED IN WESTCHESTER COUNTY on the Purchase College campus of the State University of New York and across the street from the **DONALD M. KENDALL SCULPTURE GARDEN** (see p. 136), the Neuberger Museum of Art is dedicated to presenting innovative exhibitions of modern and contemporary art, along with presenting its permanent collection, which is particularly strong in the areas of modern and contemporary American and African art.

The museum boasts high-quality works by such notable twentieth-century artists as Edward Hopper (1882–1967), Milton Avery (1885–1965), Georgia O'Keeffe (1887–1986), Stuart Davis (1892–1964), Alexander Calder (1898–1976), Mark Rothko (1903–1970), Willem de Kooning, and Jackson Pollock (1912–1956), among others. Hopper's **BARBER SHOP** (1931), a visitor favorite, offers a quiet slice of life and displays the painter's interest in studying the relationship between light and shadow. Pollock's **NUMBER 8** (1949) is an excellent example of his drip-technique where the seemingly endless spatters come together here to form a cohesive statement anchored by white, black, and green paint. De Kooning's famous **MARILYN MONROE** (1954), an abstracted interpretation of the screen icon, captures Monroe's sexuality in a very primal way by reducing her with slashes of paint to signature features like her blond hair, plump red lips, and the suggestion of large breasts.

The African art collection is also a strong focal point of the Neuberger. The museum's African holdings, particularly with regard to the art of Central Africa, received a considerable boost in 1999 when it welcomed a major gift from Lawrence Gussman, a notable collector whose interest in Africa and its visual culture was sparked by his long friendship with Dr. Albert Schweitzer, the famed medical missionary.

Highlights include **ANTHROPOMORPHIC HARP (NGOMBI)** made by the Fang peoples of Gabon in the twentieth century. The harp is highly valued by the Fang as a sacred instrument that facilitates communication between the living and the dead in religious rituals. The museum also features some extraordinary masks, including **HELMET MASK (KPONYUNGO)**, a twentieth-century zoomorphic mask made by the Sonofo peoples of the Côte d'Ivoire, designed for use by members of a secret society for initiations and funerary rituals. The helmet mask is an amalgamation of various animals, displaying the jaws of a hyena, horns of an antelope, and the tusks of a warthog. The mask essentially borrows from the most ferocious aspects of the aforementioned animals to create a hybrid creature that presumably has a kind of supernatural strength.

Although the architecture of the museum has been mostly dismissed by critics, it is worth mentioning that the famed architect Philip Johnson

(1906–2005) designed the building, which opened to the public in 1974, as well as the rest of the college campus. The museum was named for its first major benefactor, Roy R. Neuberger, a financier and art collector.

Located about forty-five minutes from mid-Manhattan, The Neuberger is open Tuesday through Sunday noon to 5 p.m. Admission fees apply. Parking available at the Purchase College Parking Lot #1; a fee applies on most weekdays from 8:00 a.m. to 6:00 p.m. Weekend parking is free.

■ NEWINGTON-CROPSEY FOUNDATION

Ever Rest, 1835
25 Cropsey Lane
Hastings-On-Hudson
PHONE: (914) 478-7990
WEB SITE: www.newingtoncropsey.com

JASPER CROPSEY (1823–1900), known as one of the principal figures in the Hudson River School of landscape painting, retired in 1885 to this residence, named Ever Rest, for the remainder of his years. The homestead was built in 1835 and he later added a studio. Though the popularity of his work had decreased with the change in taste by the 1880s, Cropsey continued painting into his later years; however, after 1893, he worked mostly in watercolor after suffering a stroke.

The foundation houses a large representative collection of works by Cropsey, including oil paintings, watercolors, drawings, and architectural renderings from throughout his life. Among the most prominent examples of his work in the collection are **NIAGARA FALLS** (1853), **CHENANGO RIVER, NEW YORK** (1856), **LAKE GEORGE** (1870), **MOUNT WASHINGTON FROM LAKE SEBAGO, MAINE** (1875), and **AUTUMN ON THE RAMAPO RIVER** (1871).

Ever Rest is a fine example of a Gothic-cottage style with typical decorative detailing and board-and-batten siding. It has been maintained in its original condition and has period décor and furniture. The primary objective of the foundation is to preserve and exhibit the work and home of Jasper Cropsey. It also furthers the historical study and cultural perspectives of the Hudson River Valley during the nineteenth century.

Guided tours are necessary to view the Cropsey Gallery and the

NEW YORK STATE

Homestead, but admission is free. The Gallery and Homestead are closed during January and August.

The Gallery is open for tours Monday through Friday from 1:00 p.m. to 5:00 p.m. The Homestead is open for tours Monday through Friday from 10:00 a.m. to 1:00 p.m. Please call at least one week in advance for tours. Unguided viewing of the grounds and architecture is allowed from 1:00 p.m. to 5:00 p.m. during the week without an appointment.

OLANA

Olana State Historic Site
5720 State Route 9G
Hudson
ARCHITECTS: William Morris Hunt (1828–1895), Calvert Vaux
   (1824–1895), and Frederic Edwin Church (1826–1900)
PHONE: (518) 828-0135
WEB SITE: www.olana.org

OLANA IS THE ARTIST RESIDENCE of Frederic Edwin Church, one of the premier Hudson River School landscape painters. Church acquired the property in 1860 and engaged the architect William Morris Hunt to create a small house for his family, which was called "Cosy Cottage." As Church's career gained momentum, he was able to add eighteen acres on the hill that overlooked the original property in 1867 and have Hunt create a French family manor house.

In 1867, Church and his family left for extended travel in Europe and the Middle East. Church became enamored of the architecture he saw in Lebanon, Israel, Palestine, Syria, Jordan, and Egypt. Upon his return, he replaced Hunt with Calvert Vaux and worked with him on transforming the house into a Persian-styled mansion, which he named "Olana." Various translations of "Olana" include "protection and strength" or "church on high" in Arabic, and the residence is supposed to have been named after a Persian fortress.

Church was deeply involved in the design of Olana and executed his own architectural sketches. It is highly personal and eclectic in its decoration, and is noted for its Victorian and Persian influences. Church and his family moved into the second story of the house in 1872 and he continued to work on the lower floor, which included a rich color palette and elaborate stencils. He had family heirlooms, which he mixed from acquisitions both here and abroad. The house continued to preoccupy Church throughout his life. In 1888 he added a studio wing and observatory and essentially completed it by 1891. The house remains largely as it looked in Church's day, and the furnishings collected by Church were intended as representative of diverse historical civilizations and religions of the world.

Two hundred and fifty acres of picturesque grounds constitute Olana's property, whose landscaping was also planned by Church with his artistic eye, giving careful attention to composition and balance. Olana was a working farm, expected to turn a profit, but he also gave careful consideration to its aesthetic appearance, with abundant plantings, planned roads and walkways, and vistas of the Hudson River and the Catskill Mountains.

There are also paintings in the collection by Church, as well as other Hudson River School artists, such as Martin Johnson Heade (1819–1904) and Arthur Parton (1842–1914), and numerous works by his close friend, sculptor Erastus Dow Palmer (1817–1904). There are also eclectic objects, furniture and works of art including Middle Eastern carpets, metalwork, ceramics, and Mexican and colonial folk art.

The grounds are open from 8:00 a.m. through sunset throughout the year. Tours are available from November to March, Friday through Sunday: 11:00 a.m. to 4:00 p.m., and are given on the hour, with the last one starting at 3:00 p.m. From April through October tours are given Tuesday through Sunday, and official Monday holidays: 10:00 a.m. to 4:00 p.m. Call (518) 828-0135 for tour information or for reservations, which are suggested. There is an admission fee.

Another related destination worth visiting is **CEDAR GROVE**, the Thomas Cole Historic site in Catskill, located at 218 Spring Street. Cole is considered the father of the Hudson River Landscape School and was Church's mentor. *Cedar Grove* includes Cole's 1815 Federal-style house, his artist's studio, and farm. There is a gallery that exhibits works relating to Cole and the Hudson River School. For more information call (518) 943-7465 or visit the Web site at www.thomascole.org.

One other historic house located close by is **CLERMONT**, the Livingston Family Estate, which dates to 1728, and is in Germantown, New York. The estate originally comprised 13,000 acres along the Hudson River and encompassed the southern third of Columbia County. Robert Livingston, or Robert of Clermont, as he was known, began construction of a brick Georgian-style countryseat, which may have incorporated an existing seventeenth-century house, between 1730 and 1750. Great views of the high peaks of the Catskill Mountain range are visible from the house, which suggest the name of the estate: Clermont means "clear mountain" in French. For more information, see the Web site: www.friendsofclermont.org or call (518) 537-6240.

SLEEPY HOLLOW COUNTRY

SUNNYSIDE, 1835
9 West Sunnyside Lane
Tarrytown
PHONE: (914) 591-8753
WEB SITE: www.hudsonvalley.org
E-MAIL: info@hudsonvalley.org

PHILIPSBURG MANOR, 1693
3819 N. Broadway
Sleepy Hollow
PHONE: (914) 631-3992
WEB SITE: www.hudsonvalley.org
E-MAIL: info@hudsonvalley.org

THE OLD DUTCH CHURCH OF SLEEPY HOLLOW, 1685
Sleepy Hollow
PHONE: (914) 631-4497
WEB SITE: www.rtodc.org

SUNNYSIDE was the home of the renowned American writer Washington Irving (1783–1859), perhaps best known for *The Legend of Sleepy Hollow* and *Rip Van Winkle*, and for such unforgettable fictional characters as Ichabod Crane and the Headless Horseman. Irving purchased the property with its breathtaking views of the Hudson River in 1835 with a vision of transforming it into the showplace it would become. "It is a beautiful spot," Irving said of Sunnyside, "capable of being made a paradise."

Irving was instrumental in designing the grounds and redesigning the house, which was originally a Dutch-style cottage, built in the eighteenth century. Inspired by his travels and in particular the architecture of Scotland, Spain, and colonial New York, Irving added stepped gables, a weathervane, and a tower resembling those found in Spanish monasteries.

The grounds, with their lovely garden paths and water features, reflect a very natural, romantic sensibility reminiscent of the best English gardens. A magnificent wisteria vine that Irving planted still grows and envelops the house. And the interior of the house features period rooms decorated with lovely early- to mid-nineteenth-century furniture and decorative items, many of which Irving himself chose and purchased. Both the gardens and the furnishings are among the best documented landscapes and period interiors in America.

Sunnyside and the surrounding community have become so interconnected with Irving and his stories that the area is generally known as "Sleepy Hollow Country." Not far from Sunnyside in Sleepy Hollow Country is the historic **PHILIPSBURG MANOR**, built by a seventeenth-century Anglo-Dutch merchant family, whose original holdings included 52,000 acres of land from Yonkers to Croton. Philipsburg Manor is a three-story, whitewashed fieldstone structure, which was constructed in two stages, with the original Eastern portion constructed in 1680. In 1720, the manor house was expanded and doubled in size. The estate is much more than a simple manor house. After it was founded, Philipsburg and its presiding family, the Philipses, headed by Lord Frederick Philipse I, rented land to tenant farmers from diverse European backgrounds and owned twenty-three African slaves, all of whom were integral to helping run the property and its various enterprises.

Today, visitors, guided by interpreters in period costume, can enter the ten period rooms in the manor house, five of which have been refurbished with reproduction objects to provide an interactive, hands-on experience. On view at the house are an array of rooms, including bedrooms, kitchen, dairy, parlor, and warehouse, all of which remind visitors that the estate served several functions, from private home to a place of business. Also on the property are a mill, a wharf, and a farm with cows, oxen, and chickens. The experience, akin to that of visiting Colonial Williamsburg, is meant to evoke another era and be instructive in raising pertinent historical, social, and political questions.

The manor rooms display a variety of seventeenth- and eighteenth-century furnishings and decorative objects from England, the Netherlands, and the American colonies, reflecting the Philipse family's many shipping and trading enterprises. On the estate grounds is a recreated slaves' garden, based on research into the gardens slaves maintained for their own use. The garden features food and cash crops as well as medicinal plants.

Located across from Philipsburg Manor is **THE OLD DUTCH CHURCH OF SLEEPY HOLLOW**, which was also constructed by the Philipses. Built with local fieldstone and completed in 1685, the church's walls are about two feet thick and its design is one commonly found in the Netherlands, particularly in the area from which Frederick Philipse emigrated. The roof displays the gambrel design common in Dutch colonial architecture, as it is a two-sided roof with two slopes on each side. The shorter, upper slope is connected to the lower slope, which is larger and much steeper. The church has undergone very few changes since the end of the seventeenth century, and, in fact, still possesses its original bell, which was cast in the Netherlands and was inscribed in Latin, "If God be for us, who can be against us?"

The Old Dutch Church's burial ground is prominently featured in Irving's *The Legend of Sleepy Hollow*, as the site where Ichabod Crane tries to escape the Headless Horseman. Adjacent to the churchyard is the **SLEEPY HOLLOW CEMETERY**, which is often confused with the churchyard, but was in fact not yet established when Irving's story was published. Irving, however, is buried at The Sleepy Hollow Cemetery. His grave is at the southern end of the cemetery overlooking Old Dutch and its churchyard. Other notable figures buried at the Sleepy Hollow Cemetery include Andrew Carnegie, Walter Chrysler, William Rockefeller, and Elizabeth Arden.

Sunnyside and Philipsburg Manor, which are both operated by the Historic Hudson Valley, have seasonal hours. In March they are open only on weekends from 10:00 a.m. to 4:00 p.m.; April through October, daily from 10:00 a.m. to 5:00 p.m. (closed Tuesdays); November through December, they are open every day (except Tuesday) 10:00 a.m. to 4:00 p.m. Admission fees apply. Guided tours are available with admission; check the posted hours on site for specific information, or call ahead for more information: (914) 591-8753 for Sunnyside and (914) 631-3992 for Philipsburg Manor.

The Old Dutch Church and its burial ground are on the right side of Route 9, across the street from Philipsburg Manor. Parking is available inside Sleepy Hollow Cemetery's south gate. Free maps of the grounds are available at the Sleepy Hollow Cemetery office about one-quarter mile north of the Old Dutch Church on Route 9 (North Broadway). In the summers the Reformed Church of the Tarrytowns, which owns Old Dutch and its burial ground, holds Sunday services at the historic church. **LYNDHURST** (see p. 144) and **KYKUIT** (see p. 140) are also right nearby and should not be missed.

■ STORM KING
Old Pleasant Hill Road
Mountainville
PHONE: (845) 534-3115
WEB SITE: www.stormking.org

LOCATED ON FIVE HUNDRED ACRES against a panorama of the Hudson Highlands about an hour outside of New York City, Storm King is a remarkable outdoor exhibition space for primarily post-war and contemporary American and European sculpture. Founded in 1960 by Ralph E. Ogden and H. Peter Stern, who at the time were co-owners of Star Expansion Company, Storm King explores the larger relationship between nature and sculpture, while also emphasizing the more nuanced connection between the characteristics of this particular stretch of land and the carefully chosen works placed upon it.

The collection began with a core group of thirteen sculptures by the Abstract Expressionist sculptor David Smith (1906–1965), an innovator who experimented with various materials and techniques and is generally credited with being the first American to use welding in creating his works. To ground, as it were, Storm King's larger collection with Smith's sculptures is particularly appropriate as its rolling landscape recalls Smith's Bolton Landing property in the Adirondacks, where he worked until his death. Smith is one of the first sculptors who became concerned with the relationship between his work and its specific location. On the Bolton

Landing property near Lake George, Smith organized his sculptures in what is referred to as an upper and lower field, sometimes arranging them in rows to emulate farm crops.

Smith's **THREE OVALS SOAR** (1960), a twelve-foot steel sculpture that seems to contradict its actual grounded quality by suggesting lightness and flight, recalls Smith's concern with achieving an almost seamless, yet original, relationship between his sculptures and the natural world. He once said, "I would like to make sculpture that would rise from water and tower in the air—that carried conviction and vision that had not existed before."

The Minimalist sculptor Richard Serra's (b. 1939) **SCHUNNEMUNK FORK** (1991) is a site-specific sculpture commissioned by Storm King. Located on a ten-acre field, Serra's work is composed of four large rectangular steel plates, sunken into the earth so that they are only partially visible. Each piece, which marks an eight-foot drop in elevation, underscores the undulating topography of Storm King.

Storm King does an extraordinary job of representing the best of post–World War II sculpture, including Barbara Hepworth's (1903–1975) musically inspired **FORMS IN MOVEMENT (PAVAN)** (1956); one of Alexander Calder's (1898–1976) last monumental stabiles, **THE ARCH** (1975), a fifty-foot biomorphic form perhaps inspired by Calder's stated desire to make immense works that would not be limited by physical constraints and where, in his words, "the sky could be my ceiling"; and Isamu Noguchi's (1904–1988) nine-part, forty-ton **MOMO TARO** (1977–78), a title that refers to the story of the ancient Japanese folk hero who was born from a peach pit, a tale that Noguchi recalled when a boulder split in half while the artist gathered materials for this sculpture.

Other highlights of the collection include three sculptures by Mark di Suvero (b. 1933) and works by Louise Nevelson (1899–1988), Alice Aycock (b. 1946), Magdalena Abakanowicz (b. 1930), Henri Moore (1898–1986), Siah Armajani (b. 1939), Ursula von Rydingsvard (b. 1942), and Andy Goldsworthy (b. 1956).

Storm King also has indoor gallery spaces to display both smaller-scale permanent collection pieces and for hosting temporary exhibitions. Call or check the Web site for hours, which change seasonally. Admission fees apply. Self-guided tram tours are included with admission.

■ **VAN CORTLANDT MANOR, BEFORE 1732**
South Riverside Avenue
Croton-on-Hudson
PHONE: (914) 271-8981 or (914) 631-8200 Monday through Friday
WEB SITE: www.hudsonvalley.org

THE STONE VAN CORTLANDT MANOR HOUSE is situated at the confluence of the Croton and Hudson rivers. The house and property has a long history that can be traced to 1697, when an 86,000-acre tract was granted to Stephanus Van Cortlandt, of Dutch background, by King William III. The manor was constructed before 1732 and Pierre Van Cortlandt took up residence there in 1749. The house remained in Van Cortlandt family ownership until 1945 and was purchased in 1953 by John D. Rockefeller, who launched his last and one of his most comprehensive restoration campaigns on the property.

Visiting the manor, one can absorb life in the Revolutionary period with demonstrations of blacksmithing, brick making, open-hearth cooking, spinning, weaving, and other crafts and tasks of the period. The manor house also offers a collection of decorative arts and furnishings from the Colonial and Federal periods, along with a fine example of a colonial kitchen with its typical wares. There is also a brick ferry house on the property that was constructed before 1750, which functioned as a tavern and inn. It has a collection of Hudson Valley vernacular furnishings. In the gardens are an array of flowers, vegetables, and herbs typically seen in late-eighteenth-century America.

The Van Cortlandts were one of New York's most prominent families and were involved in numerous entrepreneurial activities, including land development, saw and grist mills, food cultivation, and transport. They were also caught in the midst of period politics, including the slave controversy, as they were slave owners. The clever positioning of the property at the convergence of the two rivers was advantageous to the family's business concerns.

The house and property are open April to September from 10:00 a.m. to 5:00 p.m., with the last tour at 4:00 p.m.; closed Tuesdays. In October the hours are 10:00 a.m. to 2:00 p.m. and the last tour is 2:00 p.m. In November and December it is open on weekends only from 10:00 a.m. to 4:00 p.m., with the last tour leaving at 3:00 p.m. The manor is closed on Thanksgiving Day, Christmas Day, and New Year's Day. There are admission fees charged, though members and children under five are free.

VANDERBILT MANSION, 1896–99
National Park Service
4097 Albany Post Road
Hyde Park
ARCHITECT: McKim, Mead, and White
PHONE: (845) 229-9115
WEB SITE: www.nps.gov/vama/

FEATURING PRESERVED rather than recreated interiors, this Hyde Park mansion appears exactly to present-day visitors as it did to the Vanderbilts and their guests when they arrived for country getaways at the turn of the century. Designed for Frederick Vanderbilt (1856–1938) and his wife, Louise Holmes Anthony Vanderbilt (1844–1926), the palatial dwelling epitomizes the monumental opulence of the American Renaissance Beaux-Arts style. Two principals of McKim, Mead, and White, New York's preeminent gilded-age architectural firm, collaborated on the Vanderbilt project, executed between 1896 and 1899. Charles Follen McKim (1847–1909), the firm's senior partner and theoretician, designed the exterior and basic interior structure. Trained in architecture at the École des Beaux-Arts, Paris, Stanford White (1853–1906) applied his special gift for interior spaces when designing the main rooms on the first floor.

To create public rooms appropriate to his clients' status, White traveled to Europe, where he acquired antique furnishings and architectural elements from stately homes. Among his purchases for the Vanderbilts were a carved wooden ceiling and stone chimney breasts for the dining room, and Renaissance chairs for the entry hall. Also historically significant, the second floor private spaces of the fifty-room mansion are the work of other designers.

Many of the guestrooms are attributed to the New York decorator Ogden Codman (1863–1951) who coauthored, with Edith Wharton, *The Decoration of Houses* (1892). Departing from Victorian eclecticism, Ogden and Wharton recommended decorating rooms in one style. This revolutionary approach is illustrated in the lavishly appointed guest rooms, which are furnished in eighteenth-century French style. Each room has its distinct color scheme, with the motif carried into the bathroom accessories. Georges Glaenzer (active c. 1890–1910) designed Mrs. Vanderbilt's bedroom in the Wharton/Codman manner. He modeled her room on the ceremonial bedchamber of an eighteenth-century French monarch. Then he commissioned top contemporary craftsmen such as Paul Sormani (1817–c. 1877) to create replicas of period furniture. For Vanderbilt, Glaenzer took the old-fashioned Victorian eclectic approach. As a result, visitors today experience the application of two period design theories.

Although the façade and interiors of the Vanderbilt mansion evoke the aura of many generations of noble occupancy, the building techniques and mechanical systems used in construction incorporated the most up-to-date technology. The Classical style and Indiana limestone facing conceal a steel and concrete frame as well as state of the art mechanical systems—plumbing, fireproofing, central heating, and power supplied by a hydroelectric plant on the estate. The most striking improvement, considering it was built on a private property, was one of the country's first steel and concrete bridges, called the "White Bridge."

Shortly after the Vanderbilts purchased the 600-acre estate, the *New York Times* described it as "the finest place on the Hudson between New York and Albany." Visitors are still welcome to stroll 211 acres of the original parkland, where they can appreciate the centuries-old tree plantings, stunning Hudson River and Catskill Mountain views, and Italian Gardens. When the Vanderbilts acquired their Hyde Park estate, it came with a history stretching back 150 years. Rather than substantially changing the historic landscape, the Vanderbilts merely modified and restored it to its former grandeur. Consequently visitors experience not only the historic buildings and furnishings, but also the impressive settings. In 1841 Andrew Jackson Downing (1815–1852), landscape designer and theorist, wrote "Hyde Park is justly celebrated as one of the finest specimens of the Romantic style of landscape gardening in America." Downing's complimentary words recognized the work of Andre Parmentier (1780–1830) who had shaped the land into a romantic landscape for David Hosack (1769–1835) in the 1820s. Because of the vision of enlightened owners, the Vanderbilt Mansion National Historic Site showcases the plan conceived by Parmentier, one of North America's earliest landscape designers.

The Vanderbilt Mansion National Historic Site is open seven days a week from 9:00 a.m. to 5:00 p.m. by guided tour only. Guided 45-minute walking tours of the Vanderbilt Mansion include the first floor, second floor, and portion of basement. The Mansion is closed Thanksgiving, Christmas, and New Year's Day. The last tour of the day is at 4:00 p.m. Reservations are generally not necessary for individuals. Groups of ten or more are required to make a reservation. To make a reservation, visit www.recreation.gov or call (877) 444-6777. Grounds are open seven days year-round from 7:00 a.m. until sunset. Grounds are free. Admission fees apply for house tours.

WILDERSTEIN, 1852

330 Morton Road
Rhinebeck
ARCHITECT: John Warren Ritch, with Arnout Cannon,
    Joseph Burr Tiffany, and Calvert Vaux (1824–1895)
PHONE: (845) 876-4818
WEB SITE: www.Wilderstein.org

WILDERSTEIN IS A QUEEN–ANNE STYLE country house located in the Hudson River town of Rhinebeck. In 1852, Thomas Holy Suckley, a businessman and member of the noted Beekman and Livingston families, and his wife, Catherine Murray Bowne, acquired this riverfront property on which to build a country estate. They were interested in the natural pastoral features of the landscape and vistas of the Hudson River and surrounding mountains. He named the estate "Wilderstein," meaning "wild stone" in German, after a Native American petroglyph found nearby. The Suckleys commissioned a two-story Italianate villa from architect John Warren Ritch for the site.

In 1888, Stuckley's son and his wife, with the help of Poughkeepsie architect Arnout Cannon, later transformed the original structure into the Queen Anne–style now evident with the third floor addition, gabled attic, and five-story, circular turret tower.

The interiors were done by New York decorator Joseph Burr Tiffany (a cousin of Louis Comfort Tiffany) and include period rooms in Revival and Aesthetic movement styles. The landscape of the property was designed by Englishman Calvert Vaux (1824–1895) and reflects the impact of the picturesque landscape tradition that unites ideas of design and nature to create a bucolic environment. In 1850, Vaux met Andrew Jackson Downing, the prominent American landscape designer, who lured Vaux to work for his Newburgh, New York firm. He then settled in America and pursued his romantic vision in which nature and architecture are synthesized into an overall environment. His most well-known project was his collaboration with Frederick Law Olmsted in 1858 for the design of New York's **CENTRAL PARK** (See p. 5). In Wilderstein, Vaux created a romantic landscape setting with winding paths, drives, and trails with unusual tree and shrub plantings augmented with gazebos and garden seats. Later additions to the estate include the veranda and porte cochere, and outbuildings, including the turreted carriage house, Shingle Style gate lodge, and a Colonial Revival style potting shed.

Guided tours are given from May through October on Thursdays to Sundays from 12:00 to 4:00 p.m. There is a nominal admission charge to see the house but access to the grounds and trails are free.

NEW JERSEY

DRUMTHWACKET (GOVERNOR'S MANSION), 1835
354 Stockton Street (Route 206)
Princeton
PHONE: (609) 683-0057
TOURS: (609) 683-0591
WEB SITE: www.drumthwacket.org

DRUMTHWACKET IS the official residence of the governor of New Jersey and is a fine example of Greek Revival Georgian architecture. It was built in 1835 by Charles Smith Olden, who would later serve as governor. The original house design only included the two-and-a-half-story center section and may have been based on a design by architect Charles Steadman. The name of the estate references the description "wooded hill" in Scottish Gaelic.

Olden played a prominent civic role in the state, and was treasurer of the College of New Jersey (now **PRINCETON UNIVERSITY**, see p. 182). He was also a state senator and governor, elected in 1860. An opponent of secession, he offered support to Abraham Lincoln during the Civil War.

Drumthwacket Estate was acquired in 1893 by Moses Taylor Pyne, a banker and industrialist, who was also a benefactor of Princeton University. He augmented the structure and decorative gardens; the estate grew to encompass 300 acres that include greenhouses, bridle paths, a dairy farm, and formal Italian gardens. Raleigh Gildersleeve was the architect of Pyne's expansion project and also responsible for many buildings on the university campus. When Pyne died, the estate went to his granddaughter, Agnes Pyne, in 1939. The property was eventually sold to the state of New Jersey in 1966 and was designated as the governor's mansion in 1982. Prior to 1982, the governor's mansion was **MORVEN**, which is on the Princeton University campus and has now become a museum devoted to the cultural heritage of the Garden State and holds exhibitions of fine, folk, and decorative arts.

The property on which the mansion resides has important historical associations. It was where the 1777 battle of Princeton took place during the Revolutionary War and was also once owned by William Penn, the founder of Pennsylvania. In 1696, the land was acquired by William Olden, grandfather of Charles Olden, who built the mansion.

Also part of the Drumthwacket Estate is **OLDEN HOUSE**, a small white farmhouse of four rooms located across the front lawn, which was built between 1759 and 1765 by John Hill. It was purchased in 1772 by Thomas Olden, a tailor and farmer and son of John Olden, one of the six early settlers who established the Quaker community of Stony Brook. Charles Smith Olden, one of Thomas Olden's grandsons and the man who built Drumthwacket was born in Olden House in 1799. After making his fortune in New Orleans, he returned to Princeton and began the construction of the mansion Drumthwacket in 1835. As Olden House became outmoded was transformed into a rare bird aviary, and later added monkeys, for which it became known. Olden House has now undergone a careful historic restoration, which is evident in the beam mantel, handmade bricks, original floors and cupboards, and the Colonial kitchen. The house contains art and antiques and the tour highlight six rooms that focus on the cultural heritage and heritage of the main house.

Tours are scheduled for fifteen persons or more at specific assigned times on Wednesday mornings and are by reservation. Please call or check the Web site for details at least one week ahead of the visit. Parking is available on site.

■ GROUNDS FOR SCULPTURE

18 Fairgrounds Road
Hamilton
PHONE: (609) 586-0616
WEB SITE: www.groundsforsculpture.org
E-MAIL: info@groundsforsculpture.org

THE GROUNDS FOR SCULPTURE on the former New Jersey State Fairgrounds was the brainchild of the philanthropist and sculptor J. Seward Johnson II (b. 1930), who is known for his trompe-l'oeil bronze painted sculptures. Johnson wanted to establish an outdoor sculpture collection dedicated to modern and contemporary sculpture that would evolve and change over the seasons and years. The Grounds, a thirty-five-acre public sculpture park with indoor exhibition spaces, opened to the public in 1992, and its collection comprises more than 240 works by such renowned sculptors as Anthony Caro (b. 1924), George Segal (1926–2000), Beverly Pepper (b. 1922), and Kiki Smith (b. 1954).

The English sculptor Anthony Caro's **POTPOURRI** (1976–77) is a rusted and varnished welded steel sculpture composed of horizontal fragments that seem to crash together to form a large, unorganized pile of materials, suggesting destruction rather than construction and challenging any traditional expectation of finish and symmetry.

George Segal's **DEPRESSION BREAD LINE** (1999) represents five unemployed men, all slightly stooping with heads bent downward as if to suggest their burdens. The men are lined up along a wall leading to a closed door, awaiting government assistance during the Great Depression.

Works by Beverly Pepper in the collection include **UNTITLED** (c. 1968), with its highly reflective, variously angled stainless steel blocks, and the four tall, totemic forms of **SPLIT RITUAL II** (1992), part of a series of works Pepper describes as "metamorphosed tools."

Kiki Smith's deliberately provocative cast bronze **UNTITLED** (2006) is a fountain of sorts, appropriately located in the Water Garden and featuring a crouching girl urinating in a stream. Smith's work often focuses on the body, its social and political significances, and the ways in which it functions. A sculpture such as **UNTITLED** also reflects Smith's interest in issues relating to gender and sexuality; integral to such a work is the question of why it is more shocking to see a girl or a woman urinating than to see a boy or a man urinating in a stream or in a public place.

Each year, the Grounds for Sculpture presents exhibitions of new additions to the collection outdoors, as well as one-person shows held within its indoor exhibition spaces.

The Grounds for Sculpture is open year-round, Tuesday through Sunday 10:00 a.m. to 6:00 p.m. Admission fees apply. Weekend drop-in tours are offered May through October on Saturdays at 11:00 a.m. and Sundays at 2:00 p.m. No reservations are needed and the tour is free with paid admission to the grounds. Meet docents at the Reception Desk in the Museum Building ten minutes before the hour.

■ JERSEY HOMESTEADS MURAL, 1936–37
Roosevelt Public School
Roosevelt
Ben Shahn (1898–1969)
PHONE: (609) 448-2798

THE PRINTMAKER, PAINTER, AND PHOTOGRAPHER Ben Shahn, who was born in what is today Lithuania, emigrated to the United States and settled in Brooklyn, New York, with his family in 1906, a few years after his father was exiled to Siberia for alleged participation in revolutionary activities. Shahn, who is characterized as a Social Realist, often created works that addressed political, populist, and social issues and many that touched on his own Jewish heritage.

In 1933, Shahn met and served as an assistant to the famous Mexican Muralist painter, Diego Rivera (1886–1957), who was at the time working on the Rockefeller Center mural, which created an uproar and was later removed for its inclusion of the figure of the Russian revolutionary Vladimir Lenin. In 1935, along with the photographers Walker Evans (1903–1975) and Dorothea Lange (1895–1965), Shahn was hired by the New Deal's Farms Security Administration (FSA) to take social documentary photographs of the American South.

The next year, the FSA commissioned Shahn to create a mural for the

New Deal resettlement community, the Jersey Homesteads, a town partly established to assist garment workers during the difficult economic times of the Great Depression. Shahn's mural, one of his finest works, depicts the history of the Jersey Homesteads, today known as the town of Roosevelt. The town became a home for Eastern European Jewish garment workers, who escaped the sweatshop conditions they found in the city after arriving at Ellis Island to participate in forming this small cooperative community in New Jersey. In addition to Shahn, the Jersey Homesteads was early on supported by such thinkers and artists as Albert Einstein and the painter Raphael Soyer (1899–1987), both of whom are pictured in the mural, as well as the Homesteads' architects Alfred Kastner (1901–1975) and his then-assistant Louis I. Kahn (1901–1974), the renowned designer of the **TRENTON BATH HOUSE** (1954–59), Kahn's only New Jersey structure.

The Homesteads Mural is made up of three panels that are further divided by the highly effective use of architectural details like brick walls or columns and perspective variations to subtly delineate and organize various narratives and subjects within a large-scale fresco mural measuring twelve feet by forty-five feet.

Meant to be read from left to right, the mural's narrative begins with the arrival of the immigrants at Ellis Island and the subsequent lives they would find in the city, which included dark, difficult days working in sweatshops and poor living conditions in tenement housing.

Shahn also incorporates elements such as the bodies of the executed Italian-American anarchists Nicola Sacco and Bartolomeo Vanzetti to highlight the persecution and adversity that immigrant workers faced. Sacco and Vanzetti's trial, conviction, and execution for armed robbery and murder came to symbolize for many the deep roots of anti-immigrant sentiment and the corruptness of the justice system in the United States. The subject occupied a good deal of Shahn's artistic energies: in addition to its referencing in the Jersey Homesteads mural, Shahn painted twenty-three gouache and tempera paintings about the subject, including the most famous, **THE PASSION OF SACCO AND VANZETTI** (1931–32), which is in the collection of the **WHITNEY MUSEUM** (see p. 45); he also executed a mosaic mural (1967) of the subject at Syracuse University.

The central panel of the Jersey Homesteads Mural depicts the organization of labor unions and labor protests to call for the protection of exploited workers like those pictured picketing in front of the Triangle Shirtwaist Company, the site of a devastating fire that killed 146 workers in 1911 and led to the strengthening and growth of the International Ladies Garment Workers Union.

The last panel offers scenes relating to the Jersey Homesteads, most notable among them a view of New Deal government representatives and union members gathering around a blueprint for the new settlement, which would establish a farm and factory cooperative. A campaign poster picturing President Franklin Delano Roosevelt presides over the last panel.

The building that houses the mural today is the Roosevelt Public School, in Roosevelt, New Jersey. Because the mural is located at a public elementary school still in operation, it is available for viewing by the general public by appointment only. Call the school at (609) 448-2798 to schedule an appointment. When arriving at the school, have proper identification, as visitors must check in with the office.

▪ LLEWELLYN PARK, 1857

1 Park Way (off Main Street—entrance near Thomas Edison's Factory
   Complex, which is now a museum)
West Orange
ARCHITECT: Alexander Jackson Davis (1803–1892)
 PHONE: (973) 736-8402
WEB SITE: www.llewellynpark.com
E-MAIL: lpoffice@verizon.net

LLEWELLYN PARK is America's first planned residential community and was founded in 1857 by Llewellyn S. Haskell, a New York businessman and drugstore magnate who sought out noted architect and advocate of pastoral living Alexander Jackson Davis. Haskell acquired the wooded area on the eastern side of the Watchung mountain range and set out to designate it for country estates as he was also a proponent of living in pastoral surroundings.

Haskell acquired over 400 acres on the south slope of the mountain, along with eight partners, in a desirable location, only twelve miles from New York by train. He wished to create a picturesque retreat outside of the city that was consistent with his belief that righteous living could bring about the perfect existence on earth—an ideal set forth by the Perfectionists—a group to which he belonged.

Davis, in keeping with the reigning ideology of landscape architecture of the day, created a design that sets off the exclusive enclave with a gatehouse that he designed himself. A fifty-acre area called The Ramble encompasses paths and streams while prohibiting fences; there is a scheme of winding streets with period gas lamps. Many notable architects also designed homes within the 175 dwellings in the community, including Calvert Vaux, Stanford White, Charles McKim, and Robert A.M. Stern. The most notable resident of the community was Thomas Edison, whose home, Glenmont, is a historic site, and the Colgate and Merck families also had residences there. The most prominent feature of the community is the gate lodge, designed by Davis in 1860. It is the epitome of an eclectic and original vision, composed of fieldstone with round forms that are more attuned to the natural surroundings than typical angular structures. The design is so original that it suggests few historical precedents beyond parallels seen in the contemporaneous nineteenth-century British Arts and Crafts movement.

Davis was among the most noted of mid-nineteenth-century American architects. He worked extensively in New York City, Upstate New York, and Connecticut, and was known for creating structures in myriad styles. He grew up in Newark, New Jersey, and is interred in nearby Bloomfield Cemetery in Bloomfield, New Jersey.

MONTCLAIR ART MUSEUM

3 South Mountain Avenue
Montclair
PHONE: (973) 746-5555
WEB SITE: www.montclairmuseum.org

KNOWN FOR ITS AMERICAN and Native American art collections, the Montclair Art Museum, founded in 1914, was New Jersey's first art museum. The Hudson River School, early modernism, Abstract Expressionism, and twentieth-century African-American art are areas of particular note in the museum's American collection. The Native American holdings of more than 4,000 objects, including extraordinary basketry and jewelry, represent the cultural development of seven major areas in the United States, namely the Northwest Coast, California, the Southwest, the Plains, the Woodlands, the Southeast, and the Arctic. In addition to displaying Native American treasures of the past, the museum is dedicated to exhibiting and collecting works of contemporary Native American artists.

The Montclair Art Museum's collection of American art is anchored by seventeen paintings by George Inness (1825–1894), an influential nineteenth-century landscape painter who lived and worked in Montclair from 1885 until his death. The museum offers a comprehensive view of Inness's career development, beginning with his earlier, Hudson River School paintings like **DELAWARE WATER GAP** (1859), a gorgeous panoramic vista which demonstrates his mastery of naturalistic details and light. As his work matured, Inness became increasingly focused on imbuing his landscapes with a certain spirituality, and, influenced by Swedenborgian philosophy and the idea that all natural elements were connected to the spiritual world, he developed a Tonalist style where darker shades and hues dominated his now-moodier compositions. Inness's **SUNSET AT MONTCLAIR** (1892), with its very earthy palette that envelops the landscape in golden brown tones, and the predominantly gray **GATHERING CLOUDS, SPRING, MONTCLAIR, N.J.** (1890–94), are particularly strong examples of the Tonalist views he painted while living in Montclair.

Other highlights from the American collection include William Merritt Chase's (1849–1916) Spanish-inspired **A TAMBOURINE PLAYER** (c. 1886), where Chase's model/wife's physical motions and the details of her lace-trimmed white dress and golden shawl contrast sharply with the simple, dark background; Edward Hopper's (1882–1967) **COAST GUARD STATION** (1929), a landscape that demonstrates Hopper's deftness at capturing light and shadow in images that communicate stillness, quiet, and calm; Georgia O'Keeffe's (1887–1986) **SKUNK CABBAGE** (c. 1927), a breathtaking interpretation of a seemingly simple and mundane plant with its deeply saturated purples and greens; and Stuart Davis's (1892–1964) Synthetic Cubist-inspired **LANDSCAPE IN THE COLORS OF A PEAR** (1940), an abstracted landscape consisting of flattened shapes and colors that communicate a sense of energy and rhythm.

One of the most striking works in the museum's fine contemporary

Native American collection is Jaune Quick-to-See Smith's (b. 1940) oil and mixed-media collage diptych, **WAR SHIRT** (1992). Quick-to-See Smith is known for her satiric humor and political imagery, which takes on subjects such as American consumerism and the preservation of the land and culture of Native peoples. In **WAR SHIRT**, the red splatters of paint also allude to bloodshed, and the canvas's diptych format that splits the war shirt in half suggests conflicted identities and discord.

The Montclair Art Museum is open Wednesday through Sunday 12:00 to 5:00 p.m. and is closed Mondays and Tuesdays. Admission fees apply.

MUSEUM OF AMERICAN GLASS

Wheaton Arts and Cultural Center
1501 Glasstown Road
Millville
PHONE: (800) 998-4552
WEB SITE: www.wheatonarts.org
E-MAIL: mail@wheatonarts.org

BECAUSE OF THE AVAILABILITY of such natural resources as wood, sand, soda ash, and silica in Southern New Jersey, the region was an ideal birth place for the establishment of an active and thriving American glass industry. In the late eighteenth century, the earliest successful glass factory was founded in Millville, and, a century later, Millville resident Dr. Theodore Corson Wheaton, a pharmacist, began making his own pharmaceutical bottles in a glass factory. In the early 1960s Wheaton's grandson, Frank H. Wheaton, Jr., decided to establish a center that would display and celebrate New Jersey's rich heritage of glass production. The result was the Wheaton Arts and Cultural Center and its Museum of American Glass, and the complex today includes over sixty acres and twenty buildings. The Museum houses more than 6,500 historic and contemporary objects, and the center also includes a fully operational glass factory and craft studios where artists lead pottery and wood- and flame-working demonstrations.

In a series of rooms organized chronologically and thematically, the museum tells the story of American glassmaking, which had its earliest, small-scale beginnings in Jamestown, Virginia, during the seventeenth century. Casper Wistar, in defiance of English policies forbidding manufacturing in the Colonies, established Wistarburg, the first successful glass company in America near what is today Alloway, New Jersey, in 1738. In addition to Wistarburg glass, the museum also has rooms devoted to bottle design, paperweights, pressed glass, cut glass, and glass-focused period rooms such as a Victorian dining room.

Highlights include the Art Nouveau collection, featuring objects made by the foremost practitioner of the Art Nouveau style of design in American, Louis Comfort Tiffany (1848–1933), whose nature-inspired objects feature organic forms, sensuous lines, and iridescent colors. Other companies that produced exceptional Art Nouveau glassworks are also featured at the museum, and they include Quezal Art Glass and Decorating Company, Steuben Glass Works, the A. Douglas Nash Corporation, and the Durand Art Glass division of the Vineland Flint Glass Works, to name just a few.

The Wheaton Arts Center and the Museum of American Glass encourage the continued practice and development of creative glassmaking, and the museum also displays the work of renowned contemporary glass artists, including Dale Chihuly (b. 1941).

The Wheaton Arts and Cultural Center is open January through March, Friday to Sunday 10:00 a.m. to 5:00 p.m., and April through December, Tuesday to Sunday 10:00 a.m. to 5:00 p.m. Admission fees apply. A daily tour of the Museum of American Glass is offered at 2:30 p.m. and it is free with the price of admission. Other highlights of a visit to the center include regularly scheduled glassblowing demonstrations at the Glass Studio.

NEWARK MUSEUM

49 Washington Street, Newark
PHONE: (973) 596-6550
WEB SITE: www.newarkmuseum.org

FOUNDED IN 1909, the Newark Museum is the largest museum in New Jersey and houses an impressive collection, with particular strengths in the areas of American and Tibetan art. In 1990, the noted architect Michael Graves (b. 1934) completed an extensive renovation and expansion for the museum. Graves, who was first approached about the project in 1967 when he was still a struggling architect, designed a space full of light, with several small rotundas and other variously shaped small rooms that foster an intimate relationship between viewer and object.

The museum's collection of American paintings, sculpture, photography, and decorative and folk arts and furnishings is exceptional and reflects the highpoints of American visual culture. The Newark Museum offers strong examples of Colonial and early American portraiture, including John Singleton Copley's (1738–1815) **PORTRAIT OF MRS. JOSEPH SCOTT** (1765), which is vintage Copley in that it is characteristically a portrait of material possessions as much as it is one of the sitter herself, who here is turned away from the viewer, offering primarily a profile view of her face, while her clothing, accessories, and their wonderful textures are displayed to suggest her wealth and Copley's virtuosity.

Other noteworthy holdings in the American collection include first-rate Hudson River School paintings, such as Albert Bierstadt's (1830–1902) majestic **WESTERN LANDSCAPE** (1869), a gorgeous vista that demonstrates Bierstadt's mastery of representing the subtleties of geological formations, light, and water; Jasper Cropsey's (1823–1900) breathtaking and panoramic **GREENWOOD LAKE** (1871); Thomas Cole's (1801–1848) picturesque **THE ARCH OF NERO** (1846); Frederic Church's (1826–1900) **TWILIGHT, SHORT ARBITER 'TWIXT DAY AND NIGHT** (1850) with its extraordinary sky; and George Inness's (1825–1894) naturalistic **DELAWARE VALLEY BEFORE THE STORM** (c. 1865) that already hints at the moody qualities associated with his later Tonalist works like **THE TROUT BROOK** (c. 1891).

The jewel of the nineteenth-century American sculpture collection is Hiram Powers's (1805–1873) Neoclassical **THE GREEK SLAVE** (1847), one of the most celebrated and promoted American sculptures in its own day that was sent by Powers on a national and international tour. Based on classical representations of the goddess Venus, the sculpture represents an enchained nude Greek girl who has been brought to a Turkish slave market. Stressing her modesty and her role as a victim, Powers and supporters of the sculpture invented narratives to make *The Greek Slave* more acceptable to certain nineteenth-century viewers who were shocked by the unprecedented representation of nudity in a contemporary sculpture. One reviewer, for example, suggested that she was "NAKED, yet clothed with chastity." Powers made six versions of his most popular sculpture, which was seen by many as an abolitionist statement, given Powers's anti-slavery sentiments and the political climate of the time. Slightly later versions of *The Greek Slave* are also in the collections of the **YALE UNIVERSITY ART GALLERY** (see p. 209) and the **BROOKLYN MUSEUM OF ART** (see p. 108).

Late nineteenth- and early twentieth-century American painting is also well represented at the Newark Museum. John Singer Sargent's (1856–1925) **MRS. CHARLES THURSBY** (1897–98) is a gorgeously painted portrait of a "New Woman" at the turn-of-the twentieth century, who confidently confronts the viewer by placing her hands at her hips and sitting with her legs boldly crossed with one foot poking out from under her dress. The painting also demonstrates Sargent's deft handling of paint, his masterful ability to suggest various textures and to represent luxurious materials, and his keen understanding of color in details such as the contrast between the darker plum colors of Mrs. Thursby's dress and the whites of the large armchair that envelops and presents her to the viewer.

Among the best works of American Impressionism at the museum are Mary Cassatt's (1844–1926) **JENNY CASSATT WITH HER SON, GARDNER** (1895–96) and Childe Hassam's (1859–1935) **GLOUCESTER** (1899). Cassatt depicts a quiet moment between mother and son and reflects the nuances and complexities of such relationships by suggesting closeness and love in such details as the boy's head resting against his mother's chest; Cassatt also hints at the conflicts that are also natural, particularly as children mature, by painting Jenny Cassatt's hand against her son's neck as protective and loving while also potentially inhibiting. Hassam's **GLOUCESTER** is an expertly painted harbor scene that reflects the quick brush strokes, lighter palette, and fascination with light that are hallmarks of Impressionist painting.

Two particularly fine examples of work from the so-called Ashcan School, whose works tended toward a darker palette and contained modern themes and addressed social or political concerns, include Robert Henri's (1865–1929) **WILLIE GEE** (1904) and John Sloan's (1871–1951) **PICTURE SHOP WINDOW** (1907). Henri, who tackled such issues as increasing ethnic diversity in his many likenesses, offers in *Willie Gee* a sensitive and compelling portrait of a young African-American newspaper boy who delivered papers to him in New York; Sloan, whose early career was spent in Philadelphia as a newspaper illustrator, tended to paint urban genre scenes in a caricatural style that exposed such realities as the consumerism and spectacle that were an integral part of contemporary life in such works as **PICTURE SHOP WINDOW**.

The modern city and spectacle are also themes relevant to Edward Hopper's (1882–1967) **THE SHERIDAN THEATER** (1937). Hopper, who studied with Henri for a time, takes as his theme the isolation and alienation that are also integral to the urban experience by emphasizing the disconnectedness that exists between people especially in large public spaces. In an ambiguous and very quiet scene, Hopper's central figure, whose back is turned to the viewer, is depicted either watching something below the dramatic railing of the theater lobby or standing lost in private thoughts in a public place. In a space devoted to spectacle, Hopper circumvents expectation and makes the theatergoer and the spectacular architecture the key elements on display.

The highlight of the museum's strong collection of American modernism is Joseph Stella's (1877–1946) monumental mural, **VOICES OF THE CITY OF NEW YORK INTERPRETED** (1920–22), which consists of five panels, each measuring more than seven feet by four-and-one-half feet. The Italian-American Stella pays homage to the visual spectacle that is the modern city of New York in a work that reflects the influence of the Futurist movement's interest in technology and speed. The series is celebratory and offers a kind of amplified vision that pays homage to New York's energies, rhythms, and its iconic structures, as in **THE BROOKLYN BRIDGE** panel. The shapes of the five canvases are deliberately vertical, and, within each, Stella stresses verticality— strategies that visually recall the skyscrapers and immense bridges that dramatically punctuate New York's skyline. The geometries, powerfully intersecting lines and shapes, and bursts of light that

Portrait of Mrs. Joseph Scott
(c. 1765) by John Singleton Copley

make up each canvas create an aesthetic equation, positing a symbiotic relationship between modern art and the modern city.

Featuring more than 6,000 objects collected over the years, the Newark Museum also has one of the most comprehensive collections of Tibetan art outside of the Himalayas. In 1911, the museum purchased the collection of Dr. Albert L. Shelton, an American medical missionary who bartered and rescued objects from monasteries destroyed during fighting along the Tibet-China border. Since that initial purpose, the museum continued to expand its Tibetan collection, which is remarkable for its scope and quality, including both religious and secular objects such as jewelry, nomad costumes, and saddles, as well as documentary photography. Among the more religious treasures are the lovely sixteenth-century silver and partly gilded and bejeweled **VAJRAVARAHI** ("diamond sow"); a painted and gilded ceremonial crown from the fourteenth century featuring the five Buddhas; and beautiful, centuries-old paintings rendered on cloth supports. In addition to Tibet, the Museum's Asian collection also includes fine examples of art from various countries and regions including China, Japan, Korea, and Southeast Asia.

The Newark Museum also has a small but distinguished sculpture garden that includes George Segal's (1924–2000) bronze and glass **TOLL BOOTH COLLECTOR** (1980), which features the museum's former director, Samuel Miller, as a toll collector set within an actual Holland Tunnel toll booth donated to the museum by the Port Authority of New York and New Jersey.

The museum has had a long tradition of American decorative arts and has notable holdings in the area of American art pottery and glass. The museum complex also includes the late-Victorian brick and limestone **BALLANTINE HOUSE**, built in 1885 and designed by George Edward Harney (1840–1924) for Jeannette and John Holme Ballantine, of the prominent Newark beer-brewing family.

Incorporating decorative arts and furnishings from the museum's impressive collections, Ballantine House has been restored to offer a microcosmic slice of life in a series of period rooms that recreate domestic settings in America from the 1650s to the present, while also offering a glimpse of the elegant home occupied by the Ballantines shortly after they moved into the mansion at the end of the nineteenth century.

The Newark Museum is open Wednesday through Friday, 12:00 to 5:00 p.m.; Saturday and Sunday 10:00 a.m. to 5:00 p.m. from October through June, and 12:00 to 5:00 p.m. July through September; closed Mondays, except for certain holidays. There are suggested museum admission fees, and certain discounts are available. Several drop-in gallery tours are available daily and are free with suggested admission. Museum parking is available for a fee.

THE JERSEY CITY MUSEUM is located only a few miles from the Newark Museum and is primarily dedicated to presenting contemporary art and representing the diversity of the American experience. Its permanent collection includes fine and decorative arts and other materials that reflect the history of material culture in America from the colonial period to the present. Highlights include **THREE WOMEN** (c. 1975) and **MADONNA AND CHILD** (c. 1973) by the preeminent African-American artist Romare Bearden (1911–1988), most famous for his collages. The Jersey City Museum is located at 350 Montgomery Street, Jersey City; (201) 413-0303; www.jerseycitymuseum.org; open Wednesday and Friday 11:00 a.m. to 5:00 p.m.; Thursdays 11:00 a.m. to 8:00 p.m. (except during part of the summer when galleries close at 5 p.m.); Saturday and Sunday 12:00 to 5:00 p.m.

NEW JERSEY STATE MUSEUM

205 West State Street
Trenton
PHONE: (609) 292-6464
WEB SITE: http://www.state.nj.us/state/museum/index.html
E-MAIL: feedback@sos.state.nj.us

THE RECENTLY RENOVATED New Jersey State Museum was founded 1895, and its initial focus was to collect and exhibit specimens relating to natural history. Over the years, the museum's collections expanded considerably, and by 1964 its wide-ranging activities also spanned the areas of archaeology, ethnology, and the decorative and fine arts.

Today, the New Jersey State Museum's fine arts collection includes more than 10,000 paintings, works on paper, sculptures, and photographs, many with a focus on New Jersey within the broader context of American art history. Particularly well represented are the works of American modernists, many of whom were associated with the renowned photographer and promoter of modern art Alfred Stieglitz (1864–1946), including Georgia O'Keeffe (1887–1986) and Arthur Dove (1880–1946), and works by nineteenth- and twentieth-century African-American artists including Romare Bearden (1911–1988).

The strengths of the decorative arts and crafts collection of more than 12,000 objects lie in its group of works produced by New Jersey's craftspeople and industries, especially in the area of ceramics, glass, and ironmaking. The museum's first acquisition, a Belleek porcelain teacup by the well-known Trenton firm Ott & Brewer, was made in 1924. The museum also houses exceptional examples of eighteenth- and nineteenth-century New Jersey furniture, quilts, and samplers.

Georgia O'Keeffe, who married Stieglitz in 1924, painted several views from the thirtieth floor of the apartment they shared at the Shelton Hotel in New York City. O'Keeffe's **EAST RIVER FROM THE SHELTON** (1927–28) is an exceptional cityscape she painted from this location, one of the many said to have been influenced by her interest in and knowledge of photography. The upper half of her canvas, which is dominated by the bright orb of the sun and its rays, reflects the photographic occurrence of lens flare that results in the appearance of sunspots. In a work that juxtaposes form and its disintegration, O'Keeffe contrasts the light-filled haziness of the upper two thirds of the canvas with the dark silhouettes of factories and warehouses below.

Another of the museum's highlights is **AFTER THE STORM, SILVER AND GREEN (VAULT SKY)** (1922) by Arthur Dove, also of the group of American modernists associated with Stieglitz and his legendary Gallery 291. In the moody and lyrical *After the Storm*, Dove paints a simplified and abstracted landscape of horizontal bands of form and color executed on a distinctly vertical canvas.

Among the museum's sculptural highlights is Alexander Calder's (1898–1976) **EL SOL ROJO** (The Red Sun) (1968), a substantially sized black stabile punctuated by a red disk. The sculpture was an intermediate maquette for Calder's largest work, which was executed for the 1968 Olympics in Mexico City.

The Museum also boasts the complete collection of graphic works by the Social Realist Ben Shahn (1898–1969) who created images addressing political and populist themes in prints, photographs, paintings, and large-scale murals. Also at the New Jersey State Museum are the mosaic murals

Shahn initially created for an Israeli luxury liner, the S.S. Shalom, **ATOMIC TABLE** and **THE TREE OF LIFE** (1963–64), which explore the themes of science, philosophy, and religious freedom and tolerance. One of Shahn's finest works, the **JERSEY HOMESTEAD MURAL**, executed on behalf of the New Deal's Farm Security Administration-sponsored public arts projects, is located about a thirty-minute drive from the museum at the Roosevelt Public School in Roosevelt, N. J.

The New Jersey State Museum is open Tuesday through Saturday 9:00 a.m. to 5:00 p.m.; Sunday 12:00 to 5:00 p.m. Admission is free and donations are accepted.

■ OLD QUEENS, 1808
Rutgers University
New Brunswick
ARCHITECT: John McComb, Jr. (1763–1853)

OLD QUEENS, the oldest building on the New Brunswick campus of Rutgers University, is considered one of the finest surviving examples of Federal architecture. Old Queens was designed by John McComb Jr., who was the son of an architect and achieved renown for designing some of the most prominent American buildings of the period, which include **HAMILTON GRANGE** in Harlem (1802) for Alexander Hamilton; **CASTLE CLINTON** (1808) in Battery Park, Manhattan; and the New York **CITY HALL** (1802-11) (see p. 81).

The college had acquired a gift of land from the family of James Parker, of the Provincial Congress, prior to the Revolution. The property consisted of five acres bounding Somerset and George Streets, the present site of the Queen's campus, where the architectural plans of John McComb were to be realized. The building Old Queens was named after Queen's College, the earliest name for Rutgers. The cornerstone for the building was laid on April 27, 1809. The queen after whom the school and building were named was Charlotte of Mecklenburg-Strelitz (1744–1818), who was the Queen-consort of King George III, the reigning monarch at the time of the founding of the college in 1766.

The three-story Federal building is composed of ashlar brownstone on the front and sides and of local field stone in the rear, with white trim. The façade of Old Queens incorporates elegance in its balance and symmetry—typical of Federal architecture. There are classical motifs, such as Doric pilasters, pediments in low relief, and small circular windows in the pediments and the cupola. The building also boasts the original handmade glass windowpanes.

Old Queens, when first occupied in 1811, housed the academic workings of the College, the New Brunswick Theological Seminary, and the Rutgers Preparatory School, then known as the Grammar School. The building included recitation rooms on the first floor, the Chapel and the library on the second floor, and wings on each side that served as living quarters for the faculty of the College. The building was completed in 1825 due to a shortage of funds, at which time the cupola was added—a gift of Stephen Van Rensellaer, and a college bell, purchased by Colonel Henry Rutgers, that originally signaled the change of classes. The building now holds administrative offices, including that of the president of the university.

■ **PRINCETON UNIVERSITY**
■ **PRINCETON UNIVERSITY ART MUSEUM**
  McCormick Hall, 185 Nassau Street
  PHONE: (609) 258-3788
  WEB SITE: www.artmuseum.princeton.edu
■ **NASSAU HALL (1756)**
  Charles Willson Peale's (1741–1827) *Washington at the Battle of Princeton* (1784)
■ **PUTNAM COLLECTION OF SCULPTURE**
■ **PRINCETON UNIVERSITY CHAPEL (1928)**
  ARCHITECT: Ralph Adams Cram (1863–1942)
  PHONE: (609) 258-3047
■ **GORDON WU HALL (1983)**
  ARCHITECT: Robert Venturi (b. 1925)
    and Denise Scott Brown (b. 1931)

THE PRINCETON UNIVERSITY ART MUSEUM, known as the Museum of Historic Art until 1947, was established around 1882 with a collection of pottery, porcelain, casts of famous antiquities, and architectural details and ornaments. Over the years the museum's chronological and geographic range and scope have increased dramatically to include more than 72,000 objects, from the ancient through contemporary periods, including works from the Americas, Europe, Asia, and Africa.

Among the earliest European works at the museum is the collection of ancient Greek and Roman art, noteworthy for some excellent examples of Greek black-figure vase painting and marbles, bronzes, ceramics, and Roman mosaics from the University's excavations in Antioch, in what is today southeast Turkey.

Some of the best European paintings in Princeton's collection include the Italian Byzantine painter Guida da Siena's (c. 1262–1270s) lovely **ANNUNCIATION** (c. 1262–79), which simultaneously achieves drama and simplicity; a fascinating image from a follower of Hieronymous Bosch (c. 1450–1516), entitled **CHRIST BEFORE PONTIUS PILATE** (c. 1520), featuring the almost meditative figure of Christ contrasted with soldiers rendered with distorted features that are meant to be symbolic of their deplorable character and deeds; and Francisco Goya's (1746–1828) **MONK TALKING TO AN OLD WOMAN** (1824–25) is an expressive watercolor on ivory painting that reflects Goya's interest in the nightmarish and the grotesque.

The nineteenth-century European collection is anchored by such excellent works as **GYPSY WITH A CIGARETTE** (c. 1862), which reflects Édouard Manet's (1832–1883) interest in Spanish art and culture, and is a representation of an exotic woman smoking a cigarette whose body reflects a kind of liberated casualness and lack of self-consciousness; **WATER LILIES AND JAPANESE BRIDGE** (1899) is a standout from Claude Monet's (1840–1926) famous series painted at his home in Giverny; and Edgar Degas's (1834–1917) pastel **DANCERS** (1899) emphasizes the intimate, semiprivate, and corporeal while capturing dancers adjusting their clothing and stretching backstage.

Princeton's collection of American art is especially strong with noteworthy examples of early portraiture by such masters as John Singleton Copley (1758–1842), whose meticulously painted **ELKANAH WATSON** (1782) pictures a man who served as a courier to George Washington and others during the Revolutionary War. The Museum also owns other exceptional portraits by Rembrandt Peale (1798–1860), Samuel F. B. Morse (1791–1872), Thomas Eakins (1844–1916), and John Singer Sargent (1856–

1925), among others. Princeton's most celebrated example of American portraiture, Charles Willson Peale's (1741–1827) **WASHINGTON AT THE BATTLE OF PRINCETON** (1784), is located in Nassau Hall and discussed in more detail below.

Nineteenth-century American landscape painting is also especially well-represented by such works as the Hudson River School painter Asher B. Durand's (1796–1886) **KAATERSKILL LANDSCAPE** (1850), which features the naturalistic details for which he is best known; Jasper Cropsey's (1823–1900) **MORNING** (1854) evokes the act of gazing out a window to look upon a picturesque scene; **LAKE GEORGE** (c. 1870) is an elegant representation of the lake's stillness and peace by John Frederick Kensett (1816–1872); and the Impressionist William Merritt Chase's (1849–1916) light-filled **LANDSCAPE: SHINNECOCK, LONG ISLAND** (c. 1896) integrates young girls and a woman within a landscape where their clothing and hats emerge almost like flowers blossoming from the ground.

The museum's twentieth-century and contemporary collections include two strong paintings by Georgia O'Keeffe (1887–1986), **NARCISSA'S LAST ORCHID** (1940) and **FROM A NEW JERSEY WEEKEND II** (1941); the preeminent Pop artist Andy Warhol's (1928–1987) iconic **BLUE MARILYN** (1962) and **BRILLO BOX** (1964), which explore such notions as the effects of commercialization, media saturation, and consumerism; and Frank Stella's (b. 1936) sculpturally abstract **FELSZTYN I** (1971), among many others.

Princeton's photography collection is also first-rate, spanning the nineteenth century to the present and including such striking images as Edward Steichen's (1879–1973) moody, impressionistic, and almost painterly **THE POOL—EVENING** (1899); and the Cuban-born photographer Ana Mendieta's (1948–1985) **UNTITLED (GLASS ON BODY IMPRINTS— FACE)** (1972), one of a series that reflects her interest in the representation and traditional exploitation of the female body by featuring body parts pressed in deliberately contorted and misshapen ways against glass.

A highlight of the museum's fine Chinese collection is the lyrical **WINTER LANDSCAPE** (c. 1120), a monochromatic painted scroll depicting a mountain landscape enveloped in mist. The painting is the only surviving signed work by Li Gongnian, an early twelfth-century prison official. Also of note is Princeton's Pre-Columbian collection, with especially strong examples of Mayan pottery.

The Princeton University Art Museum is free and open to the public Tuesday to Saturday from 10:00 a.m. to 5:00 p.m. and Sunday from 1:00 to 5:00 p.m. The museum is closed on Mondays.

Perhaps the best-known painting in Princeton's fine collection of American portraits is Charles Willson Peale's dramatic image of the victorious **WASHINGTON AT THE BATTLE OF PRINCETON**, one of only a few portraits for which Washington posed. Peale depicts the general, dressed in a uniform noteworthy for its vibrant, golden yellow color, with his sword drawn and with the British retreating in the background. The portrait is located alongside others in the Faculty Room of **NASSAU HALL** (1756), the oldest building on the campus.

The Faculty Room, which was modeled after the British House of Commons, served as the meeting place for both the New Jersey State Legislature and the Continental Congress. Nassau Hall itself, which is depicted in the background of the Peale portrait, sustained a great deal of damage and changed hands many times during the Revolution. In 1783, the Continental Congress met for four months in Nassau Hall. The early American architect Benjamin Henry Latrobe (1764–1820), who was responsible for the reconstruction of the nation's capital after it was burned in 1814, was also responsible for rebuilding Nassau Hall after a fire in 1802 left only the outside walls standing.

Princeton displays several impressive, large-scale twentieth-century sculptures throughout the campus that are part of the **PUTNAM COLLECTION OF SCULPTURE**. They include Gaston Lachaise's (1882–1935) voluptuous **FLOATING FIGURE** (1927); Alexander Calder's (1898–1976) dynamic black stabile, **FIVE DISKS: ONE EMPTY** (1969–70); Pablo Picasso's (1881–1973) sixteen-foot **HEAD OF A WOMAN** (executed in 1971 from Picasso's maquette of 1962); Henry Moore's (1898–1986) abstract **OVAL WITH POINTS** (1971), a work that may have been inspired by Moore's study of the cavities and surfaces of an elephant skull in his studio; Louise Nevelson's (1900–1988) twenty-one foot **ATMOSPHERE AND ENVIRONMENT X** (1971), her first monumental sculpture in Cor-Ten steel; David Smith's (1906–1965) **CUBI XIII** (1963), one of a series of twenty-eight monumental abstract sculptures in stainless steel whose polished surfaces are transformed by changing light conditions; and Isamu Noguchi's (1904–1988) white marble **WHITE SUN** (1970), carved simultaneously with a gray-marble Black Sun (Seattle), which functioned together as the "White Sun of the East and Black Sun on the western shores of America."

The **PRINCETON UNIVERSITY CHAPEL** (1928) was designed by Ralph Adams Cram, whose Gothic Revival style is felt throughout the campus where he served as Consulting Architect from 1907 to 1929. In explaining the importance of Gothic sensibility to his work, Cram noted that it had less to do with specific stylistic elements than with a larger world view, stating, "Gothic is less a method of construction than it is a mental attitude, the visualizing of a spiritual impulse."

The Chapel, one of the largest university chapels in the world, is extraordinary for its architecture, sculptural ornamentation, and its incredible and numerous stained glass windows, all of which help create a sacred place of worship and meditation while allowing room for the secular to coexist. The visual programs of the sculpture and the stained glass represent biblical stories and events from the life of Christ while also depicting moments from such relevant literary epics as Danté's *Divine Comedy* and Sir Thomas Malory's *Le Morte d'Arthur*, among others.

The Chapel, which soars above the campus while remaining carefully integrated within the larger architectural plan, demonstrates the influence of Gothic masterworks like Chartres Cathedral in such areas as the tympanum on the West Door, which features an image from the Book of Revelations where Christ is surrounded by four beasts representing the Gospels and by twenty-four elders.

Throughout the Chapel, Christian imagery stands side by side with images addressing more secular pursuits. For example, the Northwest Door, which represents the Annunciation and Incarnation, is accompanied by nearby windows dedicated to art and music, where the fourteenth-century painter Fra Angelico is shown along with Saint John of Damascus, who wrote hymns and a treatise denouncing the Iconoclasm and asserting the legitimacy of making and venerating holy images and icons.

The Chapel connects to the rest of the campus and specifically to the adjacent Dickinson Hall with the **ROTHSCHILD ARCH**, a double-pointed Gothic arch that is meant to symbolize the relationship between faith and learning. And such elements as the Science Window within the Chapel itself continually reiterate that faith and science can coexist harmoniously, a message that seems particularly relevant within the specific context of a university community.

Guided tours of the chapel are available but must be arranged in advance. Please call (609) 258-3047. Self-guided tours of the Chapel can be enhanced by maps, descriptions, and downloadable audio guides available on the Chapel's web site: http://web.princeton.edu/sites/chapel/tours.html.

Robert Venturi, who graduated from Princeton in 1948, was commissioned to design a dining hall for the new undergraduate college, Butler College. According to Venturi's firm, **GORDON WU HALL**, with its long shape and central position within the college, functions as "a visual hyphen that connects the dormitories and unites them." Its brick walls, limestone trim, and strip windows visually connect it to the larger Gothic architectural scheme at Princeton. However, Wu Hall's entrance also emphatically declares that it is a product of a modern age. Set somewhat off-center, the main entrance makes a bold statement with geometric marble and granite panels. Its design also connects the modern with the past in that it recalls early Renaissance ornament, resembling an updated coat of arms.

The light-filled interior is designed to promote informal interactions among students. The grand staircase has bleacher-like seating built up along one side, to encourage relaxed study, reading, or conversation. The dining room itself in some senses reflects the grandeur of Princeton's more Neo-Gothic halls, while at the same time achieving a more relaxed feeling of intimacy and comfort. The use of natural wood, the impressive tall bay window, and the other numerous windows bring a great deal of light into the space.

Visitors who will be on campus for just one day between the hours of 8:00 a.m. and 5:00 p.m. may park in remote lot 21 near Jadwin Gym on Fitzrandolph Road. A free campus shuttle runs until the early evening. There are also metered spaces in town or commercial parking on Chambers and Hullfish streets.

NEW JERSEY

The following is a complete list of works in the Putnam Collection of Sculpture, together with their campus locations:

- Reg Butler (1913–1982), **THE BRIDE** (1961), Hamilton Court
- Alexander Calder, **FIVE DISKS: ONE EMPTY** (1970), plaza between Fine and Jadwin Halls
- Jacob Epstein (1880–1959), **ALBERT EINSTEIN** (1933), Fine Hall Library
- Naum Gabo (1890–1977), **SPHERIC THEME** (1973–74), between 1879 Hall and Architecture Building
- Michael Hall (b. 1941), **MASTODON VI** (1968), in front of MacMillan Building
- Gaston Lachaise, **FLOATING FIGURE** (1927), Compton Quadrangle, Graduate College
- Jacques Lipchitz (1891–1973), **SONG OF THE VOWELS** (1969), between Firestone Library and the University Chapel
- Clement Meadmore (1929–2005), **UPSTART II** (1970), entrance to Engineering Quadrangle
- Henry Moore, **OVAL WITH POINTS** (1968–70) between West College and Stanhope Hall
- Masayuki Nagare (b. 1923), **STONE RIDDLE** (1967), courtyard of Engineering Quadrangle
- Louise Nevelson (1899–1988), **ATMOSPHERE AND ENVIRONMENT X** (1969–70), Nassau Street entrance to the Campus near Firestone Library
- Isamu Noguchi (1904–1988), **WHITE SUN** (1966), lobby of Firestone Library
- Eduardo Paolozzi (1924–2005), **MAROK-MAROK-MIOSA** (1965), lobby of the Architecture Building
- Antoine Pevsner (1886–1962), **CONSTRUCTION IN THE 3RD AND 4TH DIMENSION** (1962), courtyard of Jadwin Hall
- Pablo Picasso (1871–1973), **HEAD OF A WOMAN** (1909), in front of The Princeton Art Museum
- Arnaldo Pomodoro (b. 1926), **SFERO** (1966), in the Lourie-Love dormitory quadrangle

- George Rickey (1907–2002), **TWO PLANES VERTICAL HORIZONTAL II** (1970), between East Pyne and Murray-Dodge
- David Smith (1906–1965), **CUBI XIII** (1963), near Spelman Hall
- Tony Smith (1912–1980), **MOSES** (1967–68), on the front lawn of Prospect
- Kenneth Snelson (b. 1927), **NORTHWOOD II** (1970), in Compton Quadrangle, Graduate College

SKYLANDS MANOR AND THE NEW JERSEY BOTANICAL GARDEN
Morris Road
Ringwood
John Russell Pope (1874–1937)
PHONE: (973) 962-9534 or (973) 962-7527
WEB SITE: www.njbg.org

SKYLANDS MANOR dates to the mid-1920s and was created by Beaux-Arts-trained architect John Russell Pope, known for his designs of the Jefferson Memorial (1943), the National Archives (1935), and the West Building of the National Gallery of Art in Washington, D.C. (1941). A prolific architect who was an advocate of Eclecticism, he worked in a variety of styles and designed many traditional homes for wealthy clients as well as civic projects, including the master plan of Yale and Dartmouth Universities.

Skylands Manor was conceived as a joint project by a widow, Helen Salomon, and her son, Clarence Lewis; she wanted a Tudor mansion as a summerhouse and he wanted extensive gardens. Lewis engaged prominent landscape architects Vitale and Geiffert to design the gardens, whose plan was executed by Feruccio Vitale (1875–1933), who specialized in private estates and whose clients included John Wanamaker, the department store magnate.

A Victorian mansion on the site was demolished and Skylands, in the style of Tudor Revival, was erected in its stead. Lewis's mother suffered from poor health and died in 1927 before completion of the house. The interior includes elaborate detailing and decoration throughout, such as paneling, frescoes, friezes, stained glass, and carvings, and many rooms include imported items and materials from Europe.

Tours of the Manor House are forty-five minutes and are given on various Sundays between 12:00 and 4:00 p.m. Please call or visit the Web site for dates and information. Group tours are available by reservation. There is an admission fee for the house, except for children under the age of six, but admission to the New Jersey State Botanical is free.

The Botanical Garden is open every day of the year from 8:00 a.m. to 8:00 p.m. There are free guided tours of the Botanical Garden every Sunday afternoon at 2:00 p.m. from May through October. The Garden closes only in extreme weather conditions.

There is a parking fee for cars on summer Saturdays, Sundays, and holidays, from Memorial Day to Labor Day. All other times parking is free.

Parking Lot A is most convenient to the Carriage House Visitor Center,

Ringwood Manor, Ringwood State Park, New Jersey

the Concert Lawn, and the Manor House. Parking Lot B provides easy access to the Lilac Garden, the Great Lawn, the Peony Garden, and the Azalea Garden. Parking Lot C is a favorite for hikers and mountain bikers with direct access to trails.

The natural topography of this area made it the center of the Colonial mining industry from the middle decades of the eighteenth century. By 1765, Peter Hasenclever made Ringwood the center of his ironmaking empire, which included 150,000 acres in New Jersey, New York, and Nova Scotia. At Ringwood there was an iron furnace, three forge operations, a gristmill, sawmill, worker's houses, stores, and farms.

Robert Erskine managed the three principal ironmaking facilities from the Ringwood headquarters. He also became General Washington's mapmaker, creating more than two hundred highly accurate maps. The Colonial Manor House at Ringwood saw at least five visits from General Washington on business. In 1807, Martin J. Ryerson purchased the historic ironworks and began building the present Manor House, which he ran for the next fifty years. Ryerson made shot for the war of 1812 and negotiated land and water rights with the Morris Canal Company for expansion of Long Pond (Greenwood Lake) and construction of the Pompton Feeder on the Morris Canal. The Ryerson Steel Company is still in operation today.

Peter Cooper of New York, a remarkable inventor and industrialist, and his young son-in-law, Abram S. Hewitt, purchased Ringwood in 1854. The properties were purchased for the iron deposits, but the Hewitts set about making the old Ringwood estate their summer home. Hewitt enlarged the manor in the 1860s and 1870s. The completed house contains fifty rooms built in a wide range of styles characterizing the Victorian Period. This impressive house features twenty-four fireplaces, thirteen bathrooms, twenty-eight bedrooms, and more than two hundred and fifty windows. The forges, mills, village, and farms that serviced the iron industry gradually turned into the Victorian summer estate of the Hewitts, who were one of the wealthiest and most influential families of nineteenth-century America.

Also worthy of mention is **THE FORGES AND MANOR OF RINGWOOD**, located nearby on Sloatsburg Road in Ringwood State Park. For hours and information, call (973) 962-2240 and for group tours, call (973) 962-2241, or visit www.ringwoodmanor.com.

CONNECTICUT

■ CHENEY BUILDING, 1875–76

942 Main Street
Hartford
ARCHITECT: Henry Hobson Richardson (1838–1886)

ONE OF HENRY HOBSON RICHARDSON'S most notable buildings, the Cheney Building is a fine early example of the unique style of architecture he pioneered, known as Richardsonian Romanesque. The Cheney Building is Richardson's only Connecticut project and it later served as a basis for one of his most famous buildings—the Marshall Field Wholesale Store in Chicago, done in 1885–87.

An eclectic style based on Beaux-Arts principles, Richardson's building uses many classical elements in his architectural vocabulary and makes a commanding statement in its corner location—though it is a transitional design in this architect's oeuvre.

The Cheney Building is composed of a façade of five stories divided into three horizontal tiers five bays wide—each crowned with a polychromed arch, a motif that is repeated in the higher levels. The higher elevations subdivide the window openings from five on the lower floor, to ten on the second, and twenty on the top floor. The building is composed of reddish brownstone complemented with contrasting light Berea limestone accents. Decorative belts, lintels, cornices, and capitals contribute to the overall dynamic exterior of the building, which is capped with low towers on the building corners that contribute to its echo of Romanesque architecture.

The building was erected by two Cheney brothers from the family that owned the Cheney Silk Mills in Manchester, Connecticut. It originally housed retail space on the ground floor and had offices and apartments in the upper lever. It was later occupied by the Brown Thomson and G. Fox and Co. department stores; it has now returned to a mixed-use building that offers retail and office space, including a hotel and café.

■ FLORENCE GRISWOLD MUSEUM

96 Lyme Street
Old Lyme
PHONE: (860) 434-5542
WEB SITE: www.florencegriswoldmuseum.org
E-MAIL: tammi@flogris.org

THE FLORENCE GRISWOLD HOUSE is best known for being the hub of the Lyme Art Colony. Shortly after Florence Griswold opened her house to boarders, the American landscape painter Henry Ward Ranger (1858–1916) arrived in Old Lyme in 1899 to work, attracted by the area's picturesque, natural, unspoiled landscape that in many ways nostalgically harkened back to New England's quieter, slower days of years past at a moment when America was becoming increasingly transformed by industrialization and urbanization.

Ranger's tonal style initially established the colony as a kind of American Barbizon, where artists produced canvases that recalled the paintings of earlier French counterparts like Jean-Baptiste-Camille Corot (1796–1875). In 1903, however, with the arrival of the noted American Impressionist Childe Hassam (1859–1935), the colony shifted its emphasis to Impressionism, making it one of the most popular destinations for Impressionists who would essentially transform the site into an American Giverny.

Artists flocked to Old Lyme and to the Griswold House to find artistic camaraderie and intellectual exchange all nestled within an inspiring landscape, where they could set up their canvases *en plein air*—in the open air. Of primary concern to Hassam and his Impressionist colleagues was the study and rendering of the way light and weather changed and affected the landscape and the various elements, both natural and man-made, situated within it.

Among the representative examples of Impressionist landscape painting at the Florence Griswold Museum are Hassam's autumnal **THE LEDGES, OLD LYME, CONNECTICUT** (1907), whose repetition of slender trees recalls Claude Monet's (1840–1926) poplar series, and Everett L. Warner's (1877–1963) sun-drenched view of **THE VILLAGE CHURCH** (c. 1910). The collection also includes Impressionist genre pictures, featuring ordinary moments from everyday life, such as Willard Leroy Metcalf's (1858–1925) **SUMMER AT HADLYME** (1914), where Metcalf's wife and daughter are shown indoors on a bright summer's day involved in quiet, domestic pursuits.

Visitors to the Griswold Museum will also see the house's beautiful gardens, which have been restored to evoke the natural setting that captured the attention and imagination of so many artists. Additionally, viewers are offered a glimpse of the working process of one of the Colony's members, the Impressionist William Chadwick (1879–1962), whose studio has been transported to the grounds from just a few miles a way. The Chadwick Studio is only open mid-May through October.

The museum is open Tuesday to Saturday 10:00 to 5:00 p.m.; Sunday 1:00 to 5:00 p.m. Closed Mondays. Admission fees apply.

Another significant site located near the Griswold Museum is the **THOMAS LEE HOUSE**, built around 1660 in East Lyme. It is one of the oldest wood frame houses in Connecticut in its original state. On the grounds, visitors may also visit **THE LITTLE BOSTON SCHOOL HOUSE**, which dates to at least 1734. The Lee house is located at 228 West Main Street, East Lyme. It is open Tuesday to Sunday 1:00 to 4:00 p.m., June to Labor Day. Special tours may be arranged at other times throughout the year. Call (860) 739-6070 for more information.

THE GLASS HOUSE, 1949

Visitor Center
199 Elm Street
New Canaan
ARCHITECT: Philip Johnson (1906–2005)
PHONE: (866) 811-4111
WEB SITE: www.philipjohnsonglasshouse.org

OFTEN CALLED the most important example of twentieth-century residential design, Philip Johnson's Glass House is an icon of modern architecture and the International Style. Based on concepts borrowed by Mies van der Rohe, Johnson created a fifty-six by thirty-two-foot symmetrical glass box residence for his own use that is elevated above ground on a platform and has quarter-inch-thick glass walls with black steel supports. Inside it is conceived as an open plan that is divided by low walnut cabinets that house the kitchen apparatus and a brick cylinder that contains the bathroom.

Sleek and elegant yet imposing, the house looks out on to the landscape and the site of forty-seven acres. There are ten other buildings on the property that were designed by Johnson from different periods throughout his life. He also completed a brick guesthouse the same year as the Glass House. He continued to live there until his death in 2005, and many of his Bauhaus furnishings remain in the house. In 1986, he donated the compound to the National Trust, which runs it as a historic property.

The additional buildings Johnson designed represent various phases in his career. A pavilion by the lake was added in 1963; there is a subterranean art gallery set into a hill with works from Johnson's extensive art collection; a sculpture gallery from 1970, which is a white brick structure of irregular geometric shapes and various levels with a glass roof; a castle-like form that is a study-library with a rounded tower of built of stucco; a concrete block tower built in 1985; a structure called the "Ghost House"; and his last structure, titled "Da Monsta," which has irregular shaped and curving walls and is dark red and purple and is a tribute to Deconstructivist architecture.

All tours of the Glass House begin at the Visitor Center located at 199 Elm Street in downtown New Canaan, directly across the street from the train station. There are various tours available, but many are booked months in advance. Visitors to the Glass House are required to purchase tickets in advance. Tours are strictly limited to ten individuals and include a half-mile walk. The tour includes access to the Glass House, Painting Gallery, Sculpture Gallery, and Da Monsta. The Brick House is undergoing restoration and will reopen after 2008. Tours begin in April and run through October. Call or visit the Web site for more information.

Also worthy of mention and a visit is a later contrasting effort by Johnson, the skyscraper **AT&T BUILDING**, which is now **THE SONY BUILDING**, in Manhattan. Located at 560 Madison Avenue at 56th Street, it was completed in 1984 and considered one of the best examples of postmodern architecture. It was designed with Johnson's partner, John Burgee (b. 1933), and it pays homage to Chippendale furniture with its ornamental top.

■ HILL-STEAD MUSEUM
35 Mountain Road
Farmington
PHONE: (860) 677-4787
WEB SITE: www.hillstead.org
E-MAIL: stanleyc@hillstead.org

THEODATE POPE RIDDLE (1867–1946), an aspiring architect, helped design her parent's Farmington country estate (c. 1898–1901) alongside an architect from the regarded New York architectural firm of Mckim, Mead, & White. Inspired by the Colonial Revival Movement and classic New England farmhouses, Riddle designed the Pope Riddle House, a carriage house, a theater, the gardens and grounds, which included a working farm, and other structures on the estate in an informally elegant style that was both aesthetically pleasing and utilitarian. Today, Hill-Stead is a 152-acre, ten-building museum complex that includes the original Pope Riddle House, featuring nineteen rooms with beautiful original furnishings and decorative objects that set the stage for an exceptional collection of Impressionist works amassed by the Pope-Riddle family.

The museum features first-rate Impressionist paintings by Edouard Manet (1832–1883), Claude Monet (1840–1926), Edgar Degas (1834–1917), and Mary Cassatt (1844–1926), as well as a fine group of smaller-scale bronze sculptures, including eight works by the animalier Antoine-Louis Barye (1796–1875).

Manet's **THE GUITAR PLAYER** (1866) features Victorine Meurent, the model for his infamous *Olympia* (1863) Musée d'ORsay. Here, Manet dresses the model of Olympia back up, and instead of depicting her as challenging, provocative, and emphatically naked, he deliberately turns her back to the viewer. Inspired by Spanish themes and paintings, Manet paints Victorine in a very full, starkly white dress that contrasts dramatically with the dark background.

The Hill-Stead successfully demonstrates Monet's range and development with such paintings as **WHITE FROST EFFECT** (1889), a work from

Edgar Degas's pastel The Tub *(1886)*

his famous haystack series, that exhibits his quick brushwork and his interest in focusing on a natural motif within a single moment and exploring the effects of light and weather on that motif; Monet's earlier seascape, **FISHING BOATS AT SEA** (1868), offers a nice counterpoint to the more mature Impressionist haystacks and demonstrates his long-term interest in painting out of doors and studying light, reflection, and weather effects.

In the tradition of Impressionist painters who focused on the modern city and its spectacles and on depicting scenes of contemporary life, Degas's **DANCERS IN PINK** (c. 1876) captures dancers backstage and not in performance, focusing instead on a relaxed moment and on the decorative effects of the fanned-out pink tutus of the dancers. Degas often depicted lower class women in private moments, as in the lovely pastel **THE TUB** (1886), which uses what is often referred to as his voyeuristic "keyhole perspective" to peek in and render a woman bent over and occupied in bathing herself.

The Hill-Stead offers a lovely example of the American painter Mary Cassatt's well-known images of mothers and children in casual, domestic settings. In **SARA HANDING A TOY TO THE BABY** (c. 1901), Cassatt, who moved to Paris and exhibited alongside the French Impressionists, focuses in a very tactile way on the baby's fleshiness and on the intimate touches, glances, and gestures that are exchanged between mothers, their children, and among siblings. In a broader view of a similar subject, the aquatint **GATHERING FRUIT OR THE KITCHEN GARDEN** (1893) also demonstrates the influence of Japanese prints on Cassatt's work.

The Impressionist masterworks are seen alongside elegant pieces of decorative art and furniture collected and used by the Pope-Riddle families. The house boasts excellent Chippendale, Federal, and Empire-style pieces, and a collection of antique clocks displayed throughout, including a French Louis XVI clock with a rhinestone-studded pendulum, modeled after a clock owned by Marie-Antoinette.

Influenced by the English countryside and especially the Cotswolds, as well as the Neoclassical Revival style of urban formal gardens, Theodate Pope Riddle was also largely responsible for Hill-Stead's grounds and gardens. Beatrix Jones Farrand (1872–1957), the only woman in the group of founding members of the American Society of Landscape Architects, designed Hill-Stead's

Sunken Garden in the 1920s and incorporated plantings that complemented the colors of the Impressionist works in the Pope Riddle House.

Located just ten minutes west of Hartford, the Hill-Stead Museum is open Tuesday through Sunday and closed Mondays. Hours are 10:00 a.m. to 5:00 p.m. May through October; November through April, the museum is open 11:00 a.m. to 4:00 p.m. June through October, the museum hosts a 1:00 p.m. gallery talk and an estate walk at 2:00 p.m. Admission fees apply. The grounds are open daily from 7:30 a.m. to 5:30 p.m.

■ LYMAN ALLYN ART MUSEUM

625 Williams Street
New London
PHONE: (860) 443-2545
WEB SITE: www.lymanallyn.org
E-MAIL: info@lymanallen.org

HOUSED IN A NEOCLASSICAL BUILDING designed by the prominent landscape designer, painter, and architect Charles A. Platt (1861–1933), the Lyman Allyn Art Museum was founded in 1932 in the city of New London in Southeastern Connecticut. The museum is known for its collection of American paintings, sculpture, and decorative art, though it also owns fine examples of art by European artists, especially in the area of works on paper.

Among the most noteworthy paintings at the museum are those by artists of the Hudson River School, including Thomas Cole's (1801–1848) MOUNT AETNA FROM TAORMINA (1844). The English-born Cole and his Hudson River School cohorts became well known for championing the painting of the American landscape. However, Cole also spent a good deal of time abroad and in Italy in particular, and this view of Taormina, Sicily, reflects his travels while offering the panoramic views and interest in ruins that are characteristic of his oeuvre.

John Frederick Kensett's (1816–1872) BASH BISH FALLS (1851), an oval-shaped rendering of a popular nineteenth-century tourist destination, offers a picturesque and highly detailed view of a site a contemporary journal described as "one of the wildest and most beautiful cascades in the country." Kensett painted Bash Bish Falls, located in South Egremont, Massachusetts, at least five times.

In the area of decorative arts, the museum has a particularly strong collection of eighteenth-century New England furniture, featuring many examples that demonstrate New London's unique contributions to the design of the period. The Lyman Allyn also owns one of the largest collections of nineteenth- and twentieth-century dolls and dollhouses in the country, and it periodically displays them, sometimes at the historic **DESHON ALLYN HOUSE**, an 1829 Greek Revival home that is also part of the museum.

As a founding member of the Connecticut Art Trail, which promotes the appreciation of the art of Connecticut through travel, the Lyman Allyn also has a fine collection of works by Connecticut Impressionists.

The Lyman Allyn Art Museum is open Tuesday to Saturday 10:00 a.m. to 5:00 p.m. and Sundays 1:00 to 5:00 p.m. Closed Mondays and major holidays. Admission fees apply. For more information on the Connecticut Art Trail, see www.arttrail.org.

THE OLD STATE HOUSE, 1796

800 Main Street
Hartford
ARCHITECT: Charles Bulfinch (1763–1844)
PHONE: (860) 522-6766
E-MAIL: info@ctosh.org
WEB SITE: www.ctosh.org

THE OLD STATE HOUSE in Connecticut is the oldest state house in America. It was designed by noted early American architect Charles Bulfinch, who was believed to be the first in this young country to practice architecture as a profession. The Connecticut State House was his first public building design, completed in 1796, and is a fine example of the Federal Style that Bulfinch popularized.

The Old State House, sited to face the Connecticut River, served as the state capitol from 1796 to 1878, and then became the city hall of Hartford until 1915. Well-known events that transpired there include Washington's meeting the French armies and the Amistad trial. Bulfinch was greatly influenced by European architecture, particularly British architects Christopher Wren and Robert Adam, who were in turn influenced by the Neoclassicism of English Georgian architecture and that of Palladian ideas, which can be seen in the refined sense of proportion, decoration, and balance as well as in the use of arches. The building form is based on the design of the Town Hall of Liverpool, England. It also reflects many of the defining features seen in Bulfinch's other building projects, including the Massachusetts State House, the Maine State House in Augusta, and the U.S. Capitol in Washington. D.C.; these features include the arched lower story, the portico with Ionic pilasters, and the entablature. President James Monroe appointed Bulfinch to succeed Benjamin Henry Latrobe as architect of the Capitol, and Bulfinch completed the wings, central portion, and the western entrance and portico.

The Old State House is composed of Portland, Connecticut brownstone, brick, and wood. The original design, which Bulfinch sent from Massachusetts, was simpler than the structure in evidence today. Later additions include the roof balustrade and cupola, though the rest of the exterior has been restored to reflect its original plan.

The building is open from Tuesday to Friday 11:00 a.m. to 5:00 p.m. and on Saturday from 10:00 a.m. to 5:00 p.m. It is closed on Sunday and Monday and major holidays

Admission is free on the first Saturday of every month from 10:00 a.m. to 1:00 p.m. and for Connecticut Historical Society Museum members and children under the age of six; otherwise there is a nominal admission fee.

Individuals and small groups are welcome to tour the building. Larger groups should make advanced reservations for tours.

■ WADSWORTH ATHENEUM, 1842

600 Main Street
Hartford
ARCHITECT: Alexander Jackson Davis (1803–1892)
   and Ithiel Town (1784–1844)
PHONE: (860) 278-2670
WEB SITE: www.wadsworthatheneum.org
E-MAIL: info@wadsworthatheneum.org

ESTABLISHED IN 1842 by the Hartford art patron Daniel Wadsworth, the Wadsworth Atheneum is America's oldest public art museum. Wadsworth envisioned not only a museum where fine and decorative arts would be displayed, but a cultural center that would preserve and make available to the general public a wide range of historical materials. He chose the term "Atheneum" to reference Athena, the Greek goddess of wisdom, a worthy inspiration for a cultural center dedicated to celebrating and fostering knowledge and creativity. The castlelike Gothic Revival building which houses this exceptional collection of American and European paintings, sculpture, and decorative arts was designed by Alexander Jackson Davis and Ithiel Town on the site of Daniel Wadsworth's family home. The Wadsworth opened its doors to the public in 1844. Over the years it has seen the addition of several wings to contain and display its continually growing collections and to host a variety of exhibitions, events, and performances each year.

The Wadsworth boasts one of the finest collections of early American portraiture, including John Singleton Copley's (1738–1815) **PORTRAIT OF A LADY (MRS. SEYMOUR FORT)** (c. 1776–80), an immaculately painted image that demonstrates Copley's mastery of representing various surfaces and materials such as lace and silk while capturing the interior life of his subjects. Here, Copley suggests Mrs. Fort's intelligence by depicting her looking out at the viewer with a keen and steady gaze while in the process of knotting a shuttle, a needlecraft-type activity popular in the day among wealthy ladies. In capturing her at work, Copley demonstrates his talents in representing hands in motion while simultaneously allowing his sitter to show off her own skills. Among the other extraordinary portraits in the collection are Copley's large companion portraits of **JEREMIAH LEE** (1769) and **MRS. JEREMIAH LEE** (1769); and the Connecticut painter Ralph Earl's (1751–1801) **DOUBLE PORTRAIT OF OLIVER ELLSWORTH AND ABIGAIL WOLCOTT ELLSWORTH** (1792), which functions as a pictorial biography of Ellsworth, a U.S. Senator who is shown holding a copy of the U.S. Constitution which he helped to draft and ratify, together with his wife, and a view of his new home in the background seen through the window of a book-filled study.

Wadsworth Atheneum

Hudson River School painting is also a strong aspect of the collection and represented by such exceptional works as Thomas Cole's (1801–1848) **THE LAST OF THE MOHICANS, CORA KNEELING AT THE FEET OF TAMENUND** (1827), a panoramic view featuring the White Mountains in New Hampshire in what is partially a "literary landscape" inspired by the work of James Fenimore Cooper. The Wadsworth's impressive collection of paintings by Cole, which also includes **KATERSKILL FALLS** (1826), **VIEW IN THE WHITE MOUNTAINS** (1827), **MOUNT ETNA FROM TAORMINA** (1843), and **EVENING IN ARCADY** (1843), among others, offers a nuanced perspective of Cole's range and varied interests in representing natural details, amazing vistas, ruins, and historical or literary scenes imbedded within larger landscapes. The Wadsworth also has several paintings by Cole's younger Hudson River School cohort, Frederic Edwin Church (1826–1900), including a spectacular view of dramatically crashing waves in **COAST SCENE, MOUNT DESERT (SUNRISE OFF THE MAINE COAST)** (1863), and steamy, tropical views that expertly capture naturalistic and atmospheric detail in paintings like **VALE OF ST. THOMAS, JAMAICA** (1867) and **EVENING IN THE TROPICS** (1881).

Other notable works in the museum's collection of American art of the nineteenth century are stellar trompe l'oeil still lifes by William Michael Harnett (1848–1892) and John Frederick Peto (1854–1907), including Harnett's masculine **THE FAITHFUL COLT** (1890). Among the Wadsworth's fine American Impressionist paintings is John Henry Twachtman's (1853–1902) **EMERALD POOL, YELLOWSTONE** (c. 1895), where Twachtman chooses to focus on a single motif rather than a vast, panoramic view by offering a cropped and almost abstracted representation of the unusual green sulfur pool at Yellowstone and the mists that envelop it. Inspired in part by Japanese art, Twachtman represents the Emerald Pool as a somewhat flattened swirl of color and energy.

Among the best of the Wadsworth's collection of works by early twentieth-century modernists are paintings by such artists as Georgia O'Keeffe (1887–1986) and Marsden Hartley (1877–1943). O'Keeffe painted **THE LAWRENCE TREE** (1929), a breathtaking image of the trunk and branches of a ponderosa pine executed during her first summer in New Mexico from the perspective of looking up from the base. The tree seems to shoot through the expressively painted, starlit night sky in a deliberately disorienting way. O'Keeffe once said, "The painting was done so it could be hung with any end up." However, she preferred that it "stand on its head," and the effect is that there is a perpetual visual shift, where sky becomes ground and branches become roots and vise versa. Along with O'Keeffe, Hartley was associated with the circle of modernist artists connected to Alfred Stieglitz's (1864–1946) famous Gallery 291 in New York City. He painted **MILITARY** (1913) while in Berlin, where he became fascinated by the pageantry associated with soldiers. In *Military*, Hartley translates that fascination into an abstracted celebration of vivid colors, shapes, and mystical numbers that explode forward and push energetically against the picture's surface.

The Wadsworth's holdings of Baroque European art are also especially noteworthy, and among the best of this group of works are Michelangelo Merisi da Caravaggio's (1571–1610) beautifully detailed **ST. FRANCIS** (c. 1594–95), which demonstrates Caravaggio's ability to suggest drama in part by manipulating the juxtaposition of light and shadows. Francisco de Zurbaràn's (1598–1664) **ST. SERAPION** (1628), depicts the twelfth-century saint, who was eventually decapitated, tied to a tree; the painting communicates a great sense of burden and weightiness, with the head, the hands, the slumped shoulders, and the extremely heavy and well-articulated drapery of the robe all drooping downward. Salvator Rosa's (1615–1673) **LUCREZIA AS THE PERSONIFICATION OF POETRY** (1640) is a striking and intense depiction of his mistress. Bernardo Strozzi's (1581–1644) gorgeously painted **ST. CATHERINE OF ALEXANDRIA** (1610–15) renders the fourth-century saint as simultaneously learned (with books at her feet), strong and courageous (holding a sword), and beautiful, with luminous porcelain skin and sumptuous clothing and jewels.

The museum's collections of nineteenth-century European art contains several remarkable works such as the Pre-Raphaelite painter William Holman Hunt's (1827–1905) highly intricate and decorative **THE LADY OF SHALOTT** (1886–1905), a painting full of swirling energy, drama, and extraordinary details and colors. The museum's **NYMPHEAS, WATER LILIES** (1904) by Claude Monet (1840–1926) is a particularly strong example from his famous waterlilies series, painted near his home at Giverny. In part influenced by Japanese art, Monet tilts the picture plane, eliminates the horizon line, and focuses on a very small portion of the pond to create an abstracted image that is not unlike the Wadsworth's previously mentioned **EMERALD POOL, YELLOWSTONE** (1895) by the American painter John Twachtman (1853–1904).

Twentieth-century highlights include important Surrealist works such as Max Ernst's (1891–1976) **EUROPE AFTER THE RAIN** (1940–42), an imagined, fantastic landscape of devastation and decay painted during the course of World War II. Ernst used a technique known as decalcomania, which involves using a smooth surface such as glass or paper to apply paint to the canvas; when the surface of choice is removed, the painter achieves various interesting textural effects.

American artists associated with the New York School are also well represented by such paintings as Jackson Pollock's (1912–1956) **NO. 9** (1949), a smaller example of the Abstract Expressionist artist's famous drip-paintings, but one that is extraordinarily revealing about Pollock's process and aesthetic vision. Pollock's very rhythmic application of white and black paint anchors the composition and contradicts any notion that his canvases are haphazard.

Other noteworthy works in the Wadsworth's post–1945 collection are Frank Stella's (b. 1936) **SINJERLI VARIATION IV** (1968), a circular painting with a certain contained energy that manipulates interlocking shapes and colors to challenge the eye; and Robert Rauschenberg's (1925–2008) **RETROACTIVE I** (1963), one of the artist's best silkscreen paintings, which responds to the role of the media in modern culture by bringing together seemingly unconnected images drawn from popular sources, including the central photograph of John F. Kennedy from a press clipping.

The museum's holdings in the decorative arts are also first-rate. The scope the American collection offers a comprehensive view of the highpoints of design in America, from early works by Connecticut craftsmen like Samuel Loomis's (1748–1814) Colchester/Norwich style furniture to giants of twentieth-century design like Frank Lloyd Wright (1867–1959) or Marcel Breuer (1902–1981). The European Decorative arts collection contains some 7,000 objects, including ancient glass and bronzes, Italian maiolica, Dutch Delft, Venetian glass, eighteenth- and nineteenth-century English pottery and porcelain, Berlin and Meissen Art Nouveau porcelain, and nineteenth-century Sèvres porcelain. The museum also owns Pre-Columbian pottery and Chinese porcelain.

The Wadsworth Atheneum is open Tuesday through Friday 11:00 a.m. to 5:00 p.m.; Saturday and Sunday 10:00 a.m. to 5:00 p.m. The museum is open until 8:00 p.m. on the first Thursday of every month. Museum highlight tours are offered on Wednesdays at 1:00 p.m. and on Saturday and Sunday at 2:30 p.m. Special exhibition tours are also offered. Check the Web site for information.

Admission fees apply; however, the museum hosts some free days throughout the year and does offer free admission to certain groups; check the Web site for qualifications. Parking is available for a fee in parking garages near the museum. Bring your parking ticket to the museum to receive a discounted rate.

Located about 5 miles from the Wadsworth Atheneum is the **WEBB-DEANE-STEVENS MUSEUM**, which operates four historic eighteenth-century houses, including the Joseph Webb House (1752), its colonial revival garden, and the Webb Barn. The Webb House served as George Washington's headquarters in May 1781, and it was purchased by the artist and photographer Wallace Nutting (1861–1941) in 1916. Nutting did extensive remodeling and redecorating and commissioned painted wall murals featuring Revolutionary scenes in the Yorktown Parlor and murals of historic houses located in the hallway and front parlors. The other homes managed by the Webb-Deane-Stevens Museum are the Silas Deane House (c. 1770), built for a Revolutionary War diplomat to France; the Isaac Stevens House (1789), which displays many furnishings original to the home and offers visitors a glimpse of middle-class family life in the early nineteenth century; and the Buttolph-Williams House (c. 1715), which features rare seventeenth- and early-eighteenth-century American furnishings.

The Webb-Deane-Stevens Museum is located at 211 Main Street in Wethersfield. It is open daily, except Tuesdays, 10:00 a.m. to 4:00 p.m. and Sundays 1:00 to 4:00 p.m. Admission fees apply and tours are available. For more information see the Web site, www.webb-deane-stevens.org, or call (860) 529-0612.

■ YALE UNIVERSITY, NEW HAVEN

YALE UNIVERSITY IS noted for a predominance of architecture in the Collegiate Neo-Gothic style. The oldest building on campus, **CONNECTICUT HALL**, was built in 1750 in the Georgian style, which, ironically, makes it appear to be of a more recent age than the Neo-Gothic buildings. The university, however, has several buildings that are considered modern architectural icons, most notably Louis Kahn's **YALE ART GALLERY** and the **YALE CENTER FOR BRITISH ART**; Paul Rudolph's **ART AND ARCHITECTURE BUILDING**; and Eero Saarinen's **INGALLS RINK** and the **EZRA STILES** and **MORSE COLLEGES**; and Gordon Bunshaft's **BEINECKE RARE BOOK AND MANUSCRIPT LIBRARY**. The University also owns a number of noteworthy nineteenth-century mansions along Hillhouse Avenue.

■ YALE UNIVERSITY ART GALLERY, 1951–54

1111 Chapel Street (at York Street)
ARCHITECT: Louis I. Kahn (1901–1974)
PHONE: (203) 432-0600
WEB SITE: www.artgallery.yale.edu

THE YALE UNIVERSITY ART GALLERY was Louis I. Kahn's first major architectural commission and is considered one of his masterpieces. Designed while Kahn was a visiting critic at the Yale School of Architecture, the building is composed of brick, concrete, glass, and steel. It was a watershed monument in terms of modern architecture, which decidedly broke with the past in terms of its conception and materials. A windowless structure, it was one of three museums Kahn designed. Kahn is revered for his analytical approach and his refined aesthetic, which emphasize geometry, light, and scale. A complete renovation, which returned the building to much the way Kahn had originally conceived it, was completed in 2006 by Polshek Partnership Architects.

The gallery is the oldest university art museum in the western hemisphere and was founded in 1832, when artist John Trumbull donated one hundred paintings of the American Revolution to the college and designed the original Picture Gallery, which is no longer extant. The encyclopedic permanent collection includes over 185,000 objects from ancient times to the present day. The permanent collection includes strength in the areas of American and European fine and decorative art, and Ancient art. Among the highlights of the permanent collection include: John Trumbull's (1756–1843), **THE DEATH OF GENERAL MONTGOMERY** (1786) and **THE DECLARATION OF INDEPENDENCE** (1786); Winslow Homer's (1836–1910), **A GAME OF CROQUET** (1866); Edward Hopper (1882–1967), **ROOMS BY THE SEA** (1951); Thomas Eakins's (1844–1916), **JOHN BIGLIN IN A SINGLE SCULL** (1874), which is an icon of nineteenth-century American realism; and Vincent van Gogh's (1853–1890) **NIGHT CAFÉ** (1888), which is the museum's most famous painting. The subject is a French café where van Gogh was living in 1888.

The art gallery is open Tuesday through Saturday 10:00 a.m. to 5:00 p.m. and Thursdays until 8:00 p.m. September through June; and Sunday 1:00 to 6:00 p.m. Closed Mondays and major holidays. Admission is free.

■   **YALE CENTER FOR BRITISH ART, 1969–74**
1080 Chapel Street
ARCHITECT: Louis I. Kahn (1901–1974)
PHONE: (203) 432-2800
WEB SITE: www.ycba.yale.edu

THE YALE CENTER FOR BRITISH ART was established by a gift from Paul Mellon in 1966 for his British art collection; it houses the most comprehensive collection of British Art outside the United Kingdom, concentrating on work from the Elizabethan period to contemporary art.

The building was designed by Louis I. Kahn and is located across the street from one of his earliest buildings, the **YALE UNIVERSITY ART GALLERY**, at the corner of York and Chapel Streets in New Haven. The Center for British Art was completed after Kahn's death in 1974, though the plan had been fully conceived by the architect. The building is composed of matte steel and reflective glass with the interior of travertine marble, white oak, and Belgian linen.

Must-see masterpieces of British art from the collection include: J.W.M. Turner's (1775–1851) **STAFFA, FINGAL'S CAVE** (1832) and **DORT, OR DORDRECHT, THE DORT PACKET-BOAT FROM ROTTERDAM BECALMED** (1818); John Constable's (1776–1837), **HADLEIGH CASTLE**

CONNECTICUT

(1829); Thomas Gainsborough's (1727–1788), **MR. AND MRS. JOHN GRAVENOR AND THEIR DAUGHTERS** (1747); and George Stubbs's (1724–1806), **ZEBRA** (1763).

The center is open Tuesday through Saturday 10:00 a.m. to 5:00 p.m. and Sunday 12:00 to 5:00 p.m. Closed major holidays. Admission is free.

■ **BEINECKE RARE BOOK AND MANUSCRIPT LIBRARY, 1963**
121 Wall Street
ARCHITECT: Gordon Bunshaft/SOM (1909–1990)
PHONE: (209) 432-2977
WEB SITE: www.library.yale.edu/beinecke/

THE BEINECKE Rare Book and Manuscript Library, designed by Gordon Bunshaft of Skidmore, Owings, and Merrill in 1963, is one of the largest buildings in the world exclusively dedicated to rare books and manuscripts. Near the center of the University in Hewitt Quadrangle, it is a windowless tower situated within a plaza. The building is windowless to protect the

Yale Center for British Art, 1969–74

collections, which are housed in air-conditioned glass stacks contained within the rectangular structure, visible once you enter the library. The exterior is composed of irregularly framed marble panels, which are cut so thin as to be translucent. During the day, a soft radiating glow of yellow light can be seen in the interior, which highlights the striated veins of the marble. At night, the lights of the building create an interior glow seen from outside. The structure is raised on concrete piers, with glass around the lower level at the entrance level, and the building's rise is five stories of uninterrupted marble panels, which appear white from the exterior.

The sunken courtyard contains geometric sculptures by Isamu Noguchi (1904–1988) said to represent time (the pyramid), the sun (the circle), and chance (the cube). Yale is home to one of alumnus Claes Oldenburg's (b. 1929) most identifiable sculptures, **LIPSTICK (ASCENDING) ON CATERPILLAR TRACK** (1969), in the courtyard of Morse College.

The library is open Monday to Thursday 8:30 a.m. to 8 p.m. and Friday 8:30 a.m. to 5 p.m. Closed major holidays.

ART AND ARCHITECTURE BUILDING (NOW KNOWN AS THE RUDOLPH BUILDING), 1958–63
ARCHITECT: Paul Rudolph (1918–1997)

PAUL RUDOLPH became dean of the school of Architecture at Yale in 1958; he remained for six years and was known as an architect of cubist buildings with complex floor plans. The Yale Art and Architecture Building, designed before he became dean, is his most famous work and is one of the best-known examples of Brutalist architecture in America, along with Marcel Breuer's **WHITNEY MUSEUM OF AMERICAN ART** (see p. 45). The Yale building has over thirty-seven floor levels in eight stories. The building is made of ribbed, bush-hammered concrete which has pronounced vertical striations created by pouring concrete into vertically ribbed wooden forms, which are then stripped away, and concrete edges hand-hammered to expose the aggregate—a favorite treatment for exposed concrete surfaces by Rudolph. Internally the building is organized around a central core space defined by four large concrete slab columns that, similar to the external towers, are hollowed out and house mechanical support of the building.

A fire in 1969 caused extensive damage to the building and during the repairs, many changes were made to Rudolph's original design. Gwathmey, Siegel & Associates has overseen a 2008 renovation, attempting to return the building close to its original design.

■ DAVID S. INGALLS RINK, 1953–58
73 Sachen Street
ARCHITECT: Eero Saarinen (1910–1961)

THIS RINK HAS OFTEN BEEN CALLED the "Yale Whale" because the arched roof design with curvilinear peak recalls a hump-backed whale with a backbone. The structure is typical of the sweeping lines often favored by Saarinen, as seen in his **TWA TERMINAL** (see p. 123), which for him was intended to recall the fluid movement of skating. It is constructed of concrete with a reinforced concrete arch from which is hung cable net that supports the seventy-foot high timber roof.

■ EZRA STILES AND SAMUEL MORSE COLLEGES, 1958–82
ARCHITECT: Eero Saarinen (1910–1961)

INSPIRED BY Yale's predominant Collegiate Neo-Gothic style of architecture and the Italian medieval town of San Gimignano, with its winding narrow streets and alleyways, Saarinen composed these buildings of a yellow aggregate with vertical bands of windows with fortress-like towers, narrow passageways, and stepped levels, which are modern yet hark back to historical architectural antecedents.

INDEX

PHOTO CREDITS